D0776963

THE ABLEST NAVIGATOR

THE ABLEST NAVIGATOR

LIEUTENANT PAUL SHULMAN, USN

ISRAEL'S VOLUNTEER ADMIRAL

J. WANDRES

NAVAL INSTITUTE PRESS
Annapolis, Maryland

Naval Institute Press
291 Wood Road
Annapolis, MD 21402

© 2010 by J. Wandres
All rights reserved. No part of this book may be reproduced or utilized in any form
or by any means, electronic or mechanical, including photocopying and recording,
or by any information storage and retrieval system, without permission in writing
from the publisher.

Library of Congress Cataloging-in-Publication Data
Wandres, J.
  The ablest navigator : lieutenant Paul Shulman, USN, Israel's volunteer admiral
/ J. Wandres.
    p. cm.
  Includes bibliographical references and index.
  ISBN 978-1-59114-952-1 (hardcover : alk. paper) 1. Shulman, Paul, 1922-1994.
2. Admirals—Israel—Biography. 3. Israel. Hel-ha-yam—Officers—Biography.
4. Israel. Hel-ha-yam—History. 5. United States. Navy—Officers—Biography. 6.
Israel—History, Naval. 7. World War, 1939-1945—Naval operations, American.
I. Title.
  V64.I752S58 2010
  359.0092—dc22
  [B]

                              2010030317

Printed in the United States of America on acid-free paper

15 14 13 12 11 10   9 8 7 6 5 4 3 2
First printing

Book layout and composition: Alcorn Publication Design

CONTENTS

PHOTOGRAPHS AND MAPS

PREFACE
Thanks for the Memories

When I hear people tell me that "writing must be such a lonely job," I smile, because I know and have experienced the thrill of constructing a book from idea to index. It is like assembling a sixty-thousand-piece picture puzzle. First, it's a huge jumble of ideas and information. Then you start to see how small groups of pieces fit together, and then these are connected to larger assemblies, until the whole tapestry is revealed before you. Set the puzzle-in-progress out on a table, and someone is sure to come by and add a few pieces. In the instance of writing *The Ablest Navigator*, people I contacted from all over the United States and in Canada, England, Italy, and Israel virtually "stopped by" to help put together the picture of Paul Shulman, Israel's first admiral. Yet, as amazing as the World Wide Web is, I am sorry that I will probably never get to actually meet most of my colleagues and contributors, many of whom are at an advanced age. But in a sense, we are like family. Speaking of family, I could never have managed this project without the steadfast belief in the project by my wife, Judi, and the support and encouragement from our extended-blended families and our many friends.

Among this group were several "first readers" who read and commented on the subject of a narrative biography about Paul Shulman based only on an early summary outline. These honest commentators included Navy colleagues Elwood "Woody" Berzins, George "Gus" Cambanes, Bill Flynn, Emmett Francois, Lawrence "Skid" Heyworth, Jonathan Leff, Steve LeShay, Don Smith, and Ken Smith. Personal friends included Guy Beardslee; Peter Bellincampi and his wife, Judi O'Keefe; Craig Birnbach; Dennis Eschbach; Sam Finley; Michael Hoffman; Michael Koss; Paul and Cyndi LaPierre; Bob Mann; Jerry and Reva Shapiro; Sy Sokatch; Justin Wandres; and Walter Zanger.

There is also a large crew of confederates who knew or served with Paul Shulman at various stations along his life and shared their memories. Paul's cousin, Albert Bildner, spent hours describing what life in the Shulman household was like. Paul's brother, Mark, as well as his wife, Peggy, and their

children, David Shulman and Judith Shulman Roth, provided pithy recollections of life with Paul. Ruth Halprin Kaslove—whose mother, Rose Halprin,
was Hadassah's president and friend of Paul's mother, Rebecca—explained
how she and Paul dashed the hopes of their Jewish "mothers" that the two
youngsters should make such a nice wonderful married couple; if only?

C. Douglas Tait, who retired as a captain in the Navy Medical Corps,
recalled the University of Virginia's Naval Reserve Officer Training Corps
(NROTC) program and Cadet Shulman. Larry Shaffer, one of Shulman's
roommates at the Naval Academy, remembered how long and hard Paul had
to study just to keep from "bilging out." Charles Sobel, also in Shulman's
class but in a different battalion, remembered Paul's features in *The Log.*
Years later, Sobel and his family, including son, Larry, would become regular visitors to the Shulman home in Haifa. Among others who recalled
the Naval Academy during the war years was Commander Jonathan Leff,
who earned his commission in the accelerated class before Paul. "Jonny"
Leff would later hook up with Kvarnit (Commander) Shulman in Israel and
serve as a gunnery instructor at the naval academy Shulman set up. Rear
Admiral Donald T. Poe, USN (Ret.), corresponding secretary of the Class of
1945 Alumni Association, added to my knowledge of his class (which also
graduated Wally Schirra, who became one of America's pioneering astro-
nauts). Much factual information about Midshipman Shulman's courses
of studies and his grade point average came from the academic archives,
courtesy of the Academy's Commander Rod Gibbons, who was then the
Academy's public affairs officer.

Many U.S. Navy ships have veterans' alumni associations. It was through
the veterans' Web site of the USS *Hunt* association that I found Bill Macy
and Don Steffins, members of the destroyer's first cruise, of 1944–45. I also
met USS *Hunt* officer Jim Wilson, who provided a look at the destroyer's first
deployment. Alan Kahn recalled Shulman's demeanor at the low end of the
table in the Wardroom. The veterans group Web site for the USS *Massey*
gave names of several men who served with and remembered Lieutenant (j.g.)
Shulman: enlisted men Ray Shilka and Carl Zinn and officers Rafael "Ray"
Mur and Martin Zenni.

It is after Lieutenant Shulman submitted his letter requesting to be released
from active duty in March 1947 that the paper trail to his life became diffi-
cult to follow. Books such as Teddy Kollek's *For Jerusalem: A Life* and Leonard
Slater's *The Pledge* give an overview of Haganah activities in the United
States after World War II. *Israel, The Way It Was,* by Haim Gershoni (aka
Hal Gershenow) provided a close-up look at how he and his volunteers and
Israeli shipyard workers put several of the derelict former Aliyah Bet refugee

vessels back in service as "warships" of the Israeli navy. At a more personal level, Marvin Broder, Dr. David Macarov, and Dr. Richard Rosenberg—each a former U.S. naval officer—filled me in on the work they did for the Haganah and their roles in helping to stand up the Israeli navy. Mimi Finard contributed to my understanding of the activities of her husband, Saunder, during and after Israel's War of Independence as well as Sandy's involvement with Paul Shulman in their company, National Engineering, Ltd.

Through an organization known as AVI—the American Veterans of Israel—I met, interviewed, or corresponded with several Americans who had volunteered to serve the cause of Zionism: David Baum; Dr. Jason Fenton, who heads up Machal West, which is similar to the AVI; Murray-Hana Greenfield; David Hanovice; Israel Kanot; Paul Kaye; Sam Klausner, the indefatigable former editor of the *AVI Bulletin*; Harold "Dov" Shugar; Philip Strauss; and Charles Weiss each contributed from his own unique memory of Paul Shulman. In the United Kingdom, Stanley Medicks, head of the United Kingdom and European section of World Machal, provided details about the Royal Navy's Palestine Patrol. Fritz "Freddy" Liebreich was generous in sharing his master's thesis about Great Britain and its fractious relationship with the Jewish Agency for Palestine as well as his observations about the Israeli leaders' fractious early attempts to manage their own affairs.

And the archives, and their amazing archivists! At the University of Florida, Gainesville, Dr. Ralph Lowenstein, professor emeritus and director of UFL's Journalism Department, has done yeoman service collecting and archiving the records and recollections of AVI members and other volunteers from abroad—the other Machal (Volunteers from Abroad). In Israel, Colonel David Teperson, director of the Machal Museum, continues to collect stories about the volunteers from Holland, South Africa, New Zealand, and Australia. Other help came from the archives at the U.S. Military Academy at West Point, New York, which holds the papers of the late Colonel David M. "Mickey" Marcus. At the National Archives in College Park, Maryland, archivist Sally Kuisel, a specialist in U.S. foreign affairs, and Barry Zerby, a specialist in modern U.S. Navy records, each helped to steer me to the archives' voluminous holdings. Eleanor Yadin, in the New York Public Library's Dorot Division of Jewish History, pointed me to a tape recording of the oral history that Paul Shulman did for the "North Americans in Israel" project sponsored by the Association of Americans and Canadians in Israel (AACI) and the American Jewish Committee (AJC). At the American-Jewish Historical Society, Susan Woodland, keeper of the Hadassah archives, helped me to understand the role that Rebecca Shulman played in her son's involvement with the Jewish Agency for Palestine as well as the work he would do to manage the reconstruction of the Hadassah Medical Center at Mount Scopus, Jerusalem. A special thanks goes to Representative Frank Pallone of New Jersey, whose letters to the Department of State helped get my Freedom of Information Act request acted upon in my lifetime.

How the Odyssey of This Book Was Launched and Evolved

What began as an afternoon's casual visit to a museum in Haifa, Israel, evolved into a six-year odyssey of research and writing, and more research, more writing, and rewriting. My wife, Judi, and I were in Israel in 1998 for the bar mitzvah of her great-nephew. Our day trip from Jerusalem to Haifa included a visit to the Clandestine Immigration and Naval Museum. This facility documents and re-creates the ordeal that scores of thousands of Jewish refugees endured as they were helped to flee Europe, in the hope that they could immigrate to Palestine—soon to be the state of Israel. The exhibits also document the heroic exploits of the Mossad le Aliyah Bet (Clandestine Immigration) and hundreds of volunteers who did everything possible to get the refugees to Palestine. The would-be immigrants were packed into barely seaworthy fishing vessels or giant, converted passenger liners and cargo ships that had to cross the Mediterranean Sea. Few of the vessels actually reached Palestine. Most were intercepted by Royal Navy warships, which were ordered by London to stop what the British government called the "illegal" immigration of the Jews. The Royal Navy towed the ships into Haifa harbor and left the derelicts to rust. Most of the refugees spent months or years in British-run internment camps on the islands of Cyprus and Mauritius, at least until the British quit its Mandatory administration of Palestine and Israel became a free nation.

At the Clandestine Immigration and Naval Museum I purchased *The Jews' Secret Fleet*, by Murray Greenfield and Joseph Hochstein. This remarkable book tells the story of the dozen or so refugee ships whose secret purchase had been funded by wealthy American Jewish business leaders and crewed in part by American volunteers. As I opened the lavishly illustrated work, I discovered that the foreword had been written by Paul Shulman. At the time, I thought that the story of an Annapolis man in the Israeli navy might make an interesting feature for *Naval History* magazine, published by the U.S. Naval Institute. When my research revealed that *nothing* had ever been written about Shulman, I immediately believed that his story deserved to be told in more than a feature article.

The Ablest Navigator is a narrative biography. It is also something of a sea story in that it attempts to re-create the time and place in which Paul Shulman operated. To give a sense of what the twenty-four-year-old Ensign Shulman, on a wildly heaving destroyer in the Pacific Ocean, must have gone through to keep the juice flowing in the USS *Hunt* during Typhoon Cobra, I called on published accounts and official U.S. Navy records. When Aluf Shulman led the brand-new Israeli navy in an attack against Egyptian warships, I started with the published (if somewhat inaccurate) account by author Samuel Katz of the raid. I then corroborated his version with official communiqués by the United Nations Truce Supervision Commission. In addition to these sources I called on the personal recollections of several American volunteers who *were* in on that raid: Murray Greenfield, Israel Kanot, Paul Kaye, Jon Leff, and Dov Shugar were witness to the Israeli naval commandos who sent the Egyptian navy's flagship to the bottom.

Telling Paul Shulman's story has been a challenge because his story does not fit easily into any clearly defined historical period. Shulman saw combat duty in the Pacific theater of operations during World War II, but his story is not about that campaign. The modern state of Israel is the subject of a seemingly unending outflow of books that try to explain this unique nation to the rest of the world. But Paul Shulman's story is not about that nation. Several well-researched books tell the history of today's IDF—the Israeli Defense Force—and how it emerged from its beginnings as the Haganah, the Jewish Agency's military force before Palestine became Israel. Because Israel's 1948 War of Independence (as well as six subsequent conflicts) was primarily a land war, there has been practically nothing published—in English—about the early years of Israel's navy and, in particular, about Paul Shulman's role in helping to launch it. Shulman's story does deserve to be told, and for a number of reasons: He was there at the beginning of the State of Israel; yet, the Haganah military leaders scorned and resented his contribution, his even *being* there. Even today the Israeli Ministry of Defense Web site does not acknowledge Aluf Shulman's contribution. In America today, the all-too-brief contribution of the late Colonel David M. "Mickey" Marcus—"accidentally" shot and killed while he was training Haganah units during Israel's War of Independence—is remembered by an annual memorial service at the U.S. Military Academy at West Point. Paul Shulman is honored with a window in the Naval Academy's Uriah Levy chapel.

How to Read *The Ablest Navigator*

With extensive, annotated chapter endnotes, a bibliography, and an index, *The Ablest Navigator* could be considered a scholarly work. It is, and it is more than that. Read it as an adventure story. Read it as the story of one man's fierce belief in an ideal—a Zionist-inspired Homeland for the world's displaced Jewish people—his people. Read it as Paul Shulman's determination to act on his ideals. As he wrote in the foreword to *The Jews' Secret Fleet*, "the men believed [that] direct action and personal involvement were morally imperative." Paul Shulman was there for it all; yet he felt denied the "thrill of victory" and recognition after the land he fought for became a nation he barely knew.

I would hope that *The Ablest Navigator* will be read as an adjunct, like a "navigational aid," to contemporary courses of study for American students of Israel's history. I hope that its thesis will spark questions and debate in and out of class because, you know, there is a saying about students of Jewish history. You get two of them to discuss an issue and you'll get three opinions. The final chapter, "The Pages of History," is intended as a précis to further readings about the nation that the European-Zionist-inspired land became during the nearly half-century that Paul Shulman called it his home. There are historians far more expert than I who have greater access to the voluminous Israeli government state archives that were declassified in the 1990s. Several of these so-called "new historians" are producing nuanced reinterpretations of Israel through lenses not so rose colored. But rather than have this work begin with an introductory chapter about Israel, without the reader knowing what or who the subject was about, I thought it wise to begin Paul Shulman's odyssey by recalling an action that marked the high point in his contribution to the new nation. Then, the course that the ablest navigator himself charted would provide markers to a view of the nation that he left when he died in 1994. This is why, at least as far as this story is concerned, the final chapter, "The Pages of History," stops in 1994.

PRELUDE
Hebrew Year 5708, 5 Iyar (1948, 14 May), 1600 Hours
Israel, Day One

A t one minute past four o'clock in the afternoon—the official end of the Saturday Sabbath—in the great auditorium of Tel Aviv's Museum, David Ben-Gurion rose at the center of the dais, amid other leaders of the Jewish Agency for Palestine. He gaveled the 250 guests into silence and began to speak. Eleven minutes later "the Lion" declared, "Accordingly, we, members of the People's Council, representatives of the Jewish Community of Eretz-Israel, and of the Zionist Movement, are here assembled on the day of the termination of the British Mandate over Eretz-Israel, and, by virtue of our natural and historic right and on the strength of the resolution of the UN General Assembly, hereby declare the establishment of a Jewish State in Eretz-Israel, to be known as the State of Israel."[1] The dignitaries erupted in a spontaneous singing of "Hatikvah," soon to be adopted as Israel's national anthem. On the streets outside, thousands of brand-new Israelis cheered, and then prepared to defend their new nation.

Chapter 1

TRUCE AND CONSEQUENCES

Paul, if you can sink them, shoot. If you can't, don't.
—DAVID BEN-GURION, FROM HIS WAR DIARY

I n the diffused half-light of dusk that spread across the Mediterranean Sea that Thursday, October 21, 1948, the two Israeli corvettes maneuvered closer in toward Gaza City. Lashed to the main deck of each corvette were two motorboats. The wood-hulled craft were seventeen feet long with a beam of six feet. Each was powered by a Ferrari marine engine, powerful enough to drive the speedboats at up to thirty knots. Israeli sailors stood at the davits, ready to lower the motorboats into the Mediterranean. Standing off a few hundred yards, another Israeli warship kept a radar eye on two Egyptian vessels anchored in Gaza bay. Farther out, a fourth Israeli vessel steamed slowly in circles to warn off any approaching enemy ships. Only a few hours before, at 1400 local time—two o'clock in the afternoon—the UN Truce Commission–brokered truce—the third such stand-down between Israeli and Arab forces since May 1948—had begun. Like the other truce periods, this one was ignored by Israeli and enemy forces.

On the bridge of one corvette, designated K-18 *Josiah Wedgwood*, was the squadron leader, an American who had graduated from the U.S. Naval Academy and had seen combat duty during World War II. Paul N. Shulman turned to his radio operator, another ex–U.S. Navy sailor. He ordered him to again contact the Israeli Defense Force High Command. "Get them to tell Ben-Gurion," Shulman urged, "Tell him that there are four of us and two of them."[1] Only static emerged from the war surplus army field radio; the attack would have to wait. The *Wedgwood* and three other Israeli ships had been shadowing the Egyptian warships for two days, and Paul Shulman was getting anxious.[2] He kept his binoculars trained on the two vessels. Israeli intelligence had identified one as a wood-hulled minesweeper. The larger vessel was a 1,440-ton sloop, the *Al Emir Farouq*. She was armed with a pair of three-inch cannons and several 20-mm antiaircraft guns.[3] More important, the warship had some five hundred soldiers embarked, waiting to go ashore to reinforce Egyptian ground units ringing Gaza City. Kvarnit Shulman paced. What was taking Ben-Gurion so long to give the order to attack?

In the six months since May 14, 1948, when David Ben-Gurion had proclaimed the State of Israel and was appointed prime minister of the provisional government, Israeli forces had chalked up impressive victories against five Arab armies that invaded Israel the day after the British Mandatory government quit Palestine. Indeed, Israel had done more than survive. The Arab invaders had not, as one Egyptian propagandist boasted in a radio broadcast, driven "the criminal Zionist bands into the sea."[4]

Ben-Gurion's Haganah-led Israeli Defense Force began with not more than 22,000 combatants. Most shouldered not much more than machine guns and homemade mortars. Only a few thousand of these combatants were in the highly trained Palmach Strike Force. Though outgunned, Israel's brigades repulsed the Syrian-Iraqi "Army of Liberation" that invaded Israel's Galilee region in the north. Jewish battalions had repulsed the British-trained Arab Legion that attacked from Trans-Jordan to the east. In the arid Negev region in the south, Israeli units pushed back the poorly led Egyptian units. The Jews, bitterly remembering the Arab blockade of Jerusalem months earlier, which came within days of starving its citizens into surrendering, were in no mood to give up even a square meter of hard-won ground.

UN Truce Commission observers in Gaza City reported: "SITUATION GAZA SO BAD SUPPLY BY SEA NECESSARY"[5] (capitals in original). The UN observers, however, were more concerned that Gaza's civilians would run out of food, water, and medical supplies. They seemed not overly bothered that the Egyptian warships waiting in the bay were evidence that Egypt was not observing the truce. Nor was Israel, for that matter. During an earlier truce, in July, the fledgling Israeli navy had thwarted an Egyptian troop carrier that was trying to land troops near Tel Aviv. Now, off the coast at Gaza, Paul Shulman waited for the order to attack. Finally, around 2030, *Wedgwood's* radio came to life. It was the voice of Ben-Gurion himself, speaking in English: "Paul, if you can sink them, shoot; if you can't, don't!"[6]

Word was passed to the other corvette, the K-20 *Haganah*. Both ships began moving slowly inshore toward Gaza City and the Egyptian warships. The corvettes' deck crews, which included several U.S. Navy veterans who had volunteered to serve Israel, lowered the motor torpedo boats into the water.[7] Each boat was armed with a 300-kilogram (650-pound) high-explosive warhead, the size of an oil drum, mounted in the bow. The fourth motorboat was unarmed; its mission was to recover the Israeli raiders from the sea. Into each boat climbed a specially trained commando, clad in a primitive, hand-made wet suit. Each boat driver eased the throttle forward. At half speed each steered toward their assigned targets at a 45-degree angle in the hope that they would not be spotted. They were. Guards on the *Al Emir Farouq*, alarmed by the roar of the motorboats' engines, switched on a searchlight and panned the water, looking for the attackers. Machine-gun fire from the sloop began to pockmark the dark waters. The Israeli ships returned fire with their 20-mm antiaircraft guns, which had been installed only weeks before. At three hundred meters out, the motorboats turned. Pushing the throttles all the way forward, each commando steered straight for its target. At the one-hundred-meter mark and traveling at top speed, each boat driver armed the warhead, locked the rudder, and then bailed out into the water. Each commando tightly clutched special gear designed to protect him against concussion from underwater explosions.

At about 2130, a dull orange explosion lit up the *Al Emir Farouq*. The Egyptian sloop began to settle. A minute later, a second motor-torpedo boat slammed into its hull and a bright orange mushroom lit up the sky. The ship broke in two and sank. The third motor-torpedo boat, locked on course and minus its driver, slammed into the minesweeper. It, too, exploded and sank. The driver of the fourth motorboat, scanning the waters lit by fires, picked up the commandos and returned them to the Israeli auxiliary ship. In addition to more than five hundred Egyptian soldiers who went down with the sloop, the Egyptian navy had lost its flagship. The Israeli naval squadron steamed back to its base at Haifa. The raid was supposed to have been a secret. A few days later, however, the English-language *Palestine Post* reported obliquely, "The Jewish vessel's anti-aircraft guns . . . poured fire into the enemy craft. The enemy was prevented from landing its cargo."[8] Nonetheless, within days, word of the Israeli navy's astonishing success was all over the streets and cafés. Foreign ears carried the news all the way to Cairo. At the time, Shulman probably was not much concerned with what Egypt thought of the action; it was only years later that he considered the possibility that it could have cost him his American civil rights and a huge fine and landed him in prison.

In a private ceremony at IDF headquarters, Ben-Gurion awarded Israel's highest military award to the commandos and their leader, Yochai Bin-Nun. A week later, on October 26, 1948, in a public ceremony at naval headquarters in Haifa, Ben-Gurion appointed Kvarnit Shulman to the position of commander in chief of the Israeli Naval Service.[9] He could now assume the title of Aluf, or admiral. Shulman was just twenty-six and a half years old. He would joke later that he was the first and only U.S. Navy officer he knew of to advance from lieutenant to admiral in three years.[10]

It would not be unrealistic to imagine a jubilant Paul Shulman looking down from Israeli naval headquarters atop Haifa's Mount Carmel as he considered the Israeli navy's success. The U.S. Naval Academy graduate had served with distinction on a U.S. Navy destroyer during World War II and survived a typhoon and kamikaze suicide aircraft attack. Now, he might well have wondered just how in the hell he had wound up "commanding" the Israeli navy, when very little in his life up to then had prepared him for this phase of his naval career.

Chapter 2

THE ABLEST NAVIGATOR

Stimulating conversation was required of us, as much as possible for
a young person.

—MARK SHULMAN, PAUL'S YOUNGER BROTHER

Paul Nachman Shulman was born in the borough of the Bronx on March
31, 1922. The federal census of 1930 shows that Herman and Rebecca
Shulman and their two children moved to the Borough of Queens, to
a modest house at 2422 Bayswater Avenue, in Far Rockaway. The Bayswater
section of "Far Rock" then—as it is today—was a quiet, safe neighborhood of
Conservative and Orthodox Jewish families.

Paul's younger brother, Mark, recalled how Paul was introduced to the
sea; well, at least to the quiet waters of Jamaica Bay. "Our Uncle Mo had a sailboat and liked to go sailing in the bay. Paul would frequently go out with him.
This was before a lot of navigation equipment. So, when Mo looked around
and didn't know where they were, my brother was told to swim ashore and find
out where they were. That was Paul's introduction to navigation."[1]

Paul's father, Herman, needed no help to see where he was or where
he needed to go. He was a graduate of Columbia University and Columbia
Law School, where he was an editor of the *Law Review*, a prestigious honor.
Herman and his college friend, Mortimer Hays, joined lawyer David Podell to
form the law firm Podell, Hays, & Shulman. Their office was at 39 Broadway,
right in the center of New York City's Wall Street financial canyons. The
partners focused on issues of corporate law. The firm and Shulman did well
enough in the 1930s to permit Herman to move his family from Far Rockaway
to a spacious apartment in Majestic Towers, a high-rise apartment building
along Central Park West at 90th street, in Manhattan's affluent Upper West
Side neighborhood. Their new home overlooked Central Park. Paul and
Mark were enrolled in the prestigious Columbia Grammar School, New York
City's oldest nonsectarian private elementary school. It was a pleasant, three-
block walk from their apartment.[2]

Paul Shulman spent his boyhood in the quiet Bayswater section of the Rockaway Peninsula, in the New York City borough of Queens. It was a safe neighborhood, where middle-class Jewish families could raise their children. PHOTO BY THE AUTHOR

Life at home was more than pleasant. Their mother, Rebecca, was by then a senior executive with Hadassah, the Women's Zionist Organization of America. "There was always some activity, some meeting going on," Mark Shulman recalled. "Our parents always had parties, but they never had time to socialize. Their only free time was weekends. So, we'd go to art galleries on Saturday afternoons."[3] Herman Shulman had an eye for art and was able to afford the works of up-and-coming French Impressionist and contemporary American artists long before their works were recognized for their artistic excellence and value as investments. Before long, Herman Shulman's art collection grew so extensive that some pieces had to be stacked against walls of the apartment.

In 1937 Podell, Hays, & Shulman gained a new client, the Loft Candy Company. Loft was trying to gain control of a soft drink company called Pepsi Cola by wresting control of its stock from owner Charles Guth. According to one friend of the Shulman family, David Podell and Morty Hays felt that Loft could not prevail. So they assigned the case to their junior partner, Herman Shulman. If Shulman's argument was not persuasive and Loft lost its bid to

Herman Shulman did well enough as a lawyer to move his family to a large apartment in Majestic Towers, overlooking Central Park along Manhattan's affluent Upper West Side neighborhood. *PHOTO BY THE AUTHOR*

acquire the stock, then Podell and Hays felt the fallout to the law firm's reputation would be minimal.[4] After a long and contentious court battle, Loft did prevail and took control of 91 percent of Pepsi's outstanding stock, or 237,500 shares. A year later, however, the law firm still had not been paid its legal fees, which, it claimed in court, were between four and five million dollars. The law firm sued Loft. After another protracted court battle, the Chancery Court awarded the law firm 13.5 percent of the shares that Loft had won in its suit. The bulk of the stock settlement went to Herman Shulman as his reward for winning the case. He was also appointed as a director of the new Pepsi Cola Company.

Paul was enrolled in DeWitt Clinton High School in September 1936. The high school was renowned for academic excellence, and its programs were like an academic petri dish for creative students. The high school's literary magazine, *The Magpie*, was highly regarded among New York City student publications for its creativity and quality of its students' writing. According to an assessment by the New Deal Network, "The [students'] depiction of teenage life—classrooms, love and friendship, and family—document[ed] the way in which they carried on their everyday lives in the face of economic uncertainty at home and growing militarism abroad."[5]

Students at DeWitt Clinton who contributed to *The Magpie* during the 1930s included writer James Baldwin, playwright Sydney "Paddy" Chayefsky, photographer Richard Avedon, and Seymour Krim, a writer and editor who would go on to chronicle the "Beat Generation" of the 1950s. There is no indication that Paul Shulman was among contributors to *The Magpie*. Still, along with his exposure at home to current events, it is not likely that he could have remained insulated from and not be aware of the mounting hostility toward Jewish people in America and abroad. Mark Shulman remembered that conversations around the dining table were always filled with events of the day, and his parents were always discussing the future of Zionism worldwide. "Stimulating conversation was required of us, as much as possible for a young person."[6]

Despite DeWitt Clinton's reputation for excellence, Paul's parents felt that it was important for their firstborn son to get not only a good education but also an education at the "right" school. Connecticut was home to many prestigious private preparatory schools—the Choate School, Kent, Hotchkiss, Loomis, and Cheshire among them. In the late 1930s, the Cheshire Academy was one of the few prep schools that publicly stated it did *not* consider a student's religious orientation as a factor in admission.[7]

Cheshire, Connecticut, is one hundred miles east of New York City. Socially and culturally the boarding school existed in a world a far remove from the energy and hustle of DeWitt Clinton. Student life at Cheshire was burnished by a patina of Old School ties, proms, and traditions passed down from one generation to the next. It is an educational institution whose graduates may feel assured of admission to an Ivy League college such as Brown, Columbia, Harvard, or Yale, places where their fathers and grandfathers studied. Notable Cheshire alumni include Gideon Welles, an early secretary of the Navy; J. Pierpont Morgan, financier, founder of the Morgan Guaranty Bank, and philanthropist; Fred Friendly, president of the Columbia Broadcasting System; and Robert Ludlum, the author.

At Cheshire, Paul Shulman did not excel academically, but he was good enough at sports to earn a place on the varsity tennis squad. He also served as assistant editor on the school newspaper, *The Academy Review*. He handled a variety of assignments such as a review of an art exhibit at the school library. As president of the Political Union, the students' debating club, young Shulman moderated a lively discussion: "Proposed: That in the event that Democracies should be losing, would the United States be justified entering the war on their behalf?" As moderator, Paul had to keep his opinions to himself. Nonetheless, in 1939 as the winds of war loomed on the horizon, it is likely that he would have argued that the United States should enter the war.

In June 1940 Herman and Rebecca Shulman drove to Cheshire to see their son receive his diploma. In *Rolling Stone*, the 1940 yearbook, young Shulman was remembered on its "Hall of Fame" page as the "least-appreciated" student. His yearbook photo showed a young man looking, without expression, off into the middle distance, as if unsure of the proper course he should set for his life. Next to his photo is a quote from Gibbon's *Decline and Fall of the Roman Empire*: "The winds and waves are always on the side of the ablest navigator." Paul's nickname was "The Admiral."

As much as Paul's father might have wanted to see his son follow him into Columbia University and a career in law, it was evident that Paul would do better at a college that would accept his average grades. He began to consider the Navy as the starting point of a career and held many discussions with his cousin, Albert Bildner. Bildner, a lieutenant in the Naval Reserve, was serving on active duty at the U.S. Navy's submarine base in New London, Connecticut. "Paul would pepper me with questions about the Naval Reserve and the submarine service," Bildner recalled. "I am proud of [my] influence in getting Paul to go into the Navy."[8]

Paul was accepted by the University of Virginia at Charlottesville. He enrolled there in part because it was among the earliest in the nation to offer the Naval Reserve Officer Training Corps preparatory course. One of Paul's classmates recalled that the course was "a strange new world of red tape, nomenclature, and ways of the sea. Seamanship became a maze of bowsprits, fantails, sternposts and quarterdecks."[9] Some UVA students saw NROTC as a quick-and-easy route to Officers' Candidate School and a Naval Reserve commission. Paul aimed higher: He saw the NROTC as a way to improve his chance of getting into the U.S. Naval Academy at Annapolis. A half-century later, he recalled, "It was the first year of the program [at UVA]. The top five cadets were asked if they would accept commissions [sic] to the Naval Academy."[10]

Shulman was not among the top five NROTC students in his class. Still, he probably did not worry that his less-than-stellar grades at UVA would keep him from getting into the Naval Academy. He knew, for instance, that each member of Congress could make up to five appointments each year.[11] Paul had hoped for an appointment from his father's friend, Senator Robert F. Wagner, a Republican from New York. The best that Senator Wagner could do that year was to list Shulman as a second alternate. By March 1941 Paul had to be content with a nomination from Representative Joseph Clark Baldwin, a Republican from New York City's Seventeenth Congressional District. This is the so-called "Silk Stocking" district that encompassed Manhattan's afflu- ent and fashionable Upper West Side neighborhood. Representative Baldwin had just been appointed to Congress to fill the term of his predecessor, who had died in office. Baldwin probably had barely settled into office when he was asked to nominate Paul.[12]

That Shulman was accepted into the Naval Academy is somewhat sur- prising. It is not because his University of Virginia grades were just average or that he had received a congressional nomination. Academy class quotas were established a year in advance. Each year the Academy received several thou- sand applications for the approximate 1,000 openings. Of those 1,000 seats in any given year, some 200 appointments were awarded to enlisted noncom- missioned officers who applied while on active duty with the fleet. Shulman had completed only two of three semesters at the University of Virginia by March 1941. As late as July 7 the UVA registrar still had not sent Shulman's final grades to Annapolis, and Paul was due to report for a physical exam two weeks later. Yet, on July 16 Shulman presented himself for physical exam and was found qualified. On July 24 he took the oath of office and was appointed a midshipman.[13]

During his high school years Paul had been friendly with Ruth Halprin, daughter of Rose Halprin, then the president of Hadassah. She and Rebecca Shulman were friends. According to Ruth Halprin Kaslove, the two Jewish mothers apparently saw the potential for a match between their children. Years later, Ruth Kaslove recalled that, unfortunately for their mothers' hopes, she was already seeing someone. Ruth knew, anyway, that Paul had met and was dating Rose Saxl, whom he met at a party at UVA. Rose Saxl came from Woodside, a middle-class section of Queens, a borough in New York City. She was the daughter of Sidney and Carmela Saxl, who, among other interests, owned a small building in Manhattan, which had street-level shops and apart- ments on the second and third floors.

The Shulman family had rented houses for several summers in Westport, a town along the Connecticut shore that was favored by artists and writers. In

In the summer of 1941 Herman Shulman bought a historic house in an exclusive, woodsy section of Stamford, Connecticut, to serve as the family's summer home. The house was photographed in 2005 by permission of the current owner. *PHOTO BY THE AUTHOR*

July 1941 Herman Shulman purchased a stately summer home in an exclusive section of nearby Stamford, Connecticut. Jazz clarinetist Benny Goodman and violinist Yasha Heifetz had homes in the area. Part of the Shulman structure, built in the eighteenth century, is thought to have been a way station along the "Underground Railway" escape route used by slaves. The house, set deep in the woods along a tree-lined country lane, had a cottage for a live-in house-keeping staff, two tennis courts, and an in-ground swimming pool. For Paul, the family's country home was an ideal place for a fast-paced game of tennis or a late-night frolic in the pool with Rose. But that summer of 1941 would be the last carefree period for "the ablest navigator."

Chapter 3

SHULMAN'S FIGHTING SHIPS

I nicknamed him "Hap" for happy, because he was always so serious about everything.

—Commander Larry Shaffer, USN (Ret.),
Shulman classmate at Annapolis

Before he arrived at the Naval Academy, Paul Shulman might have thought he had a miniscule advantage in having taken the Naval Reserve Officer Corps training preparatory course at the University of Virginia. His year at Charlottesville was scant preparation for the Naval Academy's plebe summer. Like the Marine Corps' legendary boot camp at Parris Island, plebe summer at Annapolis is not for the faint of heart. The intense program is designed to turn plebes—plebians: common men—into officers and gentlemen who can embody the Navy's character values of duty and honor. It doesn't take long for instructors and upperclassmen to spot and disqualify those who cannot meet the Navy's high standards.

Also, the almost collegial atmosphere that pervaded "the Yard" during the interwar years between World War I and World War II had all but disappeared. In 1940 the War Department told the Department of the Navy it would need to produce more officers trained and qualified to man the warships. The Navy Department directed the Academy to increase class sizes to more than 1,000 midshipmen and compress its four-year program into three years. Courses on world politics and different cultures were introduced into the curricula. Where midshipmen once had a choice of studying French or Spanish, in 1940 they could now also choose among Russian, Portuguese, German, and Japanese.

The need for increased awareness of the world's rapidly changing geo-political climate became starkly evident after December 7, 1941, following the Japanese attack on the U.S. naval base at Pearl Harbor, Hawaii. The Academy immediately went on a heightened security alert. Navy patrol craft steamed into Chesapeake Bay to scout for enemy submarines they feared

Like all students at the U.S. Naval Academy Paul Shulman discovered that "plebe" summer was not for the faint of heart, but was designed to produce officers and gentlemen who would embody the Navy's values of duty and honor to country.
U.S. NAVAL ACADEMY NIMITZ LIBRARY SPECIAL COLLECTIONS

might try to sneak upriver to attack the Academy.[1] The attack at Pearl Harbor even affected a football game. "The Washington Redskins were playing the Philadelphia Eagles that day," recalled another member of the accelerated class of 1945. "Washington pulled a 20 to 14 victory over Philadelphia, but no one cheered. We heard they stopped the game to pull senior officers out of the stands to report for duty."[2] Jonathan Leff, in the class ahead of Shulman's, recalled, "I was lying in my bunk, listening to [the] football game. The radio stopped. Then the announcer told of the attack on Pearl Harbor. Immediately the watch section was mobilized. We were issued .45-calibre pistols—with live ammunition. Our mission was to protect Bancroft hall from a Japanese attack."[3] The Academy canceled home leaves for most midshipmen over the 1941 Christmas break, but Paul was able to get a week's leave to see his family. He was also eager to see Rose Saxl, whom he had been dating since they had met the year before at the University of Virginia. While at home, Midshipman Shulman was introduced to a person who would have a dramatic, life-altering impact on his career as a future U.S. Navy officer: Among the houseguests was his mother's close friend, David Ben-Gurion, then chairman of the executive committee of the Jewish Agency for Palestine and leader of its voluntary military organization, the Haganah. In his oral history, Paul recalled: "Ben-Gurion was a guest in our home. He said that he hoped—was glad to see that Jewish boys were studying to be naval officers, and that [Israel] would need them some day in the Israeli navy. I said to him: 'I hope you had a fine navy because I was planning to spend my life in the regular American navy.'"[4]

The Naval Academy's regimen—the order, the formal training structure, the traditions and rituals—assumed a new importance for Shulman. It made sense that there was a proper way—the Navy way—to pack a seabag full of uniforms. There was a reason to learn marlinspike seamanship and knot tying. Close-order military drills and formations had a purpose. All helped to develop the leadership attributes of a naval officer. As a first-year midshipman, Shulman had to commit to memory an encyclopedia of naval history and trivia. He had to be ready to shout it out for those unexpected, up-close-and-personal moments when an upperclassman would order the plebe to "Sound off, Mister!" The underclassman would stop in his tracks, "brace up" (stand at rigid attention), then shout out his name and serial number. He would then be peppered with questions spat full force directly into his face by the upperclassman: "What were Perry's words?" "Where did Lawrence fight?" "Who is Tecumseh?" "What is a gadget?" This badgering, or "running," in yard slang, served a purpose: It taught the midshipman to be able to respond quickly and accurately to commands, and not become flustered. It was an in-your-face application of a basic rule: He who would command must first learn to obey.

During his senior year at the Cheshire Academy, Paul had been known as "The Admiral." Now, as a fourth classman at the Naval Academy, making admiral was the furthest thing from the mind of Midshipman Shulman. His primary concern was survival—mental and physical survival. He would learn to adapt to the six-day-a-week training schedule that began at 0615 and ended at 2230. If Shulman was not in class in Dahlgren, Luce, and other

Future U.S. Navy and Marine Corps warfighters jammed and crammed in the U.S. Naval Academy library in Mahan Hall. *U.S. NAVAL ACADEMY NIMITZ LIBRARY SPECIAL COLLECTIONS*

halls of learning, studying gunnery, navigation, seamanship (or "seamo"), and physics ("skinny"), as well as propulsion and electrical engineering ("steam" and "juice"), he was in the library at Mahan until taps and lights out. While marching to class or exams with his company, he might throw pennies at the bronze statue of the Indian chief, Tecumseh, hoping to land one in the chief's quiver. The replica figurehead of the Continental navy's sailing frigate, the USS *Delaware*, was also known as the "god of two-point-five." Otherwise logical and practical midshipmen believed that landing a penny in Tecumseh's quiver would somehow help them keep their grades at 2.5 or higher (out of a possible 4.0) and keep them from "bilging out" of the Academy. During his three years on the Yard, Midshipman Shulman would appeal often to the Indian chief.[5] Paul Shulman's aim might have been off, or maybe he didn't contribute enough to the tradition, because he earned below a 2.5 grade in electrical engineering and had to make up that and other deficiencies in math through reexamination.

In his youngster (second) year, Shulman was assigned to a four-person room in Bancroft Hall. Roommate Larry Shaffer recalled, "He was pretty serious most of the time, so I nicknamed him 'Hap,' for happy, because he was always so serious." Shaffer once urged Paul to take a break one Saturday evening a few days before exams, to take in a jazz concert that featured Benny Goodman, part of a Coca-Cola concert series. "I don't know whether it was because Paul owned some Pepsi stock, or because of the upcoming exams, but he wouldn't go. He thought that was wrong."[6]

Fourth classmen were not permitted to have visits from fiancées or girlfriends, who were known as "drags." The few midshipmen who married against regulations while at the Academy were dismissed if caught. Still, many upperclassmen had "wives." Wives were roommates who were responsible for order and cleanliness of their quarters. Dormitory rooms always had to be prepared for a surprise inspection. Blankets had to be tucked in a certain way. Books were arranged in a particular order on study tables. The midshipmen always had to be ready, should an upperclassman pull a surprise inspection. If the inspection revealed the dreaded "unseen dirt," the midshipmen could not earn a perfect score on the inspection, no matter how hard they worked to clean their spaces. "Above the door we had a sign that listed the person in charge," Larry Shaffer recalled. "Paul was in charge of cleanup, but I usually did most of the tidying up, at least until I got tired of it. I told Paul that he had to do it. Well, he didn't, and he got 'put on the pap' (reported to an upperclassman) for having a disorderly room."[7]

Having a disorderly room may have been less important to Shulman than trying not to "bilge out." He put in long hours at his studies but his grades seldom rose above 3.0. He may also have been affected by an unsettling undercurrent that coursed below the surface of life on the Yard: a distinct White Anglo-Saxon-Protestant, reverse "Our Crowd" mentality at Annapolis.[8] The fifty Jewish midshipmen in the class of 1945 were probably aware of it, but there wasn't much they could do about it. The overt anti-Semitism that had stained the Academy's reputation in the early 1930s had become muted by the time Shulman entered. The administration and instructors were supposed to be at least neutral to a midshipman's ethnic and religious heritage, but there was no accommodation for the Jewish Sabbath: Saturday was just another day of instruction. Yet, attendance at chapel on Sunday morning was mandatory for all. Midshipmen could attend either a Catholic service or a nonsectarian (though decidedly Protestant) service on the Yard. Those Jews who wanted to attend their own service were obliged to form a "church party," and march as a group to a Conservative synagogue outside the Academy. According to a 2002 master's thesis submitted by Midshipman Joel Holwitt: "Although the Navy did not oppose Judaism, the Naval Academy infrastructure did very little to encourage its religious inclusion."[9]

Paul Shulman did not consider himself to be an observant Jew in that he attended Synagogue on a regular basis. Rather, like his family, he saw himself more of a "secular" Jew who upheld Jewish traditions and observed the High Holy days of Passover and Rosh Hashanah.[10] At Annapolis, he was not eager to call attention to his heritage. Yet he was aware of ignorance of and an anti-Jewish bias of life at Annapolis. How, for example, could he explain to a midshipman from, say, North Dakota who'd grown up as a Lutheran, the fear and dread that Jews around the world felt on the anniversary of Kristallnacht, the Nazi's November 1938 destruction of synagogues throughout Germany?

To whatever degree these issues were important to Shulman they were a far remove from matters closer at hand: learning how to fight a naval war. Leading up to and during the first years of World War II, before the United States took an active role, the Navy's war-fighting doctrine was dominated by "battleship" admirals. These were the "blue water" strategists who planned massive set-piece battles with enemy fleets on the high seas. Shulman's 1942 summer cruise was on board the battleship USS *Arkansas* (BB-33). The old battlewagon had been commissioned in 1910 but by the 1940s was being used as a training platform. While on board Shulman learned to load and fire 20- and 40-mm antiaircraft guns, handle torpedo launchers, work in the combat information center, direct fire control, how to navigate and plot a course, how to take the helm, and how to take evasive maneuvers. He stood watches on the bridge and sweated alongside the "snipes" in the engine rooms.

During the summer of 1943, between his youngster and first-class year, Shulman passed up his annual leave. Instead, he requested a training assignment at the U.S. Navy's submarine base in New London, Connecticut. His cousin, Lieutenant Albert Bildner, was stationed there. Paul thought that this extra duty might help improve his chances of getting into the submarine service. In August Paul went aboard the SS-69, a World War I–era submarine used for training. His effort earned him an "attaboy"; that is, a letter of commendation from the submarine's commanding officer: "You displayed much interest, initiatives, and good judgment in learning the ship. . . . The Commanding Officer . . . believes you will do well in the submarine service, should you choose that branch."[11]

Back at the Yard, Shulman and Shaffer began to clip news reports from the *Washington Post, Baltimore Sun,* and other publications about innovations in the Navy. They compiled this material into feature articles for *The Log,* the Academy's student publication. Dubbed "Shulman's Fighting Ships," these features, illustrated with official Navy photographs, were filled with vivid descriptions about the Navy during war. In "Cruiser Duty," he wrote, "it must be remembered that during war no promotional examinations are given. Many new officers report to a ship with a cruise box full of books. This is not necessary." In another column, Shulman offered the following advice: "The new JO (junior officer) can best learn his duties by keeping his eyes and ears open, by hard work and application." Another feature offered the following wise counsel: "Officers country is serviced by room boys [who] should not be sent on personal errands too often."[12]

"Shulman's Fighting Ships" in The Log's Professional Notes section became popular and was widely discussed by students and instructors. Shulman wrote about the Navy's newest "aerial weapon," the Curtiss SB2C Helldiver torpedo dive-bomber. In this feature, "What Is Ahead for the U.S. Navy," he speculated on the increased role of land-based and carrier-based planes in the attacks on Japanese-held islands in the Pacific.[13] Wrapping up his stint for The Log's Professional Notes, Shulman concluded: "The same [Navy] task forces that now are in the war to secure the peace will help maintain it. The navy will be shown . . . as a symbol of national strength and potential power." When he turned over Professional Notes to his successor, Shulman was praised for his writing: "Paul's task . . . has been a demanding one . . . requiring a high degree of factual accuracy."[14] Shulman also made up academic deficiencies in math and engineering.[15]

June Week at Annapolis was filled with ceremony. While the Navy band played, the battalions marched in formation along Worden Field as they passed in review. During the graduation ceremonies, each midshipman crossed the rostrum of Dahlgren Hall to receive his diploma and commission as an ensign in the U.S. Navy or second lieutenant in the U.S. Marine Corps. After the last midshipman crossed the stage, the entire class hurled their covers— their uniform hats—into the air. Then, following tradition, many a new officer headed to Lover's Lane, to ask his "o-a-o" (one-and-only) sweetheart to pin on his ensign's bars. On June 7, 1944, Rose Saxl played her part in carrying on the Navy tradition. Lover's Lane was also the place where some new officers proposed marriage to their o-a-o. Paul Shulman was probably in a better financial position to marry than most of his shipmates. On top of an ensign's annual salary of $1,800 plus an allowance for subsistence, he could count on regular dividend checks from the Pepsi Cola stock that his father had put in trust for him until he reached the age of twenty-one.

There were, however, a few obstacles standing in the way of his hope of marrying right after graduation. There was a war on, of course, but by June 1944, there was almost a giddy hope for an Allied victory that swept America. Newspapers and radio broadcasts reported one German and Japanese defeat after another. Still, no one knew how much longer World War II would go on. And who could say who would live and who would die? Shulman felt that he and Rose would have to put wedding plans on hold for the duration of the war.

Ensign Shulman received his assignment: the destroyer USS *Hunt* (DD-674), then operating with the mighty U.S. Pacific fleet. Before he could report for duty, Shulman and half of the accelerated class of 1944 were sent on Temporary Duty for Instruction. Shulman was selected for four weeks of preflight training at the Naval Air Station in Jacksonville, Florida. The course was designed to make officers familiar with the basics of carrier-based aircraft and aerial gunnery and to see if any had the right stuff to be a Navy pilot. The students went on training flights as observers to see a torpedo-armed dive-bomber in action against a target. Ensign Jonathan Leff, in the Academy class ahead of Shulman, had been through preflight aviation training, and recalled that "duty at N-A-S Jax . . . was like a country club," compared to the highly structured regimen at the Naval Academy. Following his stint at Jacksonville, Shulman was able to take thirty days of leave, which he split between his parents' apartment in New York City and the family's country home in Stamford, Connecticut. Then, he headed west, to meet up with the USS *Hunt*.

Chapter 4

ON THE *HUNT*

We considered Paul a rather quiet fellow, but it was clear he did not lack courage.

—Alan Kahn, Lt., USNR (Ret.), torpedo officer, USS *Hunt*

While on temporary duty under instruction at the Jacksonville, Florida, Naval Air Station, Ensign Shulman's focus had to be on learning the intricacies of the Helldiver's optimal dive speed and proper glide path to enable the dive-bomber to attack enemy warships. Paul Shulman probably had little time to focus on the attack that American Zionist groups were mounting against the administration of President Franklin D. Roosevelt.

Paul was well aware, of course, that his parents, Herman and Rebecca, had become outspoken activists for the Zionists' cause. In March 1943 a coalition of Zionist, religious, labor, and peace organizations, known as the American Jewish Conference, held a "Stop Hitler Now" rally at Madison Square Garden in New York City. Herman Shulman introduced the keynote speaker, his friend, Rabbi Stephen S. Wise, president of the American Jewish Congress. To the 20,000 people packed into the Garden and another 50,000 outside listening on loudspeakers, Herman Shulman declared, "Months have passed since the United Nations [denounced] the unspeakable atrocities of the Nazis against the Jews, [but] nothing has been done as yet."[1] In October 1943 Rebecca Shulman, by then national vice president of Hadassah, delivered the keynote address at Hadassah's national convention. She called on the United States to honor the 1917 Balfour Declaration and to denounce the 1939 White Paper.[2] In February 1944 Herman Shulman was among a delegation of influential Zionist activists who testified before the House Committee on Foreign Affairs. The committee was then preparing "Resolutions Relative to the Jewish National Home in Palestine." Shulman called on the committee to have President Roosevelt join with more than fifty other world leaders in reaffirming Great Britain's 1917 Balfour Declaration.[3]

With his leave up, Ensign Shulman prepared to report for duty on board the USS *Hunt*. If a ship had an urgent need to fill a particular officer billet (position), then the Navy could authorize air travel. Otherwise, it could take weeks for an officer to reach his duty station. Apparently, the *Hunt* was not desperate for an assistant engineering officer. Shulman arrived in San Francisco, then caught a Navy transport steaming west to Pearl Harbor, Hawaii. There, he caught another ship bound for the U.S. base on the island of Guam. Only months before, the largest of the Marianas Islands had been recaptured from the Japanese, who had held the U.S. territory since 1941. At Guam Shulman got his first look at the devastation caused as a result of the two-month-long assault by U.S. Marines to retake the island. Guam was only a stopover for Ensign Shulman; he was there "FFT"—For Further Transfer—to his ship. The USS *Hunt* was then at the giant U.S. naval supply base at Ulithi atoll in the Caroline Islands. From Guam, Shulman got a hop on one of the military aircraft that made the regular 360-mile run to Ulithi, carrying "pax and sacks"— passengers and cargo.

From the air Ulithi looked like an eruption of pimples on the smooth complexion of an endless sea. The atoll's importance lay in its location: only 900 miles from the Japanese fortress on the island of Iwo Jima, and 1,200 miles from Japanese forces dug into the home island of Okinawa. The U.S. Navy's construction battalions—the Seabees—had transformed the low-lying Ulithi atoll into the Navy's largest self-contained forward-operating base in the Pacific theater of operations.

By the time Shulman reached his ship in November 1944 the destroyer had taken part in several major naval actions. The new ensign could not help but be impressed by the rows of campaign ribbons painted on the wings of the ship's bridge. The destroyer had taken part in the Marshall Islands campaign, the invasion of Hollandia in Dutch New Guinea, and the "Marianas Turkey Shoot" during the battle of the Philippine Sea in June 1944. Along with three other destroyers, she was tied up to a tender—a supply and repair ship. As Ensign Shulman crossed the gangway to the quarterdeck on November 9, he called out the traditional, "Request permission to come aboard!" He first saluted the ensign—the American flag flying at the ship's stern—then he saluted the ship's skipper, Commander Halford Knoertzer. As a lieutenant, Knoertzer had been one of Cadet Shulman's NROTC instructors at the University of Virginia. Except for that moment of familiarity, however, Ensign Shulman began as every junior officer did: at the bottom of the pecking order in the officers' wardroom.

All Navy ships, from patrol craft to battleships and aircraft carriers, are made up of several communities. Whereas land-based neighborhoods might be defined by a streetscape or the socioeconomic texture of its residents, a ship's communities are defined by rank as well as job description and location. In the small town inhabited by some 350 men that made up the USS *Hunt*'s crew, its commanding officer was the "mayor," and the executive officer, also known as "the exec" or "XO," was township manager. Senior officers were in charge of divisions such as communications, deck, supply, and engineering. Commissioned and warrant officers were addressed as "Mister." Senior non-commissioned officers were called "Chief." Those lesser-ranked than pay grade E-7 were addressed as "Petty Officer (Smith)." Officers' Country was off limits to enlisted personnel except for calls on official business. Officers slept in staterooms. They dined in the wardroom, where Filipino and "colored" stewards served meals on heavy china from nickel-plated tureens. (In an emergency the wardroom could serve as a medical treatment center, with the dining table doubling as an operating platform.) The chiefs had their own quarters, and separate chiefs' mess. The enlisted crew bunked with others from their division in sleeping "compartments." On the "mess deck," they ate "chow" dished out on metal trays.[4]

On a *Fletcher*-class destroyer like the USS *Hunt*, the radio operators, the "sparks," and the combat information teams worked one or two levels above the main deck, in the air conditioned "radio shack" and in the combat information center (CIC). These guys felt way above other ratings on board the ship because without their expertise the ship would not be able to communicate or to defend itself, attack, navigate, and know where it was and should be. The engineers, two and three levels below the main deck, felt equally superior: all the communications in the world didn't mean a thing if the "snipes" and "boiler tenders" didn't make the power that drove the ship, or evaporate the seawater into freshwater for hot showers and "joe," the coffee that was the real fuel that kept the crew going. The gunner's mates, part of the deck division, simply could not be bothered with such petty distinctions. In their view the ship's *sole* purpose was to serve as a platform for them to do their job: fire their guns at enemy shore installations, shoot down enemy aircraft, and sink enemy ships.

Back at the Naval Academy, in one of his Professional Notes columns, Midshipman Shulman had cautioned new officers reporting to the fleet not to bring textbooks with them, as they would not be needed. Shulman now saw the wisdom of his words and accepted a shipboard reality check: Yes, he was in officer in charge of E-division, the "lighting gang" that took care of the ship's 110-volt system, and the "power gang" that handled the destroyer's 440-volt direct current operating system.[5] However, he relied on the department's experienced and long-serving chiefs to get things done: They knew the ship's systems inside and out, and they knew the strengths of the guys in the division.

Ensign Shulman was also assigned several collateral duties, including running the movie projector in the wardroom. He was so new that the ensign's bars on his khaki uniform shirt collars had not had time to tarnish. Yet, his rank, "ensign, United States *Navy*" carried a certain cachet among the ship's naval reserve officers serving on active duty. Among themselves the reservists might sometime express disdain for a certain type of Academy graduate by calling him a "ring-knocker." This is because some Annapolis men liked to subtly call attention to their pedigree by occasionally knocking their Academy class ring on a hard surface. Paul Shulman was not like that; he seemed forged from different metal.

"Paul seemed to be a very serious young man," recalled Alan Kahn, the ship's torpedo officer. "The rest of us [reserve officers] were a fairly light-hearted bunch." Kahn wrote that Shulman had a sense of the seriousness of his duties. "Paul was [officer of the deck] on duty at the quarterdeck one day.[6] A man crossing the gangway from the next ship over . . . fell into the water between the ships. Paul saw the incident . . . and jumped overboard to try to save the man. Paul came into the wardroom during lunch, soaking wet, to report the incident to the captain. We considered Paul a rather quiet fellow, but it was clear he did not lack courage."[7] Shulman was unable to reach the man, but divers were able to recover the sailor's body.

By some accounts, Shulman was not the most outgoing of officers. With the men of E-division he was fair, but he required their strict adherence to "Navy regs" and insisted that his men observe Navy protocol and etiquette. He was similarly buttoned up with his peers in the wardroom. Still, he and Lieutenant James Wilson, the USS *Hunt*'s communications officer, seemed to find some common ground. "I knew of Paul's commitment to Zionism and a homeland in Israel for the Jews, but it was not something he talked about openly."[8]

Only a month after Shulman reported aboard, in December 1944, his courage and engineering skills and those of E-division were tested during Typhoon Cobra. This was the immense storm that caused the deadliest weather-related, at-sea U.S. naval disaster in more than a half century. The USS *Hunt* was part of a task force that was one component of Admiral William F. "Bull" Halsey's Third Fleet. The destroyer's primary mission was to screen and protect the battleships and aircraft carriers of the task force from enemy attacks from the sea and air and to take part in naval bombardments of Japanese warships and their island bases. The task force was about three hundred miles east of Luzon Island in the Philippine Sea after three days of attacks on Japanese positions. Admiral Halsey wanted to catch and attack a fleeing Japanese naval force.

However, many of his ships were very low on fuel. With their fuel tanks almost empty, the destroyers rode high in the water.

Despite warnings that severe weather was heading his way, Admiral Halsey stayed the course and ordered his ships to refuel. Some vessels lined up to come along side the "oilers"—the sea-going tanker ships—for the always-difficult refueling at sea. The USS *Hunt* and the destroyer USS *Spence* came along opposite sides of the battleship USS *New Jersey* to take on fuel. Winds were gusting to seventy knots per hour. Froth-whipped waves were cresting fifty feet in height. The *Hunt* was able to take on several thousand gallons of fuel. USS *Spence* took on only 1,000 gallons before thrashing seas tore apart the hose connection. Other ships were also having a rough time taking on fuel. This would have a disastrous effect on their ability to survive the typhoon. Riding too high in the water, they began to heel over up to 65 degrees from vertical. Some ships pumped seawater into their fuel tanks in the hope that this ballast would let the hull ride lower in the water. Each time the winds and waves caused the ships to heel over, tons of seawater poured down the stacks and vents into the engine spaces of the ships. This caused massive electrical short circuits, blackouts, and loss of power.

Dominic Legato, a gunner's mate on the USS *Hunt*, described the fury of the storm. "At 2130 a loud rumble and crashing sound is heard as a giant wave breaks [over] our bow and crashes full force against number one gun [mount]. We begin to ship [leak] water into the Chiefs' quarters. The repair crews take an hour and a half to stop the water. The whole side of the gun shield was pounded in as if by a super-human fist!"[9]

Up on the bridge Commander Knoertzer navigated his ship through the maelstrom. By late on December 19 the typhoon had passed on its way, but not before leaving death and destruction in its wake. The destroyers *Spence*, *Hull*, and *Monahan* had capsized and sunk with a loss of nearly eight hundred lives. The task force's aircraft carriers lost nearly 150 fighter planes. Many had broken loose from their moorings on the flight deck or below on the hangar deck. They crashed into other aircraft, causing fires and explosions.[10]

Three months later, on the morning of March 19, 1945, the task force was operating close to the Japanese home islands. Just after breakfast, the carrier USS *Franklin* (CV-13) was hit by a bomb dropped from a Japanese plane. Massive explosions and fires erupted all over the carrier, causing it to list. Hundreds of men were killed or blown overboard or jumped from the slanting deck to save their lives. Several ships, including the USS *Hunt*, moved in to recover survivors. Ensign Shulman helped to direct the crew in rescue efforts. The ship's whaleboat and its gig (captain's boat) picked up many sailors trying to stay afloat in the oil-covered waters. Several crewmembers dived into the water to help the injured get on board. The USS *Hunt* alone saved 426 of the aircraft carrier's crew. In his after-action report, Commander Knoertzer stated: "Too much praise cannot be given to the officers and men. Many men were outstanding, but the feeling of oneness came over the crew and it has remained."[11] The USS *Franklin*'s commanding officer sent a formal letter of appreciation to the commanding officers and crews of the ships for their heroic rescue efforts. The letters came with a "Bravo Zulu"—well done—along with the Navy's traditional thanks for an action well done: gallons of fresh ice cream.[12]

The USS *Hunt* put into the repair facility at Ulithi on March 25, 1945, for a much-needed overhaul, and R & R for the crew. There wasn't much rest or recreation to speak of. On Mog-Mog, the smallest of the habitable islands, Seabees had built a recreation center and three social clubs. Each club was cordoned off from the others by barbed wire fences. This was to prevent "fraternization"—commissioned officers and enlisted men socializing together. In the E-M club, each man was limited to two cans of "three-point-two"— beer with only 3.2-percent alcohol, sarcastically called "near beer." Chief petty officers had a separate club. Warrant and commissioned officers drank in the "O-Club." On Mog-Mog this was an open-sided shed with a thatched palm frond roof. The club manager at Ulithi during the war described the mood in the clubs: "The enlisted men were probably the happiest. They finished their beers then played ball or went swimming. The chiefs and warrant officers, mostly older men, were very quiet, almost contemplative. The officers, well liquored up, were quarrelsome. One explanation is that they knew what lay ahead for the men they would lead into battle."[13]

It is doubtful that Paul Shulman was among those officers who became quarrelsome. For one thing, he didn't drink. More likely, he would have found a quiet place where he could go to try and figure out what this war was all about, and what he was doing in it. While at Ulithi, Shulman marked his twenty-fourth birthday on March 31. Two days earlier Jews around the world commemorated Passover with its traditional seder, or supper. Food items on the seder plate represent the biblical salvation and liberation of Jewish slaves from the pharaoh's bondage in ancient Egypt. At Ulithi, the U.S. Navy did not have time for Passover. The Navy had the Japs to deal with. For Shulman, having to pass up Passover while on a flyspeck atoll in the Pacific Ocean must have felt like a bizarre form of personal bondage.

Following its overhaul the destroyer rejoined Admiral Halsey's forces and took up station as a radar picket ship during the massive invasion of Okinawa. It was there that a Japanese kamikaze (divine wind) suicide plane took aim at the ship. Lieutenant Jim Wilson recalled that the ship's gunners had pretty much shot up the diving Japanese plane and its pilot. "He may have been dying or dead when his Zero airplane struck the destroyer. The result was that instead of reaching its aiming point, the plane passed between the forward stack and the mast. Up in C-I-C the lights and radars went out."[14] Shulman and E-division worked around the clock to restore power and communications to the destroyer.

Shulman and the entire crew got good news on May fifth: Hitler was dead! The Nazis had surrendered! The war in Europe was over! In June 1945 the USS *Hunt* got more good news, and some bad news. The destroyer was being returned to San Francisco for a complete overhaul. The bad news was that she was to be included in the naval task force that would support a massive Allied invasion of Japan, planned for late 1945.

Paul Shulman was officer of the deck as the destroyer passed under San Francisco's Golden Gate Bridge on July 6 and tied up at Bethlehem Steel's ship repair shop near the landmark ferry terminal at the foot of Market Street. It would be four hours before Shulman was relieved of the watch. As soon as he came off duty, he found a pay phone and made two calls: The first was to his parents to let them know he was safe. The other was to Rose Saxl, asking if she would be his wife. Paul flew Rose to San Francisco and took a suite at the opulent Palace Hotel on Market Street. They got a marriage license at City Hall and arranged for a Jewish chaplain to perform a civil ceremony. Paul and Rose were married on July 18, 1945.[15] Their happiness was tinged with the knowledge that in a few weeks the *Hunt* would again sail into the gathering storm. After their all-too-brief honeymoon, Rose returned to New York and her job in a publishing company. She took an apartment at 400 East 72nd Street, in the building owned by her father. She began getting used to being Mrs. Paul Shulman, as well as the daughter-in-law of Mrs. Herman Shulman.

Rebecca Shulman is said to have been "displeased" that her son had married a woman not of his mother's liking, and not in a traditional Jewish wedding ceremony, and nowhere close to home. Whatever the magnitude of Paul's mother's displeasure, a week later Rebecca Shulman was devastated: Her husband, while playing tennis at their Stamford country home, dropped dead of a heart attack. Herman Shulman was only forty-eight. Paul was granted emergency leave to fly home for the funeral. Herman's longtime friend, Rabbi Stephen S. Wise of the Free Synagogue, delivered the memorial eulogy. Paul had lost a father. The American Zionist movement had lost a tireless advocate for the right of Jews to know that there would be a homeland for them in Eretz Israel.

Chapter 5

TWO NEW YEARS, ONE RESOLUTION

Paul hinted that if I wanted to join the Israeli navy . . . I would be welcomed.

—CAPTAIN MARTIN ZENNI, USN (RET.),
SHULMAN SHIPMATE IN USS MASSEY

The mushroom clouds that rose over Hiroshima and Nagasaki, Japan, in August 1945 had a sobering but liberating effect on Americans, including the crew of the USS *Hunt*, by then undergoing an overhaul in San Francisco. The destroyer was scheduled to take part in the naval armada that would support a massive invasion of Japan planned for late 1945.

On the afternoon of August 14, news of Japan's surrender reached America's West Coast. Victory celebrations in San Francisco turned ugly. Up and down Market Street, in the financial district, and along Chinatown's Grant Avenue throngs began rioting, looting, and wrecking storefronts. The Navy canceled all leaves and liberty (shore visits). Shulman was among several Navy officers pressed into service to help local authorities control the mobs. It was not until midnight of August 15 that the police, National Guard, and Army and Navy military police were able to restore order. Twelve persons were killed. More than a thousand people were injured.[1]

With plans to invade Japan scuttled, the Navy Department listed several warships to be decommissioned. On that list was the USS *Hunt*. In December the destroyer steamed down the California coast to the San Diego navy base to be mothballed. The crew was dispersed to all points on the compass. Some were discharged from active duty. Others were reassigned to other naval stations and ships. Paul Shulman was given orders to report to the USS *Massey* (DD-778), then at San Diego. Conveniently for Ensign Shulman, the *Massey* was being transferred from San Diego to the Atlantic Fleet, with its home port the naval operating base at Norfolk, Virginia.

The USS *Massey* had also survived the December 1944 Typhoon Cobra and had provided naval gunfire support for the March 1945 invasion of Okinawa. Now it would have a new mission. The destroyer would serve as a sea-going platform to train new officers and enlisted specialists coming to the fleet. Paul Shulman took up the same duties as he carried out in the USS *Hunt*—engineering officer—electrical. Mister Shulman also received a promotion, replacing the gold bar of the ensign with the single silver bar of the "jay-gee"—lieutenant (junior grade).

After settling in to its new home port in Norfolk, the destroyer began an intensive round of training cruises: antisubmarine warfare in the north Atlantic, gunnery practice at the Navy's bombing range on Vieques Island off the eastern end of Puerto Rico, and sonar drills in the Caribbean Sea. In April 1946 the *Massey* traveled to Annapolis to board a group of midshipmen for their summer cruise. For the "middies" it was two weeks of nonstop drills: drills to simulate general quarters for battle stations; drills to practice man overboard, repel boarders, and refueling at sea. There was no war on now, so there was no excuse *not* to do everything the "Navy way." Under the ship's commanding officer, Commander Donald I. Thomas, everything would be done "by the book," according to regulations. That was fine with Lieutenant (j.g.) Shulman.

In one instance the ship was anchored in Narragansett Bay. Mister Shulman, along with a group of midshipmen and sailors from the crew, was taking the liberty launch from the ship into Newport. When the launch reached Fleet Landing, some sailors and midshipmen jumped out onto the pier. Mister Shulman ordered them all back into the boat. He then lectured them on the proper Navy protocol for going ashore: senior officers departed first, with other officers following according to their rank. *Then* midshipmen (as future officers). The ship's crew, thus, would be the last to go ashore. Although Shulman was correct, his leadership style did not endear him to the men of the USS *Massey*. Paul, apparently, was not concerned with being endearing or popular.[2]

The constant rounds of training at sea, followed by the never-ending maintenance while in port, began to take its toll on the crew and officers. Tensions and tempers flared. Commander Thomas held Captain's Mast at least once a week, "awarding" punishments to several enlisted crewmembers for infractions of "Navy regs." One sailor was court-martialed and received a bad-conduct discharge from the naval service. An officer was found guilty of refusing to obey an order. He received an official letter of reprimand in his military record file.[3]

While the destroyer rode at anchor in Narragansett Bay, Lieutenant (j.g.) Shulman stood officer-of-the-deck watches in rotation with his fellow junior officers, including Ensign Rafael "Ray" Mur and Ensign Martin Zenni. There was no war on, so their conversations, naturally, turned to what each planned to do after they got out of the Navy. According to Martin Zenni, Paul was having second thoughts about a long career in the U.S. Navy, despite what he had once boasted to David Ben-Gurion.

During April the destroyer received five newly minted Naval Reserve ensigns, right out of officers' candidate school. They reported to the ship for a week of training to make them familiar with shipboard engineering. If their instructor, Lieutenant (j.g.) Shulman, seemed somewhat distracted when explaining the ship's electrical systems, it may have been because Paul was distracted by and focused on an event going down that week, halfway around the world at La Spezia, a war-damaged Italian fishing village along the Mediterranean coast.

Shulman liked to hang out in the destroyer's radio shack. There, he could read the Associated Press news reports that came in on the ship's teletype printer. The dispatches told how British warships were blockading two Haganah refugee vessels, *Eliyahu Golumb* and *Dov Hos*, to keep them from departing the fishing village. The two vessels were loaded with more than one thousand refugees hoping to reach British-controlled Palestine. The British refused to issue them entry visas and considered the refugees to be "illegals." The Haganah leader on board *Dov Hos* threatened to blow up the ship if the Royal Navy warships didn't back off. The warships stood fast. Then the refugees staged a hunger strike that lasted for more than three days. This too failed to move the Royal Navy. But it moved world opinion. Newspaper headlines around the world condemned the British action, giving the Haganah a publicity coup. When the Royal Navy *still* wouldn't budge, the refugees threatened to commit suicide. According to one account, on April 15, 1946, "a truce was agreed upon just before Passover. [The refugees] decided to celebrate Passover eve on board with the *seder* meal . . . and delicacies were sent to one vessel by the local Jewish community."[4] Finally, the British Foreign Office relented. It issued a thousand "emergency" entry visas and agreed to let the two vessels sail. There was a catch: the 1,014 immigrants would be deducted from that month's quota of 1,500 entry visas that the British had previously agreed to grant.

As Paul Shulman, lieutenant (j.g.), U.S. Navy, went about his official duties on board the USS *Massey*, Paul Shulman, the Zionist, began to feel that he was at sea in more ways than one. He felt emotionally and spiritually adrift from his heritage. His sense of isolation increased in July, while the *Massey* was at sea engaged in gunnery training. At home his mother and the family were taking part in the ceremonial unveiling of a memorial gravestone for Paul's father, who had died one year earlier. Paul began to think about the day when *he* would be able to join the fight for *his* people. He recalled the time when, as a midshipman home on leave, he had met David Ben-Gurion. The Jewish leader had said he was glad to see that "Jewish boys were studying to be naval officers, because some day there would be a need for them in the Israeli navy." Shulman had said thanks, but he planned a long career in the U.S. Navy.

While on board the *Massey*, Shulman kept his political beliefs pretty much to himself, but he would open up to those whom he thought might understand those beliefs. Ensign Martin Zenni, the ship's assistant gunnery officer, recalled, "More than once, Paul hinted to me that if I wanted to join the Israeli navy, I would be welcome. He knew that I was of Lebanese descent, and a Roman Catholic." In August 1946, the destroyer was at its home port in Norfolk, Virginia, when the *New York Times* ran a "Page One" story about a new British policy, which appeared to doom Jewish refugees trying to reach Palestine: "The British government has advised the United States that it will not permit any further illegal immigration into Palestine and will henceforth ship all such immigrants temporarily to the island of Cyprus. . . . It was learned today that this new ruling would apply to about 7,000 Jews held on ships and in camps in the vicinity of Haifa. . . . It is evident that, since the Zionist underground bombed the British military headquarters in the King David Hotel in Jerusalem, British policy has stiffened."[5] In the same article, the *Times* reported that the Jewish Agency for Palestine asked twelve European nations to challenge the British position, which was that the Foreign Office considered illegal the immigration of Jews to Palestine. President Harry Truman is reported to have listened to his Department of State and declined to intercede on behalf of the Jewish Agency.

A sense of helplessness began to fester like an abscess within Shulman. Apparently, it began to affect his military performance. His FitRep (Fitness Report) was less than a stellar endorsement of his military qualities: The most enthusiastic comment that Commander Thomas could muster up about the ship's engineering officer was that "Lieutenant Shulman has a good, all around knowledge of wartime destroyer duty. . . . A very capable Officer of the Deck underway."[6]

Shulman's growing disenchantment about following a career in the U.S. Navy came to a head during an incident at the end of September 1946. The USS *Massey* was serving as plane guard for the aircraft carrier USS *Leyte* (CV-32). The plane guard ship follows astern of the carrier in order to be able to pick up the pilot of a plane that "splashes," or misses the flight deck and crashes into the sea. On September 30, The Leyte's pilots were doing "touch-and-go" flights. They would make an approach to the flight deck, touchdown, and then roar up and back around for another practice run. Lieutenant (j.g.) Shulman had the 0800-to-1200 OOD watch on the bridge of the Massey. One of the carrier's planes missed the flight deck, splashed, and began to sink. The destroyer closed on a parachute floating in the water and dispatched two swimmers to see if the pilot was alive. One swimmer, Ensign Zenni, reported back that only the pilot's upper body and arms remained and were tangled in the parachute's lines. The rest of the body was missing.[7] Shulman was required to record the incident in the ship's deck log. He wrote: "Stopped amidst plane's debris. Dismembered remains of pilot observed under parachute. Remains insufficient to warrant recovery. Sank parachute with weights."[8]

Paul Shulman was not a particularly observant, that is, a "religious," Jew. But the incident happened on his watch at the beginning of the Jewish High Holy Days. The evening before, or erev Rosh Hashanah, signals the beginning of the Jewish New Year. The first day of October 1946 would begin the Jewish year 5706. In synagogue during this High Holy Day service, congregants silently read a meditation: "Let us proclaim the sacred power of this day; it is awesome and full of dread. Now the divine judge looks upon our deeds, and determines our destiny." Then, aloud, the congregation reads the prayer. In English it is "On Rosh Hashanah it is written, on Yom Kippur it is sealed: 'How many shall pass on, how many shall come to be; who shall live and who shall die. . . .'"[9]

Like all regular Navy (not Reserve) officers Paul Shulman had signed a contract that obligated him to serve for six years, or until March 1950. However, his commission stated that he "served at the pleasure of the president." At the end of August 1946, the Navy had 80,300 commissioned officers on duty and planned to release 23,700 of them by the end of 1947. Lieutenant Shulman intended to be one of those officers. He had accumulated enough points by virtue of his active duty and because he was married—Rose was his legal dependent—to be eligible for discharge.[10] Shulman wrote a letter to the secretary of the Navy requesting permission to be separated from active duty. His request was approved by Commander Thomas and forwarded up the chain of command.

While Shulman waited for a reply—and hoped-for approval—the USS Massey and three other U.S. Navy warships went on an official goodwill cruise to Chile and Peru in November.[11] Following, the destroyer resumed its schedule of training maneuvers, then put into the naval shipyard at Charleston, South Carolina, for an upgrade to its communications equipment. The ship was scheduled to stay in port until late January 1947. Paul called Rose to ask if she would like to celebrate New Year with him in Charleston. However, for Mr. and Mrs. Shulman the New Year celebration was anything but joyous. "Rose came down from New England and they went to check in to a big hotel downtown," Martin Zenni recalled. "Because they were Jewish they were refused. We officers went down there and raised hell."[12]

The USS Massey's deck log shows that Paul Shulman stood his last watch on January 23, 1947, while the ship was still in Charleston. He was transferred to the Naval Receiving Station at the Brooklyn Navy Yard for separation from active duty. On or about February 28, 1947, he walked out the gate, onto Flushing Avenue, now just Mr. Paul Shulman, civilian. He joined Rose in the apartment she had set up as their home at 400 East 72nd Street, at the corner of First Avenue, in New York City. Paul also put their names on the list for an apartment in Peter Cooper Village, an immense housing complex that stretched from 20th to 23rd streets along New York City's East River. The high-rise development, built and managed by the Metropolitan Life Insurance Company, gave preference to veterans. Then, for the first time in his adult life, Paul Shulman went looking for a job.

Chapter 6

HOTEL FOURTEEN

At the time we were not thinking so much about a navy.

—SHLOMO RABINOVITCH, DIRECTOR, THE HAGANAH'S NEW YORK OFFICE

Even before World War II was over, in January 1945 the Jewish Agency for Palestine had opened up an office in New York City in order to mobilize American support for a Jewish national homeland in British-controlled Palestine. The Jewish Agency operated from offices on East 66th Street, near Madison Avenue. The agency's executive committee was made up of the heads of all the major Zionist organizations in America, including Hadassah. The executive committee's director was David Ben-Gurion. Its secretary, Lois Slott, wrote that the committee "dealt with strategy, tactics and planning such as how to reach delegates of those countries that were on the borderline in their support of our cause." The Jewish Agency's activities were open and quite public. In fact, the organization even put out a regular newsletter. As Slott would recall many years later, "Side by side with the political scene were the 'cloak and dagger' boys. The Haganah had a team of men [in the United States] to work with the American fundraisers and with the underworld of gun runners."[1]

As visible as the Jewish Agency's activities were, the Haganah maintained a discreet office in a residential hotel at 14 East 60th Street, just off fashionable Fifth Avenue. The stately Hotel Fourteen "befitted its location, genteel and sheltering, [and was] attractive to elderly widows of means and breeding."[2] The hotel was owned and managed by Rudy and Fannie Barnett. They were described by one source as a "pleasant couple in their sixties." Behind their smiling demeanor they were ardent Zionists and did what they could to help the cause. From his position at the front desk, Rudy Barnett controlled access to the hotel's upper floor. Fannie Barnett registered the Haganah operatives and their guests under fictitious names, should someone suspicious ask about the hotel's "guests."

The Haganah's Mossad le Aliyah Bet group operated out of Hotel Fourteen, 14 East 60th Street, just off fashionable Fifth Avenue, in Manhattan. In the same building was the famed nightclub, the Copacabana. The Mossad jokingly called their top floor headquarters "Club Copa*Haganah*." *PHOTO BY THE AUTHOR*

However quiet and unassuming the hotel might appear, the building attracted a crowd every night like moths buzzing around a lightbulb. A separate entrance next door, at 10 East 60th, led from the street down a flight of steps to the Copacabana, the famous supper club for New York's café society. Lena Horne and Frank Sinatra were among entertainers who performed at the "Copa" in 1947. The Haganah jokingly called their Hotel Fourteen headquarters "Club CopaHaganah." In fact, the hotel served as a nerve center to arrange for the collection and disbursement of supplies, armaments, and funds for Haganah forces in Palestine. According to one account, Frank Sinatra is believed to have helped the Zionist cause in its drive toward setting up the State of Israel.[3]

The Haganah's secure apartment on Hotel Fourteen's top floor allowed Zionist leaders in New York to stay at no cost (hotel rooms in Manhattan were scarce right after the war) and to hold meetings away from spying eyes. They didn't merely assume that their phones were tapped and that they were under constant surveillance. They took it for granted and tried to work around it as best they could. According to former CIA agent and author John Loftus, the surveillance was all-encompassing: "It [was] not American intelligence that mounted an intensive surveillance operation against Ben-Gurion's arms purchases in the United States. It was *British* [emphasis in original] intelligence that wiretapped American Jewish citizens without warrants and leaked the information to the FBI. The truth is that the British had been eavesdropping in the United States for a very long time."[4] This arrangement, Loftus wrote, let FBI Director J. Edgar Hoover insist that the Bureau was not spying on Jews in the United States. Maybe the Bureau was not, but the G-men were not ignorant of the Jewish Agency's urgent need to bring refugees to Palestine and defend itself against the threat of an Arab invasion.

In early March 1947 Paul Shulman, newly discharged from active duty with the Navy, found employment. Through a family friend's connection, he was hired by Zigfrid Komarsky, a Zionist supporter who ran a small import-export company in New York City. Soon, however, Paul found himself becoming more involved with the Haganah and its Mossad le Aliyah Bet—the secretive group working to bring refugees and Holocaust survivors out of Europe. "The Haganah kept asking me every week to do something. . . . Each time I had to take a vacation from my new job. So, the owner of the company paid me for several months while I did volunteer work for the Haganah."[5]

It is likely that Paul's influential mother, Rebecca, had already made a call here or sent a personal note there to help further her son's ambitions. Rebecca Bildner Shulman's connections were invaluable. She and David Ben-Gurion had been close since before the war. Ben-Gurion and Golda Meyerson (later Meir) were among the few she allowed to call her "Billie," her pet name as a girl. Both "B. G." and "Goldie" were among friends invited as house-guests at the Shulman apartment in Manhattan and at their country estate in Stamford, Connecticut.

Paul Shulman was introduced to Shlomo Rabinovitch, then head of the Haganah's New York operation. Even at their first meeting at Hotel Fourteen, Shulman asked Rabinovitch if the Haganah had yet started to plan for a naval force. Years later in Israel, Rabinovitch would recall, "With all due respect to ourselves, at that time we were not thinking so much about a navy."[6] Rabinovitch directed the former U.S. Navy lieutenant to report to a certain room at the Hotel Breslin, at Broadway and 29th Street. There, he was to ask for "Kieve." Akiva "Kieve" Skidell headed up an organization called Land and Labor for Palestine. Ostensibly, Land and Labor was looking for volunteers to do agricultural work on Kibbutzim (communes) and Moshavim (collective communities) in Palestine. The reality was that Skidell was hoping to recruit military veterans who could advise or serve in the Haganah and its Strike Force brigades.[7]

Through a sympathetic contact in Washington, D.C., the Haganah acquired a list of hundreds of Jewish veterans who had served in the American Army, Navy, Air Corps, and Merchant Marine. The purloined list gave name, rank, branch of service, and the veteran's home address. Jewish Agency representa-tives in cities across the United States contacted these veterans. Those who were selected were given a bus ticket to New York City. There, they were inter-viewed again by someone from their branch of service, because Skidell needed to see how the Haganah could use their military training and experience.[8] They were also queried as to their commitment to establishing a state in Palestine for Jews the world over. Getting the volunteers to Palestine was a challenge. If an American volunteer stated he was going to Palestine as a volunteer to per-form "agricultural" work, he could usually obtain a visa that got around the U.S. embargo on "travel to or within Palestine."

Volunteers signed a time-specific contract and were paid a stipend plus an allowance for room and food. If they had skills urgently needed by the Haganah, they might be flown to Palestine. Others went by ship to France, to the Haganah's operations center near Marseilles. There, they waited for pas-sage, usually under an assumed name, often on one of the vessels that had been converted into refugee carriers. Later volunteers were called Machal, an acro-nym for the Hebrew name that translates as "volunteers from abroad." The later volunteers were paid a salary and provided life insurance and medical benefits. Of the estimated nine hundred Americans who volunteered, some two hundred had served in the U.S. Army, Army Air Corps, Navy, Coast Guard, or Merchant Marine service.

Paul Shulman's volunteer involvement came about in a somewhat different manner. Shlomo Rabinovitch alerted Skidell and others who Shulman was and what expertise he could bring to the table. It was obvious that Shulman's Naval Academy training and duty as an engineering officer on a warship in a combat zone made him a very valuable volunteer. And he was willing, able, and eager to serve.

Shulman, was legally *still* in the U.S. Navy, and would remain with the Naval Reserve until March 1950, though in an inactive status.[9] Shulman must have been aware of his legal obligation to the Navy. Just as important, he may have been at least familiar with Title 18 of the U.S. Code of Federal Regulations. This body of law, whose origins began during the United States' own war of independence from the British crown, spells out punishments for citizens who violate U.S. foreign policies. Several sections of Title 18, as well as the 1937 Neutrality Act, prohibit American citizens from enlisting in and serving the military forces of another nation. Punishment, if convicted, can include loss of passport and civil rights, a fine, and a jail term up to three years. Until the 1970s punishment could mean loss of U.S. citizenship. Shulman apparently felt that serving the Zionist cause of a Jewish homeland did not violate U.S. laws. Skidell passed Paul on to Ze'ev "Danny" Schind. Danny worked with the Mossad le Aliyah Bet (not to be confused with the Mossad, Israel's secret intelligence service). *Mossad* is Hebrew for institute or department. *Aliyah* is return to the homeland, literally, "going up to Jerusalem." *Bet* is the second letter of the Hebrew alphabet, that is, Plan B. The Jewish Agency's Plan A would have been the legal immigration of Jewish refugees. However, up until June 1944 the British Foreign Office let only 1,500 Jews a month enter Palestine, and then no more. The British considered the refugee sealift illegal. The Mossad called Aliyah Bet merely "clandestine"; in any event, they preferred the term Haapalah, which means to go to Israel (up to the biblical Jerusalem) in force. Schind's mission was to obtain vessels to transport refugees from Europe to Eretz Israel (as the Zionists called Palestine). Schind operated out of a nondescript building at 24 Stone Street, a grungy section of lower Manhattan overshadowed by Wall Street's financial towers.

Another organization was the loosely structured and equally secretive Sonneborn Institute. Its members included influential Jewish business owners and financiers, who collected and managed the vast sums of money needed to purchase and convert vessels into refugee carriers. The organization, headed by influential financier Rudolf Sonneborn, moved contributions through a labyrinth of bank accounts, and used the funds to buy everything from combat

Ze'ev "Danny" Schind's "headquarters" was in a grungy brick building at 24 Stone Street (end of street, left), in the shadow of Wall Street financial towers. Today, Stone Street's cafés and boutiques are popular with noonday shoppers. *PHOTO BY THE AUTHOR*

boots to the Aliyah Bet boats. Of the dozen vessels obtained in the United States and Canada, several were declared surplus by the U.S. and Canadian governments, and were for sale "as is."

Under Danny Schind, the Mossad set up several legal but essentially shell companies, each of which purchased one vessel before the company was dissolved. Each company was established in a different state and listed a president and officers on its letterhead. Among vessels purchased through a Mossad corporation was the former Chesapeake Bay passenger liner, SS *President Warfield*. The U.S. Navy had conscripted the vessel in World War II to serve as a communications ship during the June 1944 invasion of Normandy. Later, the ship ferried Allied reinforcements from England to Europe. After the war, the U.S. Maritime Commission struck the *President Warfield* from the register of active vessels. When acquired by the Mossad, the ship had been towed to Pier Four of the inner harbor at Baltimore, Maryland. The ship was barely seaworthy.

Historian David C. Holly, author of *Exodus 1947*, asserts that Paul Shulman was called on to help evaluate the seaworthiness of the *President Warfield*: "This assessment (*Warfield*'s possibilities outweighed her disabilities) was echoed by Paul Shulman who arrived in Baltimore to check on her condition and capability to carry large numbers of passengers."[10] Whether or not Shulman was involved with the *President Warfield* is not relevant here. But he was becoming more and more involved with Danny Schind's operation. The letterheads for the Mossad's shipping companies now included Caribbean Atlantic Shipping; Montrose Shipping; Pine Tree Industries; Ships and Vessels, Ltd.; and Weston Trading Company. In December 1945 Weston Trading had purchased a pair of two-year-old, war-surplus Canadian submarine chasers, the HMCS *Norsyd* and the HMCS *Beauharnois*. Each of the 900-ton, 208-foot-long, twin-screw vessels was in excellent condition, but had been stripped of their armaments, as well as their radar, as a condition of sale for civilian use as private yachts. The corvette-type patrol vessels were designed to carry a crew of eighty-three men and officers. Each vessel had cost $350,000 to build. The Mossad acquired both for $75,000.

In March 1947 Schind took Shulman to look at a surplus U.S. Coast Guard cutter, the USCG *Northland*. She had served valiantly in World War II and was still in good shape. The purchase was so secretive that the *New York Times* reported that the ship "suddenly became a mystery, whose whereabouts was unknown." The *Times*' intrepid reporter initially was unable to find a telephone listing for a Weston Trading Company. Even after he used his pull with the telephone company to get a number, he wrote, "A spokesman, who refused to be identified, said that [Weston] was virtually out of business, and that Nautical Shipping and Servicing company was winding up Weston's

CORVETTES
and
"Q" BOATS

These units of the fighting fleet are undergoing conversion for peace time uses, at our yard.

Your requirements of all kinds can now be taken care of by our excellent facilities.

FOR SALE
42' Chris-Craft Cruiser in A-1 condition.

The Mossad le Aliyah Bet purchased the two ex-Canadian navy subchasers (rear, left) for $75,000. After being converted to carry thousands of refugees to Palestine, the ships were intercepted by the Royal Navy's Palestine Patrol and interned in Haifa harbor. One became Shulman's flagship, the K-18 *Josiah Wedgwood*. COURTESY CITY ISLAND, N.Y., HISTORICAL SOCIETY

affairs."[11] Now, in March 1947, Danny also brought Paul Shulman up to speed on the Mossad's plans to purchase two more vessels for the Aliyah Bet "fleet." It was a purchase that would change the dimension of the refugee sealift. It would also cause Paul Shulman to make a major tactical error in the turbulent sea of Zionist aspirations.

Chapter 7

THE *PANS* AS PAWNS

Even a "rich, eccentric American" like the young Paul Shulman
. . . found it hard to explain why sheep needed . . . so many showers
and toilets.

—ZE'EV VENIA HADARI, IN *VOYAGE TO FREEDOM*

P aul Shulman had barely settled in to the apartment that Rose had set
up for them when he plunged into working with the Mossad le Aliyah
Bet. Danny Schind wanted to take him out to Brooklyn, to the Bush
Terminal piers that jutted into Upper New York Bay, where cargo ships were
loaded and unloaded. He wanted to show Shulman the two vessels that the
Mossad was negotiating to buy. The SS *Pan Crescent* had just arrived from
Havana. Its sister ship, SS *Pan York*, was due to arrive in New York in a couple
of weeks. Longshoremen were already unloading fruit from the *Pan Crescent's*
huge cargo holds when Danny and Paul went aboard.

The usually taciturn Schind was excited.[1] The 360-foot-long, 4,570-ton
reefer (refrigerator) ship had carried bananas for the United Fruit Company.
The *Pan Crescent* and *Pan York* were for sale by their owner, the Waterman
Steamship Company. Though more than forty years old, both ships' propulsion systems were in good shape. The vessels had sophisticated air-handling
systems to keep their perishable cargoes from spoiling. Schind explained that
the mammoth cargo holds could be converted into huge dormitories, each
capable of holding thousands of refugees. Each ship had sixteen feet of freeboard; that is, the main deck was sixteen feet above the waterline. If the ships
were intercepted by British warships while crossing the Mediterranean Sea,
this high freeboard could make it difficult for Royal Marines to board and take
over the Aliyah Bet ships.

When the Mossad resumed the so-called "clandestine immigration" refugee sealift after World War II, they preferred small vessels such as trawlers
and fishing boats. They were plentiful and cheap. However, most were not

well suited to crossing the open Mediterranean, and some were barely seawor-thy. The first Aliyah Bet vessel to sail after the war was a converted fishing trawler, the *Dalin*.[2] She departed on August 28, 1945, from an Italian fishing village and was able to land 35 refugees in Palestine at a beach near the old Roman seaport of Caesaria. Over the next four months seven more Aliyah Bet boats made the Med crossing, landing another 1,032 refugees. Still, the Jewish Agency began to put pressure on the Mossad to deliver a greater number of ref-ugees. Ben-Gurion had visions of hundreds of thousands of Jews, languishing in European displaced-persons camps, being brought out to Palestine; besides, he needed more male individuals of military age who could be trained to serve with the Haganah fighting forces.

Purchase of the two *Pans* marked a major change in the way the Jewish Agency intended to bring refugees to Palestine. The solution seemed to lie in using larger ships, but they were not cheap. The War Shipping Administration had mothballed scores of the Navy's obsolete warships, troop carriers, amphib-ious landing ships, and patrol craft. Getting them past the U.S. embargo would be difficult. Though skeptical, Ben-Gurion was persuaded of the potential for propaganda victories by using larger ships. According to Fritz Liebreich, a British researcher who has studied the politics that drove the Clandestine Immigration project during this period, "The Zionist intentions were mani-fold: there was the aim to flood, engulf and thus overwhelm the Cyprus intern-ment camps. . . . And there was, certainly, the intention to influence the United States and European public opinion. The decision to transfer to a 'big ship' policy was deliberately taken to coincide with the debate in the United Nations General Assembly, and the work of a new United Nations Special Committee on Palestine."[3]

In New York, negotiations to buy the *Pan Crescent* and *Pan York* had taken months. The Mossad agreed to pay $440,000 for the reefer ships, know-ing that it could cost another half million dollars to convert them into float-ing dormitories, each capable of holding thousands of refugees. In March Danny Schind had to form yet another shell company to purchase the ships, and this new "company" would need a president and officers. David Macarov, who was involved with Schind in the purchase of the *Pans*, recalled how they came up with a name for the new company. "It was at the end of a long, tir-ing, smoke-filled session. [We] needed names for five corporations to own the ships. We had just about given up on finding the fifth, neutral, non-Jewish, non-revealing innocuous name."[4] The winning company name selected was "F. B. Shipping." Now they needed a president. Danny turned to Shulman and asked him to head up the new company. The choice of Shulman was obvious. He was an American citizen and a former naval officer. So, of course, his new business venture as a shipowner would appear totally legitimate. On March 17, 1947, two weeks before his twenty-fifth birthday, Paul Shulman became president of "F. B. Shipping" and owner of a pair of 360-foot-long refrigerator ships. When asked what the initials "F. B." stood for, in public he would say, with a straight face, "Far Better Shipping." To the Mossad, the initials meant "Fuck Britain."[5]

The next problem Schind had to deal with was how to charter the vessels. A perfectly legal corporate entity had purchased the ships, but Schind knew that they probably could not meet the stringent safety requirements mandated by the U.S. Maritime Administration and would be refused registration under an American flag. This meant that the U.S. government would refuse to let an American-flagged vessel carry anything vaguely resembling military hardware to Palestine. This didn't stop the Mossad, but it made registering the ships a little more expensive. Schind went looking for a more sympathetic nation that would register the ships under its maritime "flag of convenience." Liberia, Honduras, and Panama were such nations that were not terribly picky about safety concerns. Dealing with such nations could be made much easier and go more smoothly if "incentives" were offered. Schind was introduced to Sam Zemurray, president of United Fruit and a staunch supporter of a Jewish homeland in Palestine. He knew how and where to employ such incentives. He advised Danny as to which Panamanian officials to approach and how much of an incentive to offer each. Bulging, unmarked envelopes filled with greenbacks changed hands, and the vessels soon sported the red, white, and blue-starred maritime flag of Panama flying from their jackstaffs.

The *Pans'* true mission was supposed to have been cloaked in secrecy. But Shulman, Schind, and others involved with the purchase went to Philadelphia for a gala benefit hosted by Jewish supporters in the City of Brotherly Love. According to one account, the Zionist supporters "put on a gala entertainment evening in a magnificent ballroom. The event featured a high-stakes fundraising *tombola* lottery. From time to time the master of ceremonies would joyously announce, 'Mr. X has donated 30,000 cans of meat [for the refugees on their voyage to Palestine], and Mr. Y has pledged to equip a [medical] operating theater on the ship.'"[6]

The *Pan Crescent* sailed from New York on June 6 bound for Marseilles. Along with its commercial cargoes, loaded into her holds were the medical "operating theater" and the "30,000 cans of meat," as well as cooking stoves, pots and pans and other kitchen and dining table equipment, galley tables and seats, shower stalls and toilets, and quantities of wooden beams and planks. The *Pan York* arrived in New York on March 31 and had departed on May 22 for Gibraltar, similarly loaded.

Meanwhile, the SS *President Warfield* had arrived in Marseilles, where its once-elegant staterooms and plush lobbies were ripped out and replaced with sleeping shelves for thousands of refugees, On July 10, 1947, jammed with more than 4,500 women, children, and men, the overloaded ship sailed from Port du Bouc, near Marseilles. Out in the Mediterranean the ship was renamed *Haganah Ship Exodus 1947*, and the captain hoisted the blue and white Star of David flag. Three ships of the British Royal Navy's Palestine Patrol took notice and, at first, kept a respectful distance as they tailed the ship. As the wallowing ship neared Palestine, she was ordered to stop. The captain refused. The British warships closed on the overloaded vessel. When the captain still refused to bring the engines to All Stop, the warships came alongside. Royal Marines swarmed aboard and battled refugees who fought back with anything not bolted down—tools, cans of food, potatoes. The second mate of *Exodus 1947*, an American volunteer named Bill Bernstein, was bludgeoned and later died.

The British never let the refugees off the pier at Haifa. Under armed guard, they and their belongings were hustled onto British "comfort" ships. The British were determined to teach the Haganah a lesson by sending the refugees back to where they came from—France. When the British ships arrived at Marseilles, the French government refused to let the refugees disembark. The Jewish Agency, of course, had already alerted the press and accused Great Britain of "inhumane" treatment of the refugees, many of whom had survived the Holocaust. Soon, the plight of the immigrants held on board *Exodus 1947* was a "Page One" story around the world. Humiliated and infuriated, the British Foreign Office ordered the vessels to continue on to Hamburg, Germany. Great Britain's foreign secretary, Ernest Bevin, threatened to confine the refugees in former German concentration camps. The *refuseniks* refused to disembark and stated they would rather starve to death. In the face of world condemnation, the British backed down. The refugee-laden ships sailed again, not back to Palestine, but to internment camps on the British-controlled islands of Cyprus and Mauritius.[7] The refugees did not make it to the Promised Land then, but their determination let the Jewish Agency and David Ben-Gurion claim a moral victory for the Zionist dream.[8]

Deeply humiliated by the *Exodus* debacle, the British put increasing pressure on Italian authorities to stop helping the Mossad with its clandestine immigration program, or at least try to be more strict about letting the Aliyah Bet vessels depart from Italian ports and fishing villages. The Mossad sent orders to the *Pans'* captains: After each had offloaded its commercial cargo, the ship was to avoid Italy and steam directly to Costantza, a Romanian port and industrial complex on the Black Sea. The Mossad determined that it would be safer to convert the ships and board the refugees there. At that time, the British had neither the legal right-of-passage through the Turkish-controlled Bosporus Straits, nor had Great Britain established diplomatic relations with the newly installed Communist Romanian government. En route from Marseilles, the *Pan Crescent* developed trouble with its steering gear. On its next leg, the ship developed engine trouble while crossing the Mediterranean. Reluctantly, the Mossad directed her to Venice to make repairs. The ship entered Venice lagoon on the first of August and limped into the Guidecca shipping channel.[9]

The head of the Mossad's Italian section sent a cablegram to Danny Schind in New York, asking that Paul Shulman, the ship's owner, be sent to Venice to oversee repairs to the *Pan Crescent*. Shulman flew to Paris, where he was briefed at the Mossad's European headquarters. From there he traveled by train to the organization's operations center near Marseilles.[10] Then, most likely traveling on his U.S. passport as an American shipowner, Shulman arrived in Italy. After being briefed at the Mossad's Italian headquarters in Milan, Shulman made his way to Venice. The former naval officer now found himself with a new title: naval aide to the Mossad's new Italian section chief, the redoubtable Ada Sereni. The former U.S. Navy engineering officer was expected to provide Sereni with technical advice on the *Pan Crescent*'s situation. When he arrived, he found that repairs were being held up. Sereni had not been able to find a ship repair facility that was willing to endure sanctions by the British. So, she employed her considerable network of contacts, along with a substantial monetary "incentive," and persuaded a private facility to berth the 360-foot vessel so repairs could be made there.

The Cantiere Pagan boatyard was on the small island of Sacca Fisola, across the main shipping channel from the familiar and famous Venice that tourists were once again beginning to visit. The boatyard's waterway was barely able to accommodate the *Pan Crescent*'s 36-foot draft. What was more vexing to the Mossad was that a British naval facility shared the waterway with the boatyard. This gave British intelligence agents an excellent vantage point from which to keep tabs on what was going on aboard the ship.

Shulman was set up in an apartment near the boatyard so he could oversee the work, although there wasn't much he was required to do. This was probably a good thing, because he also found himself serving as host and tour guide for his mother. Rebecca Shulman had been in Jerusalem overseeing work at the Hadassah Medical Center on Mount Scopus. On her way to Basel, Switzerland, to attend a conference of the World Zionist Organization, she stopped off in Venice to see her son. In his oral history, Shulman recalled, "I couldn't tell my mother everything, of course . . . but she more or less knew

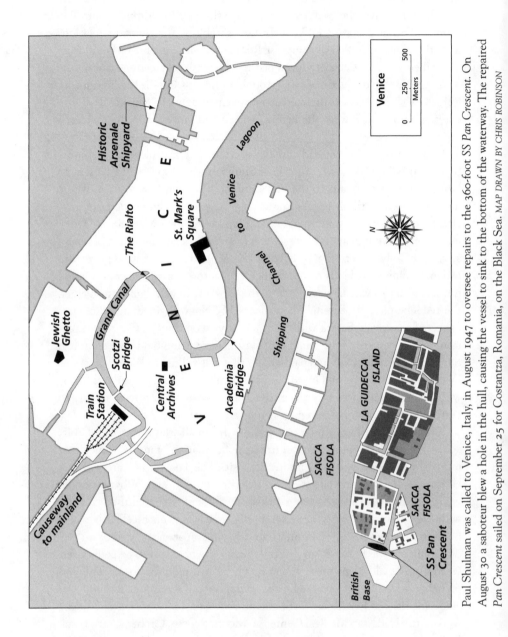

Paul Shulman was called to Venice, Italy, in August 1947 to oversee repairs to the 360-foot SS *Pan Crescent*. On August 30 a saboteur blew a hole in the hull, causing the vessel to sink to the bottom of the waterway. The repaired *Pan Crescent* sailed on September 25 for Costantza, Romania, on the Black Sea. MAP DRAWN BY CHRIS ROBINSON what I was doing."[11] And so did the British and Italians. As he recalled in *Voyage to Freedom*, Ze'ev Hadari wrote:

> The Italians . . . did not investigate Paul Shulman's story about need-ing extensive alterations to prepare the ship to carry flocks of sheep from Australia. They might have been convinced if it had been only a question of providing numerous water containers and ventilation in the enormous holds. They might, with difficulty, have believed that the layers of bunks were required for the comfort of the sheep. But even a "rich, eccentric American" like the young Paul Shulman, who acted as the shipowner, found it hard to explain why the sheep needed advanced [medical] operating theaters and so many showers and toilets.[12]

The Mossad posted guards on the main deck of the *Pan Crescent*, but secu-rity was lax. On the night of August 30, 1947, around 0330, a loud explosion shook the neighborhood. By day's first light, a crowd of curious spectators had gathered to see the *Pan Crescent*, now settled into the muck of the waterway. Two days later a headline in *Gazzettino di Venezia* read: *"ESPLOSIONE SU UN PIROSCAFO IN CANTIERE ALLA GUIDECCA."*[13] In English, the headline meant "explosion in a steamship in [a] boatyard on Guidecca [ship-ping channel]." It was the kind of sabotage that immediately caused tongues to wag and fingers to point. The news account, quoting "official" (that is, British) sources, accused "Palestina Araba" for the sabotage. The Mossad accused the British of being behind the explosion. They suspected that the legendary British naval commando, Commander Crabb, had planned or actually carried out the sabotage.[14]

Ze'ev Hadari, who worked with the Mossad's Italian section and was involved with salvage of the ship, recalled the mood as the Mossad gathered to assess damage to the ship: "There was an oppressive atmosphere at the meeting. They had all seen the sunken ship but only a few grasped the tech-nical implications [of salvaging the vessel]. The only 'professional' was Paul Shulman, who was not steeped in the same traditions of improvisation and dedication as the Israelis. According to others at the meeting, he threw up his hands and declared that the ship was lost."[15] Ada Sereni agreed with her naval aide that the ship was not worth saving, but Mossad leader, Shaul Avigur, vig-orously disagreed. With him at the meeting was Binyamin Yerushalmi, head of the organization's Greek section. Yerushalmi was not a man of the sea, but he had studied shipbuilding and ship repairs.[16] He was contemptuous of the Italian section's lack of professionalism in maritime matters. Yerushalmi spoke five languages fluently. English was not one of them, but he made it very clear to the American naval officer that he, Yerushalmi, could not understand why the "naval expert" was willing to give up on the ship so easily. Yerushalmi volunteered to resurrect the sunken hull. "I had no patience for this kind of attitude," he would write many years later. "I went to the owner of the dockyard and hired divers. We fixed wooden plates on both sides of the hole . . . and began to pump the water out."[17]

Shulman's problem, apparently, was that he could not see beyond a standard solution to the salvage problem. As an engineering officer (electrical) on board one destroyer in the U.S. Navy, he never had to deal with such situations; there were always trained and experienced Navy repair specialists or civilian shipyard experts able to fix a problem like a hole in the hull. Ada Sereni once again found a dry dock that would make the necessary repairs to the hull but told the Mossad that the facility's day rate would be exorbitant. There was no other choice. There was another problem. Once repairs on *Pan Crescent* were completed, the Mossad had to figure out a way to get the ship out of dry dock, and under way for Costantza.

The British Foreign Office in London was putting intense pressure on the British Legation in Venice to use all possible legal means to block the vessel from sailing. The legation was ordered to try to hold up the *Pan Crescent*'s sailing permit. London demanded that Panama lift the ship's registration and flag. The *New York Times* reported that the Panamanian Consul told the British, "There was no record that the [*Pan Crescent*] had 'habitually engaged in contraband or illicit commerce or piracy,' and therefore, the Panamanian government had no reason to pull the ship's papers."[18]

The stalemate became an economic nightmare. Repairs to the *Pan Crescent* were complete, but the ship was prevented from sailing because of a Royal Navy warship inconveniently anchored near the dry dock. Every day that the reefer ship stayed high and dry, the dry dock owners charged the ship's owner. Shulman's F. B. Shipping Company refused to pay. Charles Weiss, an American volunteer crewmember of the *Pan Crescent*, recalled Shulman's frustration. "Paul Shulman was down on the dock, giving orders, doing everything possible to get the ship ready to sail."[19]

Again, Ada Sereni came to the rescue. As the story was told in *The Jews' Secret Fleet*, British authorities had compelled the mayor of Venice to declare that because the Haganah had planned to blow up a British warship in retaliation for the *Pan Crescent* sabotage, the cargo ship's sailing would be delayed until a full and thorough investigation could be completed and a final report was made. The mayor, between the devil and the deep blue sea, had no choice but to publicly refuse to allow the *Pan Crescent* to sail. Sereni, however, knew that the mayor was not entirely pro-Britannia. She is said to have persuaded him to host a lavish cocktail reception and dinner party for the warship's captain and officers in a club within the Arsenale, the historic Venice shipyard. While good Italian vino flowed into the officers, water flowed into the dry dock. Late at night on September 25, the *Pan Crescent* slipped its lines, navigated around the anchored battle cruiser, escaped through the narrow shipping channel of the Venice lagoon, and steamed into international waters. Paul Shulman stayed behind in Venice.[20]

The *Pan Crescent* set a course south by east through the Adriatic Sea, then steamed due east through the Aegean Sea and Dardanelles archipelago, then made a transit of the Bosporus Straits. She arrived in Costantza on October 2. The *Pan York* arrived on October 11. At Costantza, a workforce of ship fitters began to install refrigeration, sanitation, ventilation, water tanks, cooking facilities, and upward of 7,500 wooden sleeping shelves in each ship. Even as the ships were being converted, thousands of refugees from all over Eastern Europe were being organized, processed, and transported to Romania by another Haganah organization known as Bricha. Meanwhile, the Royal Navy warships could do little more than steam around in circles in the Aegean, waiting for the two *Pans* to reappear in free world waters.

Coming to a boil beneath the surface of the political waters was a showdown between the Haganah and the Mossad, which was increasingly following an agenda not always aligned with the policies for the Jewish Agency for Palestine that David Ben-Gurion laid down. He was most insistent that the *Pans* not sail, because he did not want to risk a repeat of the *Exodus 1947* debacle. Yet, according to Israeli historian Idith Zertal, "The Zionists had never intended to actually bring the 4,500 [*Exodus 47*] refugees onto the shores of Palestine, and such an effort had no chance of success, since the *Exodus* was a show project from its inception."[21] Ben-Gurion was also afraid that, despite the condemnation heaped on Great Britain for its inhumane treatment of the *Exodus* refugees, the Jewish Agency would possibly lose favor in the United Nations, which was then debating a resolution over whether or not to partition Palestine into separate Jewish and Arab enclaves. Ben-Gurion feared that a repeat of the *Exodus 1947* affair could backfire on his leadership and cause a vote in the United Nations that would consign Palestine to being governed as a UN trusteeship. Ben-Gurion had staked his reputation and political future in having Palestine recognized as Eretz Israel—the Greater Israel.

The Mossad, perhaps more activist driven than Ben-Gurion's Mapai political organization, insisted that the ships *would* sail. If challenged by the Royal Navy, they would fight being taken over. However, ugly rumors circulated that certain refugees on the ships were secret Haganah members and would try to dynamite and sink the vessels—with the loss of thousands of lives—rather than let the ships fall into British hands. Paul Shulman was put in a bind. On the one hand loyal to and perhaps feeling beholden to Ben-Gurion and the Zionist leader's faith in him, Shulman could not publicly endorse the sailing. Yet he may have found it necessary to salvage his reputation with the Mossad, especially in the wake of his "expert" pronouncement that the Pan Crescent was not worth salvaging. As owner of the vessels, but on his own, Shulman sent a telegram to Moshe Shertok at the Jewish Agency in New York. "[Shulman] suggested that, on behalf of the Mossad in Europe, the ships' crews declare themselves mutineers. In this way, the whole matter would be taken out of the Mossad's hands."[22] Shulman did not have authority to send the telegram, and it suggests that he may have been out of the loop with regard to the internal struggles between the Mossad leadership and Ben-Gurion's organization.

Conversion of the two ships at Costantza was completed in late November 1947. However, at Romania's insistence, the ships were moved to Burgas, a Bulgarian port on the Black Sea. There the first of thousands of refugees were beginning to arrive from all over Eastern Europe. Meanwhile, the British Foreign Office circulated a rumor that "hundreds if not thousands" of the refugees could be Communists intent on taking over Palestine. The New York Times dutifully reported, "British officials [in London] expressed . . . the 'liveliest apprehension' that Communist agents might be filtered into the ranks of unauthorized immigrants to Palestine. However, at the [British] Colonial Office, officials conceded that no evidence of any . . . Communists in the early shipments of immigrants had been found."[23]

Much of the international diplomatic posturing was lost on the refugees. Whatever their national loyalties, they were focused mainly on their own personal dreams of reaching Palestine. One eleventh-hour glitch almost scuttled the sailings. Many among the two ships' crews had been "spooked" by the sabotage of the Pan Crescent and feared it could happen again, at sea. Though each ship had sleeping shelves, showers, and toilets for the refugees, neither of the ex–banana boats carried life rafts and life vests for up to 7,500 refugees on each ship. Charles Weiss and the other American volunteers among the crew, as well as the Spanish captain and crew, refused to sail from Burgas until F. B. Shipping doubled their pay for the short voyage to Palestine, or to Cyprus, whichever came first.[24] Shulman, as the company president (which is to say, the Mossad), had to agree.[25]

On December 30, 1947, the two Aliyah Bet ships—now lying much lower in the water with their totals of 11,951 persons—5,089 males, 4,266 females and 2,596 children—emerged into the Aegean and encountered the British warships that would escort them. A deadly showdown at sea was averted when

In July 1948 the SS *Pan Crescent* and the 4,570-ton *Pan York* carried a total of nearly 12,000 refugees from British internment camps on Cyprus to Israel. *U.S. HOLOCAUST MEMORIAL MUSEUM*

both ships' captains radioed to the British that they would not attempt to reach Palestine, but would consent to be escorted directly to Cyprus. Each vessel was tailed by three destroyers and a frigate. Almost at midnight on New Year's Eve 1947, Ben-Gurion, said to be "furious" with the Mossad's defiance of his opposition to the sailings, was nonetheless persuaded to agree to the sailing; in any event, the vessels were already under way for Cyprus. Ben-Gurion sent a message to the ships' captains. Henceforth, the *Pan Crescent* could be called *Atzmaut*, meaning "Independence." The *Pan York* could become *Kibbutz Galuyot*, meaning "Ingathering of Exiles." But, in a fit of pique, possibly, Ben-Gurion refused to let the ships add the prefix "*Haganah Ship*" to their Hebrew names. It was the only way he could hold back his full endorsement of the sailings. The *Pans* did reach Israel, but not until July 1948, steaming into Haifa harbor, carrying thousands of *legal* immigrants to Israel, many crying and singing the Israeli anthem, "Hatikvah."

With the episode of the *Pans* now over, Paul Shulman was sent back to Mossad headquarters in Paris, to help with the continuing problems of moving refugees and Machal volunteers to Palestine. One American who came through Paris in January 1948 was David M. Marcus. "Mickey" Marcus had graduated from the U.S. Military Academy at West Point in 1924. As a colonel, he had taken part in the D-day invasion of Normandy, then served on General Dwight D. Eisenhower's staff in Europe. Marcus retired from the Army and set up a law practice in Brooklyn, New York. There, he was visited by Shlomo Rabinovitch and asked if he would be willing to find a retired U.S. Army general who could help train the Haganah's Palmach strike force. When Marcus could find no general officer willing to undertake the task, he agreed to do it himself. He and Rabinovitch flew to Paris. There, the West Point graduate met the Naval Academy graduate. As Paul recalled their meeting, "We kidded each other, claiming to have attended the finer military academy."[26]

Shulman's movements from January to March 1948 are not known. He probably returned to New York City to be with Rose, who was expecting their first child. What is known is that Ben-Gurion had placed the Haganah on high military alert, stockpiling arms and supplies for a war that they anticipated would begin as soon as the British quit Palestine. On March 2 Ben-Gurion sent an urgent cablegram to Moshe Shertok at the Jewish Agency in New York. "Can you send two or three shipping experts? Can Paul Shulman come at once?"[27]

Chapter 8

THE "BATHTUB CORPS"

Despite his youth and inexperience [Paul] did an outstanding job in converting a rag-tag bunch into the nucleus [of an] effective fighting force.

—Dr. Richard Rosenberg, professor emeritus, Haifa University; former instructor, Israeli navy.

P aul Shulman was among the twenty or so passengers on board the Pan African Airways plane making its initial approach to Haifa in April 1948. The twelve-hour night flight from Paris in the twin-engine DC-3 had been arduous, because the cabin was neither pressurized nor heated.[1] The aircraft descended as it flew north along Palestine's west coast that faced the Mediterranean. Soon the Plain of Sharon and fertile Jezreel Valley gave way to Cape Carmel and its namesake, the 500-meter (1,600-foot) Mount Carmel. The plane banked around the headland as it made its approach to Haifa.[2]

If Shulman had looked out the window that morning as the sun rose in the east he would have seen Mount Carmel's outstanding landmark, the nineteenth-century Carmelite Monastery and Stella Maris lighthouse. As the plane began its final approach to Haifa's Michaelis airfield, Shulman would have looked down on a city of three- and four-story buildings that stepped down from the Carmel heights to a commercial center close by a magnificent harbor, whose most prominent feature was a long breakwater that arched into the bay. The former U.S. naval officer might also have spotted several small vessels tied up in the protected anchorage behind the breakwater. What he could not have known from the air was that by April 1948, Haifa had become an all-but-abandoned city.[3]

Six months before, in October 1947, when Great Britain announced that it would quit its Mandate, the British High Commissioner for Palestine began turning over operation of municipal services to non-British citizens employed by the Mandatory government. By April 1948 nearly every British security unit had pulled out of its position in Palestine and was getting ready to return to England. Whatever the British could not take with them, they sold, or disabled, or destroyed.

The Jewish Agency for Palestine, of course, had not just stood around waiting for the Mandate to end to begin gearing up for the war that everyone expected would commence as soon as the British finally lowered the Union Jack.[4] Knowing that the Mandatory administration was preoccupied with clearing out on schedule, Ben-Gurion now directed the Haganah to launch the notorious "Plan Daleh." Haganah units began clearing Arabs from towns and cities near Palestine's northern borders with Lebanon and Syria. Many villages were bulldozed into rubble. In the Arab quarters in cities throughout Palestine, non-Jews closed the doors on their retail businesses and walked away from civil service jobs. Haifa's merchants, many of whom were Arabs, fled despite being reassured by Palestinian leaders that they would be able to return, after the Arab armies were victorious. Few believed that they would be able to return and resume doing business as usual in the new nation. By April 22, 1948, after the Haganah's Carmeli Brigade had occupied Haifa, fewer than 10,000 of the city's 146,000 Arabs remained. In *The Birth of the Palestine Refugee Problem*, Israeli historian Benny Morris wrote, "Arab municipal and Mandate employees feared that in the Jewish state they wouldn't have any chance of advancement in their careers because precedence would be given to Jews. This feeling was reinforced by the fact that most Arab officials lacked fluent Hebrew."[5]

It was into this paralyzed city that Paul Shulman descended to carry out *his* mandate from Ben-Gurion: to set up an academy to train officers for Israel's new naval service. Shulman was met by a delegation from the Jewish Agency, and then driven to Tel Aviv, to naval headquarters in the old San Remo Hotel.[6] There he was welcomed by Ben-Gurion. Yaacov Dori, the Haganah chief of staff, introduced Shulman to Gershon Zaq, a civilian, whose title was deputy minister of defense and director of naval affairs. Zaq was to be Shulman's superior. Shulman was given the title of chief of staff for naval training.

Back in Haifa, Shulman began to lay plans for the school that would become the Israeli naval academy. It was not as if he had to put up "I Want You" posters, hoping that if he built it they would come. There was no shortage of cadets. Five years before, at the end of 1943, the Palmach had established a naval company known as the Palyam.[7] By the time the Mossad-run clandestine immigration sealift resumed after World War II, the Palyam operated a secret training base near the ancient Roman seaport of Caesaria, about thirty-five miles south of Haifa. The first commanding officer was Avraham Zakai, whom Shulman met in Venice in 1947 during the salvage operation

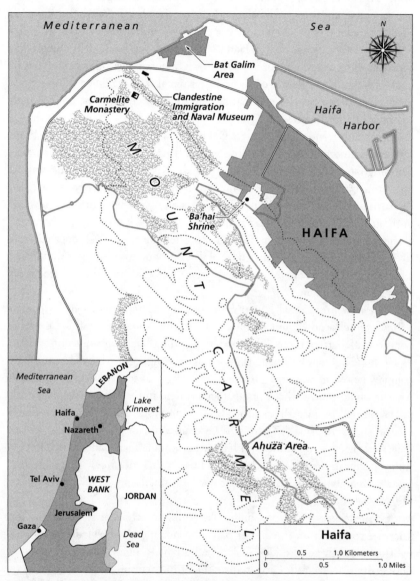

Months before there was a State of Israel Ben-Gurion called Shulman to Palestine to be chief of staff for training for the new navy. From naval headquarters at the Carmelite Monastery atop Mount Carmel, Shulman began with no official rank, no proper uniform, not even training aids. *MAP DRAWN BY CHRIS ROBINSON*

of the SS *Pan Crescent*.[8] Shulman kept a low profile as he got the naval training school ready to open its doors, because the Royal Navy's autonomous
Mediterranean Command was still operating from its headquarters at Stella
Maris, atop Mount Carmel in Haifa.[9] As a U.S. Navy officer Shulman was
accustomed to just filling out a request for supplies and getting them. Now, in
Haifa, Shulman was dismayed to find that naval training aids were nonexis-
tent and that Sea Service commander Gershon Zaq had no idea of how and
where to obtain them.

On the afternoon of May 14 David Ben-Gurion proclaimed the State
of Israel. Later, at midnight, the British high commissioner, Sir Alan
Cunningham, left his keys on his desk at the King David Hotel and walked
away from the territory Great Britain had administered since September 1922.
By dawn five enemy forces began their invasion of the new nation. It was not
until after the Royal Navy had struck the Union Jack on May 30 that Ben-
Gurion could motor up from Tel Aviv to celebrate the British departure. In
his war diary, he wrote: "I reached [Haifa] at 6:15 and went straight to the port
where celebrations were taking place." Ben-Gurion's war diary does not say if
he met with Shulman.[10]

The new provisional government had already commandeered the Ben
Yehuda Hotel atop Mount Carmel, and Shulman and his staff set up temporary headquarters there. The modern building had a magnificent view of
Haifa, but Shulman had little time for sightseeing. As he looked at the port
complex below, he was trying to see where the naval academy would train and
what it would train with. A one-paragraph item in the *New York Times* dutifully reported: "An Israeli naval academy is to be established soon 'somewhere
on the shores of Israel.' There will be courses for ordinary seamen, mates,
engineers, wireless operators and harbor personnel. The academy will have a
training ship in addition to school buildings."[11] It is not likely that Shulman
saw the item, but if he had he might have muttered some 1948 equivalent to
"Yeah. Right!"

Shulman appointed Avraham Zakai to be his chief of staff, because he
knew he could rely on the former Palyam commander's knowledge of its war-
fighting capabilities. Besides, Zakai had studied engineering at Columbia
University in New York City and was fluent in English. Shulman planned to
use Israel's famous technical institute, the Technion in Haifa, to hold some
classes. In addition, the academy would need facilities close to or within the
port complex and access to piers. Shulman began with almost nothing. He had
no textbooks or training aids. He had no uniforms for himself, his instructors,
or the students. Somewhere Zakai found a cache of cast-off Palestine police
uniforms, which Shulman and his staff wore, sans badges of rank. In fact, Paul

The former U.S. Coast Guard cutter *Northland* sailed as the refugee vessel *Haganah Ship Jewish State*, with nearly 2,700 refugees jammed on board. After being intercepted, she collided with and heavily damaged one of her warship escorts, which was towed into Haifa harbor. *Northland* joined the Israeli navy as the auxiliary ship, A-16 *Eilat*.
COURTESY DAN SHUGAR

himself had not been assigned an official rank yet, because those for the navy had not been established. He was given the provisional rank of an Israeli army Kvarnit, equivalent to a U.S. Navy commander.[12]

As for a training ship, Shulman decided to use the former U.S. Coast Guard cutter *Northland*. He and Danny Schind had looked her over in New York the previous March and he knew her history. Even before the United States entered World War II, in September 1941 while serving as an icebreaker with the Coast Guard's Greenland patrol, the crew had captured and destroyed a German weather-reporting station on Greenland. The Mossad purchased her the day after she was stricken from the naval register in March 1947. The ship was converted into a refugee carrier. Renamed *The Jewish State*, she boarded nearly three thousand persons and made one trip to Palestine trailed by three British destroyers. Before Royal Navy marines could board her, the crew disabled the steering gear and slashed the diesel fuel lines to the engines. Powerless, the cutter collided with one of the destroyers, causing damage to the warship, but the ship's reinforced bow suffered only a dent. The British had to take the ship under tow all the way to Haifa harbor. In May 1948 the ship was commissioned as the Israeli navy's auxiliary ship A-16, *Eilat*. Many years later, Shulman was asked why he needed an icebreaker. He replied, "That's what we could buy."[13]

The Israeli Naval Service now had its training ship but no one to command it. Somehow, Shulman had heard about Harold "Dov" Shugar, one of about three dozen Americans using the GI Bill to study at Hebrew University in Jerusalem. Shugar was trying to learn to speak Hebrew without it sounding like it came out of the hills of his native North Carolina. Like several of the American students at Hebrew University, he had been recruited by the Haganah and assigned to a Palmach mortar crew.

"I don't know how Shulman knew about me," Shugar recalled. "But he heard that I had been a U.S. Navy gunnery officer. Right on the spot he offered me command of the *Eilat*. I did not know enough Hebrew and didn't want the responsibility." Shugar did agree to serve as the ship's gunnery officer. His first task was to install the *Eilat*'s armaments—a pair of 20-mm pedestal cannons, which were bolted to the foredeck. The ship's main gun was a World War I–vintage 65-mm French army field artillery howitzer. The wheels were removed and the gun carriage mounted on a platform bolted to the main deck. The *Eilat*'s gun crews nicknamed it "Napoleonchik."[14]

Shulman initially recruited instructors from among former Royal Navy officers, some of whom were not Jewish, but who *were* sympathetic to the Zionist cause. According to one of the American instructors, Richard Rosenberg, "While there were several Palestinian Jews who had served as officers in the British Navy during World War II, all of them had served ashore, primarily in technical functions. The British navy did not permit Jews to serve afloat."[15] The "Brits" included David De Lange, who became the academy's chief of operations. Allen Burke, who commanded a Royal Navy corvette during World War II, taught seamanship and navigation. Harvey Miller was experienced in radar. With scrounged electronic parts, he built and installed a radar unit atop the new Israeli naval headquarters at Stella Maris.

Courses were usually taught in English because few of the instructors spoke Hebrew and most of the students understood some English. Also, Hebrew had a noticeable lack of technical and nautical terms. As a consequence, the pace of instruction was slow. The Palyam cadets, used to lightning-quick, hit-and-run commando raids, were impatient with the didactic method that the instructors used: classroom lectures followed by practice, practice, and more practice. According to Richard Rosenberg, some students derisively referred to the new Israeli navy as Cheyl Haambatya—the "bathtub corps."[16]

Shulman and his instructors understood the challenge of getting the former naval commandos fired up and working as a cohesive team. They had been used to carrying out small-group raids. Now they were being trained to operate not as individual sabotage cells, but as crew members of a warship, subordinate to a commanding officer, whose vessel would be part of a larger squadron conducting tactical operations at sea. The ideas of mutual cooperation and interdependence, so crucial to manning a warship and engaging an enemy at sea, were foreign to many of the future officers. Developing esprit de corps took time; Shulman knew this from his three years at Annapolis and his fifteen months serving in two U.S. Navy destroyers. He was well aware that the Israeli navy did not have three years; Shulman did not have even three months. He was already under pressure from Ben-Gurion and Yaacov Dori to deliver officers and trained crews.[17]

Shulman knew, and Ben-Gurion had to concede, that there were no officers in Israel who had experience in naval command and control. Israel had never had a navy; there was not even a Hebrew word for navy. So, Paul persuaded Ben-Gurion to let him go to the United States to recruit "foreign" officers to teach at the Israel naval academy. The reality is that Shulman felt more comfortable around officers who had been trained by and served in the U.S. Navy and could teach "the Navy way." In July 1948 he flew to New York City, where he met with Teddy Kollek, then running the Haganah office at Hotel Fourteen. While in New York Shulman also helped to arrange for the purchase of three more former Canadian submarine chasers for the Israeli navy.

He was invited to address a lunch meeting of the Sonneborn Institute. This was the New York–based group of influential and wealthy Jewish business owners and investors who had worked assiduously to collect and contribute the millions of dollars and war surplus needed to fund the State of Israel and equip its military forces.[18] Rudy Sonneborn introduced Shulman as "Commander Shaul Ben-Zvi" of the Israeli navy. This was the Hebrew name that Shulman chose for himself, after Ben-Gurion insisted that each Israeli military commander should take a Hebrew name when he accepted a commission in the Israeli Defense Force.[19]

Shulman/Ben-Zvi described the difficulties that the Israeli squadron faced in trying to defend Israel's long coastline with only two patrol craft and an ex–Coast Guard cutter. They were up against vessels of the forty-five-ship Egyptian navy, which included numerous former Royal Navy warships and whose officers and crews had been trained and equipped by the British. Shulman also presented a shopping list of supplies and teaching materials that the academy needed. His want list included five hundred copies of *The Bluejacket's Manual*, which is the U.S. Navy's basic guide for sailors, and fifty copies of the *Watch Officer's Guide*. Shulman also asked if someone could find a "telescope for use by a high ranking Israeli officer." When asked why he wanted a telescope and not high-powered binoculars, Shulman replied that it was for General Moshe Dayan, who had lost one eye in combat. Shulman admired Dayan, who seemed to know how to navigate around the stifling bureaucracy, the turf battles that were typical of Israel's fledgling provisional government, and the Israeli military's intensely competitive commanders.

While in New York, Shulman himself did not recruit the instructors. He had neither the time nor contacts. Instead, he called on Teddy Kollek and his network to find and recruit former U.S. naval officers to serve as volunteer instructors. Shulman's other mission was to help his wife, Rose, close up their New York City apartment and get her and their three-month-old son, Tzvi, ready to travel to Israel.[20] The Shulmans returned to Israel in mid-August and to the Ben Yehuda Hotel. There they shared communal cooking and housekeeping with the other American volunteer instructors and their wives and families.

The first American instructors to arrive from the United States were Richard Rosenberg and Marvin Broder. Both had been working with the Mossad in New York City. Richard Rosenberg recalled: "My function had been to evaluate [candidates to see] whether they were kooks, or spies or were really suitable. Then I was called in and told that I was needed to set up the [Israeli navy's] communications and electronic warfare unit." Rosenberg protested that he had been a junior officer in the U.S. Navy and didn't know very much. "They told me, 'Yes, we know you don't know very much, but we have no one else.'"[21]

Lieutenant Commander Marvin Broder had served as a damage control officer on a U.S. Navy aircraft carrier during World War II. As a civilian, he had volunteered to help Akiva Skidell at Land and Labor for Palestine, interviewing candidates for service in the Haganah. He too answered the call, and, with his new bride, was sent to Israel. Like Shulman, Broder was still in the U.S. Naval Reserve (in an inactive status). He refused a commission in the Israeli Defense Force but served as a civilian instructor for about six months. Broder remembered the day he reported to naval headquarters at Stella Maris. "Two sailors were slouched on the couch in the outer office. I said to one, 'Could you tell Commander Shulman that Marvin Broder is here.' One sailor turned to the other and said, 'Go tell Paul there's a guy to see him.' That wasn't the navy I was used to." As Broder saw it, the cadets had little regard for protocol and not much respect for their professional appearance. "Shortly after the cadets got their uniforms, I saw one walking down the street with his uniform jacket open to the waist. I told him to button it up. He said, 'but it's a hot day.'"[22]

The third ex–U.S. Navy volunteer who reported to Shulman was Saunder "Sandy" Finard. During World War II, he had held the rank of lieutenant commander in the U.S. Navy's submarine service. After the war, he was working for DuPont in Wilmington, Delaware, when approached by Kollek. Bored with the pace of civilian life, he was eager to help the Zionist cause and resigned from his job. He and his wife, Miriam (who had gone to high school in Palestine), sold their house and prepared to go to Israel. Years later, Mimi Finard recalled, "At the last minute, Teddy Kollek gets a telegram from Gershon Zack [sic], then head of the Israeli Navy, telling him to cancel the three Navy specialists. It was internal politics, and Teddy Kollek had the good sense to disregard the cable and send us all on our way."[23]

Jonathan Leff showed up in September 1948, but arrived by a different route. He had graduated from the U.S. Naval Academy the year before Shulman and knew about Paul from his "Shulman's Fighting Ships" articles published in The Log. Following his naval service, Leff volunteered as third mate and navigator on one of the Aliyah Bet ships, an ex–U.S. Navy patrol craft that the Mossad renamed Yucatan. In Marseilles the ship was converted into a refugee transport and took on an Israeli crew for the voyage to Palestine. Leff learned that Shulman was running the Israeli naval academy. He got word to him—did he need an experienced gunnery officer who was eager to come out to Israel? Upon his arrival, Leff was named head of the navy's "Department of Ordnance and Gunnery of the Army of the Sea." The odd-sounding name, Leff recalled, was because "there was no biblical Hebrew word for 'Navy.'"[24] Like Dick Rosenberg and Marvin Broder, Jonathan Leff was dismayed at the lack of professionalism he found among the future officers. "The first time I went aboard one of the ships I found an officer standing near the gunpowder magazine holding a lighted cigarette."[25]

Also crowded into the Ben Yehuda Hotel with his family was Harold "Hal" Gershenow, a graduate of the Massachusetts Institute of Technology. He was not an instructor, but the work he did was crucial to the Israeli navy being able to operate. While Shulman and his staff were trying to drill seamanship into the heads of the former naval commandos, Gershenow and his team of "ex-pats," along with Israeli and Palestinian Arab shipyard workers, worked around the clock to get the Bat Galim port complex and the derelict Aliyah Bet vessels back into operation.

In his memoir, Israel: The Way It Was (published under his adopted Hebrew name, Haim Gershoni), Gershenow recalled that Gershon Zaq seemed incapable of making a decision on what to do first. "One of Zaq's first moves was to consult with experts. . . . The first two experts were shown the refugee ships. . . . Their reaction was to throw up their hands in despair and

The former HMCS subchaser *Beauharnois* made one refugee trip, then sat in Haifa harbor for two years before being purchased for the Israeli navy. As the navy's "flagship," the K-18 *Josiah Wedgwood* sailed with no radar, no radio, minimal armaments, and no crew quarters. Those had been torn out for 1,250 sleeping shelves for the refugees. COURTESY AMERICAN VETERANS OF ISRAEL ARCHIVE

go home. The third expert suggested a navy based on high-speed motor torpedo boats. . . . The only trouble with all the expert advice was that it did not fit the conditions."[26] The "conditions" under which Gershenow and his crews worked were primitive: "The British had, as a matter of policy, closed down and refused to hand over various services to the new authorities. Whatever was worth having they took with them. . . . Hardly a navy yard, but a start."[27]

Gershenow's other mission was to get the former Aliyah Bet vessels ready for service. There was the former U.S. Coast Guard cutter *Northland*, which had attempted to land more than 2,700 refugees. Close by was the former U.S. Navy patrol craft *Cythera II*. As the once-private luxury yacht *Argosy*, it had been purchased by the Irgun-sponsored American League for a Free Palestine. As the refugee carrier *Abril*, the vessel had attempted to land 660 refugees. (For the story of the *Abril*'s history and its role in the clandestine immigration, see the appendix.)

With their hulls stained and rusting were the two former Canadian subchasers, HMCS *Norsyd* (2,678 refugees) and HMCS *Beauharnois*. The Mossad had designated *Norsyd* as K-20, *Haganah*, and *Beauharnois* as K-18, *Josiah Wedgwood*, during the sole Aliyah Bet voyage that each made.[28] The *Wedgwood*, designed for a crew of eighty-five, was intercepted trying to land some 1,250 refugees. On June 26, 1946, a British destroyer intercepted her as she approached Palestine. The crew disabled the diesel engines, which forced the British ship to tow the vessel into Haifa harbor. Stretched across *Wedgwood's* bridge was a banner: "We survived Hitler. Death is no stranger to us. Nothing can keep us from our Jewish homeland."[29] Now Paul Shulman determined that as soon as the *Wedgwood* could be made seaworthy, she would serve as the navy's flagship.[30]

According to Hal Gershenow, the vessels had been looted and stripped of anything valuable. None had radar or radios; communication initially would have to be by war-surplus army field radios. There were no crew's quarters— the bunks had been torn out and replaced by sleeping shelves when the vessels were converted into refugee carriers. For the first few months the crews had to sleep on mats thrown down on the steel decks. The shipyard workers managed to get three of the vessels shipshape enough so that they could depart from Haifa not looking like derelicts. The ships were finally accepted into the new Israel navy and given hull numbers. "Gray paint converted the three naval vessels to warships," Hal Gershenow recalled, "and high numbers painted on their bows, such as K-20, K-18, and A-16, gave the impression of a large fleet."[31]

Shulman, the former U.S. Navy lieutenant (junior grade), had been in charge of a highly trained, well-disciplined group of enlisted specialists who maintained the electrical systems on one U.S. Navy warship. Now, as squadron commander, he was deeply frustrated by the disrespect shown by the former sea commandos for the training. He felt overwhelmed as head of an entire training facility, trying to teach a corps of officer candidates who seemed to need some serious attitude alignment. Lack of respect and professionalism was not limited to the cadets as individuals or even as a student body. The chaos seemed everywhere. Fritz Liebreich, a former British naval officer who served in the Israeli navy, wrote his master's thesis on the early years of the Israeli navy. His research showed that "the administrative chaos was considerable and orders were received from many directions. One headquarters settled itself in Tel Aviv's San Remo hotel and issued orders. But orders also emanated from [naval] headquarters in [Stella Maris] . . . and finally, there was the Mossad le Aliyah Bet in the lower town of Haifa, to whom the Palyam was supposed to report, and they also issued instructions."[32]

Shulman also found himself caught in the crosscurrents of competing Israeli policies and practices, and buffeted by counter-conflicting personal and public agendas within Tel Aviv's several political factions. Prime Minister and Minister of Defense David Ben-Gurion himself was acutely aware of the difficulties of creating a unified military force. He constantly battled entrenched

fiefdoms of formerly powerful military commanders. Israel Galili, commander of
the Haganah Central Command, sent Ben-Gurion memos "urging," "insisting,"
and "demanding" that control of all military war fighting assets be under control of the Haganah; that is, himself. Ben-Gurion retaliated by disbanding
the Haganah's separate command structure and then folded its units into the
Israeli Defense Force. Nonetheless, Ben-Gurion preferred leaders he could
trust and were loyal to him, as was Paul Shulman. In his war diary Ben-
Gurion wrote that he often had to lecture his fractious military leaders about
the importance of unity. He knew that a unified command could not be established merely by issuing an order: "It was impossible to change the attitude
of the Haganah at one fell swoop . . . it had been an underground organization for thirty years. Many Haganah members had experience in the Jewish
Legion of World War I. Many more served in Jewish units of the British Army
in World War II. And finally, there were officers with considerable battle
experience—men like Colonel David 'Mickey' Marcus and Paul Shulman of
the American navy."[33]

The twenty-five-year-old Shulman often felt over his head when it came to
the political infighting that dominated the early provisional government. When
he and his chief of staff, Avraham Zakai, drove to Tel Aviv to attend General
Staff meetings, Zakai doubled as his translator and interpreter. Zakai once told
him, "You're fortunate that you *don't* understand Hebrew, so you don't have to
listen to all the (expletive) that goes on." Some strategy meetings degenerated
into shouting matches among the various military-political factions. According
to Fritz Liebreich, "One top-level meeting at Naval Headquarters was dedicated
exclusively to the problems of sailors' headgear and badges."[34]

Funding for the Israeli Naval Service was a constant battle. Each of
the service commanders had to compete for limited funds available from
the stretched-thin budget of the provisional government, which was trying
to pay down a drawer full of IOU chits for arms and munitions purchased
from war surplus brokers all over Europe. Access to and *control* of funds, if
not the money itself, was powerful currency in the military. Shulman had to
argue with Gershon Zaq for funds with which to keep the navy operating.
Zaq, whose civilian background was in educational administration, is said
to have been more interested in promoting culture. One academy instructor
described what Shulman had to do just to complete work on a communications station: "All requests for an allocation to complete [a radio transmit-
ting station] were rejected. One officer suggested a solution, [which was] to
request money for a cultural centre. The governing powers approved it immediately, but the money was 'misappropriated' and used to complete the vital
communications centre."[35]

At several levels, communications, or its lack—or at cross purposes, or issued by various power cliques—seemed to be the Achilles' heel of the nascent Israeli navy. While Shulman pleaded for money to complete a communications station that could broadcast messages far out to sea, a small group of naval Machal volunteers was planning to broadcast their message only as far as Tel Aviv. Foremost, they wanted to know who was, or should be, at the helm of the Israeli navy. The group included one of the American "ex-pat" officers who was an instructor at the Israeli naval academy and who served with Shulman on board his "flagship," the K-18 *Josiah Wedgwood*. The protesters hoped to present their complaints to Yaacov Dori, the IDF's chief of staff. The complaint began, "We, the undersigned, consider that the temporary establishment prepared by the Naval Staff is proof of inadequate experience in matters pertaining to the sea [and] the failure to cooperate with the few professional captains and officers we have. . . . We as seamen find the idea [unacceptable] that command of battleships [sic] is given to persons without seagoing experience."[36] The complaint is referring not to "persons" such as Aluf Shulman but to the Gershon Zaq, the civilian head of the Naval Service, and others of the Haganah Central Command. Paul was not blind to the problems he faced, but as the navy's operational leader, there was little he could do. The group of dissidents was able to deliver its five-page gripe sheet to Dori, who passed it on to Ben-Gurion, who appointed a commission to investigate the allegations. The commission was headed by Baron Marcus Sieff, Ben-Gurion's adviser on transportation and supplies for the Israeli Defense Ministry. Baron Sieff visited eleven naval establishments and interviewed more than three dozen enlisted men and officers. *Not* interviewed was Paul Shulman. Among conclusions of the Sieff report was: "There is no one in Israel available either with operational experience in Naval staff tactical and operations or in Naval Command at Sea."[37]

Chapter 9

THE CONSEQUENCE OF TRUTH

The Haganah was limited to land forces. There was no possibility of creating units to operate [in] the air or on the sea.

—DAVID BEN-GURION, FROM HIS WAR DIARY

Buried somewhere in the voluminous archives of the Israeli Defense Force or the Haganah may be the "truth" as to why Paul Shulman was not called by the Sieff Commission to talk about unrest within the navy. Shulman had more than a few detractors, but he may have benefited from the Israeli custom of *protectzia*—that is, he was shielded by Ben-Gurion, who probably told Marcus Sieff to lay off.

Among Shulman's supporters were Richard Rosenberg and Marvin Broder. Rosenberg was an instructor at the naval academy. Before he came out to Israel he had told Teddy Kollek in New York that he knew little about electronic communications. Yet in Israel he taught communications and would later be named to develop and manage the new Israeli navy's communications systems. "While it is true that [Paul] had much less sea-going and much less combat experience than the rest of us, I think he did a very creditable job of organizing the navy. And that wasn't so easy given the opposition of the Palyamniks."[1] Marvin Broder, who taught shipboard damage control, said of Shulman, "He was not a magnetic type. [The instructors'] dedication was to Israel and the navy rather than to Paul personally. . . . Paul was more of an administrator than a leader. What was in his favor was his total dedication to what he was doing in Israel."[2]

Nearly all of the military and civilian leaders of the new nation had come to Palestine as young men and had matured politically within the socialistic ideals of the Kibbutz movement. Their philosophies were driven by the desire to forge a new nation and to bring closure to what some modern Israeli historians called the "Diaspora mentality." They yearned for their own place, their homeland on Earth. Whatever their country of origin, in Israel the Kibbutzniks felt that they had paid their dues. They had earned a certain right to call themselves Israelis. Some of these leaders and military commanders were suspicious of outsiders, in particular, the Machal volunteers from abroad. Certain of the military commanders thought that Shulman, whom they derisively dubbed "the New York Jew," should go back home to where he came from and let "real" Israelis run the country. The problem, of which Ben-Gurion and his chief of staff, Yaacov Dori, were only too well aware, was that there were few so-called native-born commanders who knew how to get the job done. In his oral history Shulman recalled that he had been called to Israel "nominally to be the adviser to the navy. But within two or three days I was called by Ben-Gurion. He said: 'You are no longer the adviser. You are the first Commanding Officer.'"[3]

Shortly after Shulman raised the Israeli flag over Stella Maris, he realized that there was no one other than, possibly, Allen Burke—who had commanded a Royal Navy corvette during World War II—who could take the fledgling navy into action. The four-ship Israeli squadron lacked a command, control, and communication system, because there had been no time to teach and practice "C-3" ship handling. Even to get his ships under way Shulman had to temporarily suspend classes at the naval academy: whether or not the men were trained, he needed the instructors and cadets to man the ships. Armaments on the two former Canadian submarine chasers and the former U.S. Coast Guard cutter consisted of an ancient army field cannon, 20-mm cannons, and handheld machine guns. Ammunition was in such short supply that there was almost none available for practice. Diesel fuel had to be purchased on the commercial market. The ships had no radar, and their commanders had to communicate with the Haganah ashore by using war-surplus army field radios. Jonathan Leff, gunnery officer on one of the Israeli vessels, recalled that even language was a barrier. Because he spoke little Hebrew, he had to write his messages in English. His Israeli counterpart translated and broadcast them in Hebrew to the Haganah; the reply in Hebrew had to be translated back into and written in English before Shulman or the other American officers could carry out an order or take action.[4] There were no crew's quarters to speak of. As refugee carriers, bunks in the officers' and crew's sleeping compartments had been torn out and were replaced by wooden sleeping shelves for the refugees. Despite all these deficiencies, the Israeli navy went into action against hostile forces that threatened the new nation.

On June 4 Shulman in his flagship, the K-18 *Josiah Wedgwood*, along with the training ship, A-16 *Eilat*, steamed into action from its base at Haifa port toward Tel Aviv. There, the armed Egyptian troopship, *Al Emir Fawzia*, was attempting to land soldiers. The Egyptian squadron included corvettes and patrol craft the British government had sold to Egypt. The ships were faster and better armed. They had better communications and radar.[5] As the Israeli ships steamed south, Sea Service commander Gershon Zaq sent a radio message to the captain of the *Eilat*. He ordered the old cutter with the reinforced bow to ram the Egyptian troopship. The *Eilat*'s captain radioed back with apologies, but explained that his barnacle-fouled vessel's top speed was nine knots—at best. There was no way he would be able to catch the much faster and better-armed Egyptian ship, and even if he could, he was not willing to ram the enemy vessel. As for shelling the Egyptian warship, the CO explained, that would be next to impossible. The training vessel's main deck cannon was still stuck at a 45-degree angle. It could neither be raised nor lowered nor could it traverse from side to side.

As the *Wedgwood* and *Eilat* stood off from the *Al Emir Fawzia*, Shulman climbed down into his flagship's motorboat. He came alongside the Egyptian warship and aimed his only weapon—a handheld loud hailer—at the bridge. He called up to the captain, and in English informed him that the Egyptian warships had illegally invaded the territorial waters of the sovereign nation of Israel. Shulman instructed the Egyptian captain in no uncertain terms that it would be best if his ships took their departure. The Egyptian captain did the right thing. He and his escorts turned about and steamed out beyond Israel's territorial three-mile limit. The next day, the *Palestine Post* duly noted: "Four Egyptian warships approached the coast [and] were met and engaged by the Israeli navy, while Tel Aviv coastal defense went into action."[6] It would not be the Egyptian navy's last attempt to reinforce its ground forces.

Back in Haifa Shulman reopened the naval academy. Now, instead of having to contend with Egyptian naval incursions, the Israeli navy had to deal with UN Truce Commission observers: The first truce period had gone into effect and would run from June 11 to July 9. The multinational force of UN observers fanned out to hotspots all over Israel. Their task was to take note of violations of the truce and report these to the respective Israeli and Arab leaders. On loan to the UN Truce Commission were three U.S. destroyers, which were to patrol the coastal waters looking for seaborne violations of the truce. It was largely a symbolic show of force, because the Israeli Defense Force prohibited UN inspectors on board the destroyers, citing the danger of the observers being in a "war zone."

Assigned to the Truce Commission headquarters in Haifa were seven U.S. Navy officers whose duties were to observe the port and coastal areas. Their task was effectively stymied because Israeli port security officers denied them access to what they deemed as "sensitive" areas, and the Israelis found other ways to block the observers' view of port areas. It was not likely that former Lieutenant (j.g.) Shulman put out the welcome mat for his fellow officers—some of whom were Annapolis graduates. In any event, they had been briefed by U.S. naval intelligence about Shulman and knew where to find him—if they needed to.[7]

Despite being under the watchful eye of the United Nations, even before the truce ended on July 9, the Israeli navy sallied forth into Lebanese waters on its next raid: shelling a Syrian supply depot in the Lebanese coastal city of Tyre. The *Eilat*'s gunnery officer, Harold "Dov" Shugar, had to coordinate the firing of "Napoleonchik" with the up-and-down wave motion of the ship and hope that the shells hit something. The cannon made a huge noise, but the shells did little physical damage, except to astonish the hell out of those in Tyre who didn't think Israel even had a naval force.

It may have been a boost for the morale of the officers and men of the upstart Israeli navy to face down those forces that were, clearly, Israel's enemies. One confrontation, in which the "enemy" was not so clearly defined, affected Paul Shulman deeply. The Irgun, headed by Ben-Gurion's longtime political rival, Menachem Begin, had purchased a war-surplus amphibious tank landing ship, an LST that had served the U.S. Navy.[8] At a port in France, Begin loaded the *Altalena* with war-surplus weapons, ammunition, and vehicles. The ship also took on about nine hundred refugees, of whom about eight hundred were male individuals of military age, or "MIMAs," as the UN peacekeepers called them.[9] Monroe Fein, a former U.S. Navy officer, was the *Altalena*'s commanding officer, whose crew included several American Navy veterans. Begin's plan was to sail the *Altalena* to Israel and use the weapons and ammunition to reinforce Irgun units. The MIMAs would join Irgun units and fight alongside Haganah forces. But Menachem Begin had his own separate agenda. He was also fighting to win the hearts and minds of the Jewish people and take control of Israel's government. Ben-Gurion and his Mapai-dominated military commanders were just as determined to thwart Begin's ambitions.[10]

The *Altalena* reached the coast of Israel on June 21. Ben-Gurion let Begin believe that the munitions and men would be welcomed. He didn't tell the Irgun leader that most would be assigned to Haganah forces, not Irgun units. As the vessel approached Tel Aviv, Ben-Gurion ordered the Israeli navy to intercept the amphibious landing ship before it could offload its explosive cargo. As officer in tactical command of the Israeli squadron, Kvarnit Shulman did as he was ordered. The *Wedgwood* intercepted the vessel off Tel Aviv. Shulman sent its captain a radio message that ordered the *Altalena* to stop, turn about, and head back out to sea. What followed could have turned into a tragedy of epic proportions, which would have done irreparable damage to Ben-Gurion's credibility.

In his book, *Genesis 1948*, Dan Kurzman described the action: "[*Wedgwood*] approached to within 150 yards of *Altalena* and made radio contact with [the commanding officer, Monroe] Fein. 'You are in the territorial waters of Israel,' Shulman said. 'You are ordered to move west, out to sea.' There was a long wait before a reply came back from Fein: 'I haven't enough fuel to head out to sea.'" According to Kurzman's account, Fein had his radioman send a string of meaningless radio messages to Shulman and the Haganah command ashore, as a stalling tactic. When *Altalena* didn't turn about, Ben-Gurion ordered Shulman to fire on the vessel. *Genesis 1948* continued: "Shulman fired a cannon, hitting the ship's bow and wounding several people. With Tel Aviv in sight, Shulman received urgent orders to stop the ship at any cost before she reached the beach. He fired again, but [*Altalena*] was now heading into the deeper water of the harbor. In a last desperate effort, Shulman finally swung his corvette round between the LST and the shore and fired, but he missed."[11] Ben-Gurion's account is somewhat different. In his war diary he would later write: "While the [Israeli naval] ships were sailing, Shulman asked the *Altalena* whether it needed medical help. He received a negative reply. He ordered the *Altalena* to move to the west. When his orders were not obeyed Shulman told his men to fire over the ship. As the [*Altalena*] was moving toward the shore [Shulman] was instructed to prevent it, at all costs, from reaching Tel Aviv, but it was already too late. Our ships did not fire a single shot all through the day. They were three to four miles from the shore."[12]

Ben-Gurion wrote his war diary account soon after the incident. Kurzman's book was published in 1992 and supposedly had the benefit of interviews with both Irgun and Haganah veterans who remembered the incident. Nonetheless, both Kurzman's and Ben-Gurion's accounts are inaccurate and seem self-serving, although for different reasons. For one thing, the *Altalena* was not "heading into deeper water," because it could not. Photographs show why Monroe Fein was unable to obey Shulman's order to head out to sea: the shallow-draft amphibious landing ship had run up over and was stuck on the submerged hull of an Aliyah Bet ship sunk years before by the British. While the LST was trying to back down off the obstacle, a Haganah shore battery opened up on the *Altalena*. As hundreds of people along the shore and from hotel balconies watched in horror, several shells struck the ship, causing fires. Menachem Begin, still on board, was screaming to fire back, but he was hustled into one of the *Altalena*'s motorboats and taken ashore. There were fires all over the ship, but it remains a mystery as to why the floating arsenal didn't explode in a giant fireball.[13] Paul Shulman had carried out Ben-Gurion's order, but he had been ordered to fire not on only Jews but on

The Irgun vessel *Altalena*, loaded with ammunition for Irgun units, almost reached the beach off Tel Aviv, when it was shelled by Haganah shore artillery. Ben-Gurion commanded Paul Shulman, in *Wedgwood*, to prevent the LST from landing its cargo, even if he had to fire on the *Altalena*, with its American captain and crew. COURTESY *THE JABOTINSKY INSTITUTE*

Americans—U.S. Navy veteran volunteers—who, like himself, were helping in the fight for a Jewish homeland.

Following the *Altalena* incident, Monroe Fein and several of the American crew members let it be known that they wanted to join the Israeli navy. One of Shulman's friends, Lee Harris, arranged a secret meeting in his Tel Aviv apartment so that Fein and the others could meet with the head of the Israeli navy. According to Harris, Shulman was in favor of letting the Americans join the navy. "Paul said okay, and he went back to Haifa, [but] this political commissar, (Gershon Zaq) just overruled him. . . . [Fein and the crew] wanted to come in as a group . . . but Paul didn't have the power to insist that they be taken in."[14] A week after the *Altalena* incident, on June 27, at the headquarters of the new Israeli Government in Tel Aviv, Ben-Gurion, as minister of defense, swore in the first officers of the Israeli Defense Force army, air force, and navy. Shulman is known to have been there, but it is *not* known if he raised his right hand and recited the following oath: "I hereby pledge to remain faithful to the State of Israel, its laws and its legally constituted authorities, to accept unconditionally the discipline of the Israel Defense Forces, to obey all orders and instructions given by authorized officers and to devote myself, even unto death, to the defense of the Homeland and of Israel's freedom."[15]

In mid-August the Israeli navy again went into action. Acting on intelligence from the Mossad's Italian section, K-18 *Wedgwood* and its sister ship, the K-20 *Haganah* (the former HMCS *Norsyd*), steamed westward toward the Greek island of Crete. In an operation code-named "Pirate's Booty," they intercepted a coastal steamer, the *Argiro*. According to intelligence, the *Argiro* was carrying munitions to Syrian forces. After ordering the vessel to stop, the *Wedgwood* came alongside the wooden vessel, and the crew boarded her. The Israelis transferred 6,000 rifles and eight million rounds of ammunition as well as other small arms. They put the *Argiro*'s crew ashore, then sank the ship.[16]

By September 1948 the War of Independence had entered what Israel called the war's fourth phase. IDF units had pushed Arab forces off the heights that flanked the only road from Tel Aviv to Jerusalem. Now, with access to the besieged city, the Israelis were able to bring relief to the starving population. In the northern and eastern sectors of the country, Haganah units had pushed back Lebanese, Syrian, and Jordanian forces. Israeli forces strengthened their stranglehold on Egyptian forces in the arid Negev that were fighting to hold a line around Gaza City.

As successful as the Israeli brigades were, Ben-Gurion understood their limitations. In his war diary, he praised the fighting done by the Haganah, but cautioned, "The Haganah, as an underground movement, could not operate regular military schools. . . . There was no possibility of training at anything higher than the company level. . . . The Haganah was limited to land forces. There was no possibility of creating units to operate [in] the air or on the sea."[17] On August 31 Ben-Gurion made a rare visit to naval headquarters at Haifa. Along with Shulman he toured one of the ships and the naval base, which was now operating in the Bat Galim section of the port complex. He wrote in his war diary, "Our naval personnel make quite a good impression, but there is insufficient equipment. There is not a single naval gun, and the few pieces of ordinary artillery are not suitable for use on ships. There is no antiaircraft defense and only one gunnery officer."[18]

The navy, which had been derisively referred to by some of its detractors as the "bathtub corps," finally got the respect it was due. Naval personnel also got ranks. And uniforms. And naval guns and antiaircraft guns. And radar. Shulman and his instructors began delivering officers and ship's companies that could function as well-trained crews in the navy's four ships-of-the-line. Paul Shulman began an aggressive campaign to acquire larger, faster, newer warships. In New York, Danny Schind was behind a scheme to purchase the former aircraft carrier, USS *Attu*. The plan was to register the auxiliary flattop

In a rare visit to naval headquarters in Haifa, Ben-Gurion inspected one of the navy ships. Saying that the naval personnel make "quite a good impression," the prime minister conceded that the warships had "not a single naval gun." *COURTESY THE AMERICAN VETERANS OF ISRAEL ARCHIVE*

under a foreign maritime flag of convenience, load it with warplanes and arms, then sail it to Israel. The Mossad did purchase the vessel, but Ben-Gurion scuttled the idea. He said that it would be impossible to get the huge ship past the U.S. arms embargo. Schind was forced to sell the carrier to a scrap dealer. Shulman wanted submarines. Israeli intelligence learned that Italy was preparing to sell two of its World War II U-boats to Egypt. Ben-Gurion vetoed a scheme to intercept them at sea, which would have been an act of piracy. The subs reached Alexandria, where they sat out the war, rusting away at pier side at Egypt's naval base.

The Israeli navy had proved its worth. Paul Shulman's role was acknowledged, on October 26, 1948, following the raid on the *Al Emir Farouq*. Shulman's official promotion to be commander in chief of the navy conferred other rewards. The provisional government finally found a house for him and his family. At last, Paul and Rose and their infant son, Tzvi, could move out of the Ben Yehuda Hotel. The house was located in the elegant French Carmel neighborhood up on Mount Carmel. The building, at Number 5 Bashir Street, had been commandeered by the Mandate as quarters for senior British naval officers. Its owner was an Arab merchant who elected to flee during Israel's takeover of Haifa. The house, built in the Turkish Ottoman tradition, featured a wide, front-to-back central hallway that let cooling breezes pass through, but whose windows high up could be closed off from the harsh sun by wooden shutters. The house had two amenities that were most welcome. One was a kerosene-fired cooking stove. The other was running hot water, which had been installed by the former Arab occupants. Water flowed from a tank down through a coil heated by a kerosene burner, and into the sink.

By the end of 1948 it was becoming evident that an Israeli victory was in the air. Yet it was becoming apparent to the navy's commander in chief that there would be no recognition of the role he had played in the nation's victories. Shulman's nemesis seemed to reside in the person of Israel Galili, former commander of the Haganah Central Command. Galili remained adamant that the Israeli Defense Force senior command, and *not* Minister of Defense Ben-Gurion, should have absolute authority on all matters that dealt with the military. The army, air force, and navy should be led by Israelis, and certainly *not* by foreigners.

Lee Harris, who had been among the group to welcome Shulman to Palestine and supported him all along, had also become an essential liaison between the government and scores of Machal volunteers. Many were trying to return to the United States. Some were trying to stay in Israel. All were having problems with the government over matters of pay, release from their contracts, and the increasingly obvious fact that they were being discriminated against, simply because they were "foreigners." Harris wrote in his own letter to Yaacov Dori, "there are considerable and persistent complaints [by the Machal] in the navy that appointments are not made . . . on the basis of experience and merit."[19] Along with this were complaints by the small group within the navy's key American personnel. Their five-page, typed manifesto also leveled criticism at the Israeli naval leaders: "Most officers are political appointments—[They] may be (a) nice fellows, (b) brave, (c) right party, (d) distinguished in other fields," but "most have no idea of what a naval officer does or how he conducts himself."[20]

Hostilities with Israel's enemies had ended, but hostilities within the Israeli military establishment continued for Shulman. Yet he personally would not speak out. Even in his 1993 oral history, he was almost noncommittal about the problems he faced: "I managed to get along. The navy, although it was integrated into the Central Command more or less, had its own direct access to Ben-Gurion and the Minister of Defense. We did a great many things independently, [but] we were all fighting for the same budget, and personnel."[21]

By July 1949 the new Israeli government had signed armistice agreements with its enemies. At a special ceremony in July 1949, the heroes of the war were honored with a victory parade in Tel Aviv. Standing in the rear of a Jeep in his dress white uniform was Aluf Paul Shulman. A *New York Times*

Israel marked the new nation's first year of independence with a parade. The Israeli navy was represented by a contingent of sailors and its *first* commander in chief, Paul Shulman, riding in a Jeep. COURTESY MIRIAM FINARD

account of the event reported, "The main parade in Tel Aviv had everything that parade lovers could wish for. Even before the parade started, the Israeli navy, [was] augmented by an imposing destroyer, [which] maneuvered in the adjacent waters. The vessels displayed streamers of lights looking very much like an inverted V for Victory. . . . Before the parade had passed the reviewing stand, decorations for valor were presented for the first time. Ribbons representing Israel's Medal of Heroism were given to eight outstanding heroes and posthumously to the relatives of others."[22]

It is not known whether the late Colonel David M. "Mickey" Marcus or Paul Shulman were singled out for special honors. In any event, for Shulman the celebration was a prelude to his farewell; yet he sensed there would be little in the way of the traditional send-off as in the U.S. Navy, where the retiring officer is wished "fair winds and following seas." Ben-Gurion, bowing to his military commanders and political ministers, now had little choice but to direct Aluf Shulman to stand down from his position as commander in chief of the navy. To soften the humiliation, perhaps, he named Paul to be his special naval adviser. In Shulman's oral history, recorded nearly a half century later, his voice clearly shows how he still felt about being "kicked upstairs": "When Ben-Gurion told me that I was being replaced, he told me the names of the officers he was considering to take the job. They were both army officers. . . . I was not enthusiastic about it, but I couldn't pick a fight with Ben-Gurion's choice. So, he asked me who did I think would be good. I said, 'Moshe Dayan.' And [Ben-Gurion] said, 'Well, he's the best officer in the army. Why did you pick him?' And I said: 'With one eye he's half a Nelson to begin with.'"[23]

Ben-Gurion, ever the political pragmatist, ran true to form. He selected a party faithful, the apparatchik Shlomo Shamir (nee Rabinovitch) as the next naval commander in chief. Shamir, the former major in the British army, had run the Haganah office in New York City. The fact of his subsequent, less-than-stellar command of the Seventh Mechanized Brigade in the Battle of Latrun, and obvious fact that he had no experience in managing a naval force, seemed not to concern Ben-Gurion. Shamir's elevation to head up the navy did worry Paul Shulman: "I'm not sure how much that the man who relieved me, the Admiral, was prepared to put into practice. He was not very enthusiastic about Volunteers from Abroad. . . . I think he was a hindrance not a help to me in my job."[24] Shulman served as Ben-Gurion's naval adviser for a few months. Ben-Gurion turned down Paul's request to be transferred back to the navy as its director of plans and policies. Still, he managed to pass on to the ships' commanding officers his ideas about how the navy should be run: "We distributed all the work that I did to the various commanders of the ships, and I know that they put that into effect well before it was an official document."[25] Not long afterward, Paul Shulman launched the next phase of his life—as a civilian— and as a business owner trying to make a living in Israel.

Chapter 10

PASSPORT PROBLEMS

Obviously his services for the Israeli government were not in the interests of the United States.

—W. H. YOUNG, U.S. STATE DEPARTMENT

TITLE 18 UNITED STATES CODE:
Crimes and Criminal Punishments
CHAPTER 45: Foreign Relations

§958: *Commission to serve against friendly nation*:
Any citizen of the United States who . . . accepts and exercises a commission to serve a foreign . . . state . . . in war, against any . . . state . . . with [which] the United States is at peace, shall be

§959: *Enlistment in foreign service*: (a) Whoever, within the United States, enlists . . . or go[es] beyond the jurisdiction of the United States with intent to be enlisted, or enter in the service of any foreign . . . state . . . as a soldier or as a marine or seaman on board any vessel of war shall be

§ 960 *Expedition against friendly nation*:
. . . knowingly begins or . . . furnishes the money for, or takes part in, any military or naval expedition . . . against the territory or dominion of any foreign . . . state . . . with [which] the United States is at peace . . . shall be fined or imprisoned not more than three years.

America's Neutrality Act of 1794 made it a felony for any citizen to take part in any military action against a country with which the United States was not at war, or to "enlist or hire himself, or hire or retain another person to enlist or enter himself, or to go beyond the jurisdiction of the United States with the intent to be enlisted in the service of a foreign prince or state."[1]

Historically, at least since the middle of the nineteenth century, Americans by the thousands, however, had served nations other than the United States. They did so out of personal or moral conviction, or for adventure, or money (or both), or because they were acting covertly on behalf of an American governmental agency. Americans fought alongside British Royal Marines against Imperial Russian forces in the Crimean War during the 1850s. American pilots flew with France's Lafayette Escadrille squadron during World War I. Colonel John Stonewall Jackson "Clare" Chennault recruited American pilots to serve with the Flying Tigers of the Chinese air force, to help stem the Japanese incursion into China in the early 1940s. Before the United States entered World War II, scores of Americans swore allegiance to Great Britain so they could fly with the Royal Air Force's Eagle Squadrons. In this instance, because their show of solidarity with England threatened the fiction of America's "neutrality," scores of Yanks were charged and convicted. It took many of them twenty years and a U.S. Supreme Court ruling to get back their citizenship.[2]

After World War II, it became imperative for leaders of the Jewish Agency for Palestine to recruit volunteers, in particular those who had special skills, that is, who had served in the American military. It also became evident to the Haganah that they would have to come up with ways to get around U.S. nationality laws as well as the government's trade and travel embargoes. In cities where American Jews were recruited, the local Haganah leader gave prospective volunteers specific instructions on how to apply for a passport and a travel visa. Potential "agricultural volunteers" were advised not to all go to a passport office at the same time, or all put down the same dates and reasons for travel abroad.

Paul Shulman needed no such subterfuge. As soon as he was separated from active duty with the Navy in March 1947, he applied for a passport, which was issued on May 23, 1947. He was working for a staunch Zionist, Zigmund Komarsky, in his import-export company. By then, Shulman was already involved with the Haganah and had been named president of F. B. Shipping Company. His application for a visa may have stated that his reason for travel to Europe was for business on behalf of his company, and that he intended to visit France and Italy.

His actual itinerary was somewhat different. During the summer of 1947 Shulman is believed to have met with the Mossad le Aliyah Bet leadership at its offices in Paris, as well as with the Italian Mossad, in Milan, Italy. He is known to have been in Venice from mid-August to at least September 25, during the period of repairs to and salvage of the *Pan Crescent*. Shulman is thought to have returned to Paris until late January 1948, at which time he met Mickey Marcus, who was on his way to Palestine to train Palmach units.

Sometime in late March or early April 1948, Ben-Gurion called Shulman to Palestine, which was then still under British control. Traveling on his U.S. passport, his arrival in Haifa probably would not have been questioned by British officials, who, anyway, were preoccupied with closing down operations in time for the May 14 end of the British Mandate. Even if asked, it is not likely that Shulman would have advertised that his purpose for being in Palestine was to set up an academy to train officers for Israel's navy. According to David Macarov, an American who had worked with the Mossad on the purchase of the two *Pan* ships, "The fact that Palestine was not a nation . . . made it possible for many operations to be undertaken, and many people to do things that would not have been possible if [Palestine] were a foreign nation."[3]

Yet, even before the State of Israel existed, the U.S. government was looking suspiciously at American veterans who were merely studying in Israel on the GI Bill. In their book, *I Am My Brother's Keeper: American Volunteers in Israel's War for Independence*, Jeffrey and Craig Weiss wrote, "The U.S. Consulate asked the president of Hebrew University if Americans were still engaged in university studies. The president replied, 'They are studying just as much as the other students are.' On January 30, 1948 the Consulate announced that the United States would recall the passports of any Americans found taking part in the fighting, to be returned only for a trip back to the United States. . . . However, the threat was intended to express the U.S. government's disapproval of such activities without putting too much real pressure on Americans."[4]

It was after May 15, 1948, that Americans had to be more evasive about why they were traveling to the new State of Israel. According to Jason Fenton, an American who served in the Israeli army, "There was a concern by American volunteers that our passports [should] not include any entry stamps indicating our presence in Israel. . . . The Israelis complied with our wishes and stamped our entries and exits to and from Israel on a separate document."[5] Such subterfuges aside, the U.S. government had a pretty good idea of how many Americans had volunteered to help Israel, despite whatever their stated purpose for being in Palestine/Israel. Consular officials had the benefit of dossiers developed by a variety of federal agencies. In Shulman's case, in particular, it would have been nearly impossible for him to keep his activities below the United States' diplomatic radar. His elevation to the position of navy commander in chief in October 1948 had been made at a ceremony attended by a former U.S. secretary of the Treasury. Shulman's participation in Israel's first Independence Day military parade in May 1949 was hardly a clandestine act. In his oral history, he explained what he thought was a rationale for the legality of his Israeli service: "You could not pledge allegiance to a foreign state.

You could pledge allegiance to carry out the orders of the army . . . we [volunteers] all undertook to comply with the laws of the army. But when it became against the law the rest of us resigned. And I guess I was ready to resign."[6]

On Friday, June 27, 1949, Paul Shulman was invited to pay a visit to the American consul in Haifa, but it was anything but a social call. He had been directed to turn in his American passport. Vice Consul Thomas S. Bloodworth was acting by order of the State Department's Division of Passport Services, on behalf of Secretary of State Dean Acheson. The order for Shulman to appear followed an investigation, classified SECRET, which informed the State Department that Shulman was known to have served, or was still serving, as "chief of staff" of the Israeli navy. Shulman was invited to explain his actions.[7]

Following the meeting, Vice Consul Bloodworth wrote to the secretary of state that Shulman "was rather evasive as to what specific assignment he held in the Israeli Navy, although he did not deny that he had been serving in an active capacity with that organization. . . . [Shulman] also stated that he had not taken an oath of allegiance to the State of Israel and that the position which he held with the Israeli Navy was not one which was reserved for nationals of the State of Israel."[8] Shulman did not turn in his passport; in fact, he also presented the vice consul with a request for a two-year extension of his visa. The extension, he explained, would let him continue to reside outside the United States in order to pursue his business interests. He and Sandy Finard had already begun planning their company, National Engineering, which would bid on large-scale civil engineering projects in Israel and the Middle East. Paul had already sent Sandy to Canada where surplus earthmoving and dredging equipment were for sale.

The vice consul asked Shulman to provide documents that would show that he had not taken an oath of allegiance to Israel. The next morning, a Saturday and the Jewish Sabbath, Shulman drove to Tel Aviv, to the home of Paula and David Ben-Gurion. The following Monday Shulman was back in the consul's office in Haifa. He presented a note, typed in English, on Ministry of Defense letterhead. The note, addressed "To Whom it May Concern," confirmed only what Shulman had said, that he had neither taken an oath nor voted in an Israeli election. The note added: "In appointing Mr. Shulman to his various positions, this Ministry was aware and accepted the fact that he was of foreign nationality." The note was dated, "Ha'kirya, June 28, 1949," and signed by David Ben-Gurion, minister of defense.[9]

What is curious about the outcome of the inquiry from Vice Consul Bloodworth is that there are no notes extant of that meeting. It is not known, for example, if Bloodworth asked Shulman when, how, and for what purpose he first came to Israel. Bloodworth's report does not mention whether or not Shulman was asked about his contractual obligation to the U.S. Naval Reserve until March 1950. The report does not show that Bloodworth advised Shulman that his service to a foreign government violated terms of that contract. The State Department's response, under the authority of Secretary of State Dean Acheson, was swift, but it was also equivocal: "Advise Shulman that it is universally accepted rule of international law that a person who voluntarily enters military or naval service of a country owes that country temporary allegiance and cannot look to any other country for protection. Thus by entering and serving in Israeli Navy Shulman placed himself in a position where he cannot look to United States for protection and consequently cannot properly bear passport as national of United States . . . and establishes beyond doubt that he has performed no act entailing loss of American citizenship."[10]

The State Department's response is revealing more for what it did *not* say. It did *not* allege or charge that Shulman violated the 1794 Neutrality Act, or the Nationality Act of 1907, or the 1937 Neutrality Act (as amended), or Title 18 of the U.S. Code, or any other laws that proscribed Americans' involvement in the affairs of other nations. The State Department merely issued an advisory, which showed that, by his actions, Shulman had placed himself beyond the protective arm of the United States. The reality of the situation was that the U S. State Department had long been ambivalent toward American citizens who chose to support, join, or fight with the armed forces of foreign nations.

In his 1993 oral history, Paul Shulman asserted: "Just before I left [the] Israeli navy the American government asked for my passport back, because they had received complaints from Egypt that I had conducted the battle that attacked the flagship of the Egyptian Navy."[11] The State Department may or may not have received such a complaint; in any event, it apparently was not terribly relevant to their inquiry into Shulman's affairs.

Other American volunteers who served in the Israeli navy were not bothered as much. U.S. Navy lieutenant commander Marvin Broder was one of the officers recruited by Teddy Kollek to serve as an instructor at the Israeli naval academy. As soon as he reached Israel Broder reported to the U.S. consul in Haifa. He said that he was still in the U.S. Naval Reserve but would be serving as a *civilian* volunteer. He refused a commission in the Israeli navy and returned to the United States as soon as his contracted services were no longer needed.[12]

Richard Rosenberg, conversely, had a close call with U.S. laws. He, too, had been recruited by Teddy Kollek and taught radio communications at the naval academy. To disguise his actual reason for traveling abroad, Rosenberg said that he obtained letters that stated he would be traveling throughout Europe on business for his employer. He and his wife sailed to France on the SS *America* and then flew to Palestine. Following his stint as an instructor he was appointed to the position of chief of communications and electronic warfare for the Israeli navy. By then, he and his wife decided to make Israel their home. In 1951 they planned to return to the United States for a visit. Now, he had to apply for a new passport, which would include their child who had been born in Israel: "We were aware of some of the problems some of the Americans in the [Israeli] air force had encountered, so I got a letter from the Ministry of Defense saying that I had been drafted and that I had not signed an oath of allegiance. . . . As I was about to take the oath [to uphold the Constitution of the United States], and swear that I had never served in the armed forces of a foreign nation, the U.S. consul produced a file which had all the details of my Israeli navy service." Years later Rosenberg could joke about that day in the consul's office. "The Consul's Israeli secretary said with a smile, 'You know, it's amazing that you were drafted one day, and the next you were promoted to the rank of Commander.'"[13]

Not all Americans got off with a smile and a wink. The U.S. government came down hard on two individuals, Hank Greenspun and Adolf W. Schwimmer. Greenspun was publisher of the fledgling *Las Vegas Sun*. Through his contacts he was able to obtain large quantities of U.S. government war surplus. Al Schwimmer, who had an extensive postwar career in aviation maintenance, helped to "export" to Israel a dozen war surplus aircraft, which included B-17 bombers and C-46 transports. To get the aircraft out of the United States, Schwimmer and Greenspun set up an airfreight company, which was chartered and registered in Panama. They used the war-surplus planes to actually ship food supplies by air from Florida to Puerto Rico. After delivering the goods, however, the planes were refueled, then continued on across the Atlantic Ocean, stopping in the Azores for fuel. They then flew on to Czechoslovakia, where they loaded cargo destined for Israel. This included arms and ammunition for Israeli ground forces and Czech-made Messerschmitt ME-109 fighter planes for the air force. After the B-17 bombers reached Israel, they were accepted into the Israeli air force and were flown by volunteer American veteran pilots who had served in the Army Air Corps.[14]

Hank Greenspun was charged along with Schwimmer with violating the U.S. arms embargo and exporting military goods without a license. Greenspun pleaded guilty and paid a $10,000 fine. Schwimmer opted for a trial, was convicted, fined $10,000, and lost his civil rights. Neither man lost his U.S. citizenship. Hank Greenspun was pardoned in 1962 by President John F. Kennedy. Al Schwimmer was pardoned in 1991 by President Bill Clinton.[15]

Shulman may or may not have believed he was doing anything illegal by volunteering to serve Israel's fight for independence. He was following his own moral imperative. As he would write many years later, in the foreword to *The Jews' Secret Fleet*, "The men whose stories are found in this book were not satisfied with the mere giving of money. . . . They believed direct action and personal involvement were morally imperative."

Still, the State Department's order for Shulman to turn over his passport came as an unwelcome surprise. He had no intention of returning to live in America. He was determined to do whatever was necessary to forestall making the one-way trip back to the United States and face possible prosecution. His case dragged on. In June 1951 he renewed his request for a visa extension. In a long, rambling "Supplementary Affadavit" he made many of the same points he made in his 1949 request for an extension. However, the way the affidavit reads suggests that Shulman was not entirely forthright in describing his presence in Israel or service in the Israeli navy. He did not account for his duties and responsibilities in the Israeli navy up to the time of his resignation. He also stated that he "entered the Israeli Armed Forces in October 1948." This curious choice of words flies in the face of the ceremony in Haifa October 26, 1948, at which David Ben-Gurion personally appointed him commander in chief of the Israeli navy.[16]

Shulman's renewed application and affidavit were forwarded to Ruth B. Shipley, chief of the Passport Division. Mrs. Shipley was not a person to be trifled with. In a *New York Times* profile she was reported to have had ninety assistants but insisted on examining every passport application herself. "She never seems hurried. The door to her office is always open and any applicant with a grievance can see that she is in there, and can walk right in." The *Times* described her as "a handsome woman with iron-gray hair and a gentle manner which is deceptive. . . . She is completely immovable, however, once a decision has been reached."[17] Although "immovable" in her decisions, Ruth Shipley was not autocratic. In Shulman's case she sought a ruling from W. H. Young, a deputy undersecretary. Young advised: "I cannot see that Shulman has improved his case by remaining in Israel. Obviously his services for the Israeli government were not in the interests of the United States . . . when a citizen of the United States lends his talents to a foreign government which is waging intermittent war against countries which are friendly to the United States."[18]

On July 24, 1951, Young sent a secret cablegram to the American consul in Haifa, directing that Paul Shulman's passport be canceled, except for travel back to the United States.[19] Still, Aluf Shulman continued the fight, although now in the United States. He and the family returned to their New York

STANDARD FORM NO. 64

Office Memorandum • UNITED STATES GOVERNMENT

TO : Mrs. Simpson   DATE: July 11, 1951.

FROM : Mr. Young

SUBJECT:

       I would adhere to the original authorization in
this case. I cannot see that Shulman has improved his
case by remaining in Israel. Obviously his services
for the Israeli government were not in the interests of
the United States. The interests of the United States
are not furthered in any way when a citizen of the United
States lends his talents to a foreign government which is
waging intermittent war against countries which are friendly to the
United States. Shulman subordinated his allegiance to
the United States to allegiance to the New State of Israel.
I suggest you inform Haifa that a passport only for travel
to the United States is authorized and that extension of
this passport for return to Israel will be considered when
Shulman applies therefor and submits evidence showing his
connections with American firms.

130- Shulman, Paul Nachman
PD:WHY:meo

Deputy Undersecretary of State William H. Young was referring to Paul Shulman as the "citizen" who "lends his talents" to a "foreign government" (Israel) that was "waging *intermittent* warfare against countries [Egypt] which are friendly to the United States." The U.S. and Egypt had trade agreements. *U.S. DEPARTMENT OF STATE, VIA AUTHOR'S FOIA REQUEST*

City apartment in September, but listed "11 Haviland Road [sic], Stamford, Connecticut," as his legal address.[20]

Shulman went to Washington, where he took advantage of Ruth Shipley's open door to press his case. In his oral history he recalled that he had "a big fight with Mrs. Shipley." Again, his recollection is at odds with what happened. Shipley was on leave, and Shulman met with Undersecretary W. H. Young, then acting director of the Passport Division. Paul conceded that he had "no further intentions to participate in the Israeli armed forces." In arguing to keep his passport, he explained that National Engineering was an American Corporation, with American officers and stockholders, but that it did business in Israel. For good measure he added, "Having investments and working in Israel will continue to promote good will and understanding of the people of Israel toward the people of the United States."[21] Having an American presence, of course, could qualify National Engineering for American foreign aid.

Details remain classified as to the outcome of Shulman's arguments before the State Department. Nonetheless, in July 1952 Paul, passport in hand, civil rights and citizenship intact, returned to Israel along with Rose, four-year-old Tzvi, and two-year-old David. Paul and his family would remain in Israel another four decades, but he never became a citizen of Israel—a country that was more of a home for him than his own nation.

Chapter 11

FORTY YEARS

What struck me was that [Paul] never forgot the human cost.
He didn't have a lot of respect for people who were "hawks."

—MARK SHULMAN, JULY 22, 2006

After the roar of war has subsided, it sometimes seems to take time for the sounds of peace to be heard. The day after Israel signed an armistice with the last of its invaders, in July 1949, there were the sounds of Israel beginning to build its new nation—the long-dreamed-of homeland for the world's dispersed Jews.[1]

But now, it seemed, the new government had no time and no thanks for the nearly three thousand volunteers—the Machal—among them about twelve hundred Americans and Canadians—who had joined in and, in some instances, led the fight for Israel's independence. Former U.S. Army colonel, the late David M. "Mickey" Marcus, had advised and trained the Palmach brigades that reopened the road to Jerusalem. Colonel Marcus was killed in an incident of questionably "friendly" fire. Paul Shulman had trained and led the fledging "bathtub corps" navy against the more powerful Egyptian navy. He was "kicked upstairs" by Prime Minister David Ben-Gurion and had to stand by, watching, as a fractious Haganah command fought to take the reins of authority.

Lee Harris was an American civilian who had been working in Palestine since February 1947 and was among the delegation that met Shulman when he first arrived in Palestine. Now, in 1949, he saw how quick the new Israeli leaders were to forget the contributions of the Volunteers from Abroad: "The accusations against Machal usually are that because they cannot speak the language they are, *ipso facto*, of very little use. The fact remains that were it not for the English-speaking Machal there would have been no Airforce in the skies. There would have been no ships on the sea. There would have been darned little Armoured units."[2] Harris, himself an ex–U.S. Navy officer, did not serve in the Israeli navy. Yet he saw how *protectzia*, indifference, and bureaucratic bumbling in the provisional Israeli government hobbled the navy. This, he believed, favored "incompetent Israeli personnel when there are experienced Machal men available. The situation in the Navy is a prime example. The navy is filled with experienced and excellent Machal personnel, who cannot do a job because of three or four Israelis who are determined to hold the power in their hands."[3] Because of *protectzia*, Harris observed, "In the Navy, Paul Shulman is being pushed around by Gershon Zaq, the undersecretary of the navy, who is the pal of Ben-Gurion. . . . I think [the Ben-Gurion government] was worried about having a young American in [command] there and they put in somebody who was, in effect, a political commissar. . . . Paul wasn't strong enough to have the guy keep his nose out of his business."[4]

According to another American volunteer, David Macarov, who worked with Danny Schind on acquiring ships for the Aliyah Bet clandestine immigration, it was not surprising that Shulman was ostracized by Ben-Gurion's inner circle: "If you hadn't come from Europe at the beginning of the twentieth century (even by way of America, as per Golda) you were an outsider, not to be trusted. . . . We [volunteers from abroad] learned that anyone who came to Israel expecting, 'Thank God you came,' could not but be disappointed when the attitude was, 'Where the hell have you been?'"[5]

Following Israel's armistice with Syria, officially ending the War of Independence, the Israeli government began a massive reallocation of properties once owned by Arabs.[6] Shulman was able to purchase property in Haifa's Ahuza section, a wooded, sparsely built-up area on the western slope of Mount Carmel. It was an ideal place to start a house and home. The property, with unparalleled views of the Mediterranean Sea below, caught the afternoon sun; cooling breezes washed up the slopes. To the east were the fertile Jezreel valley and the Hula marshlands.

Now officially detached from the Israeli Naval Service, Paul and Saunder Finard went full speed ahead at their company, National Engineering, Ltd. It was chartered in Israel but most of its investors, including Paul's mother, were Americans. Paul saw an opportunity for National Engineering to become involved with the Jewish National Fund's plan to drain the marshy areas around Lake Hula, a 177-square-kilometer (115-square-mile) region northeast of Haifa that had abundant freshwater. The plan called for digging channels and dredging feeder streams to funnel water into the Jordan River, which fed Lake Kinneret (the Sea of Galilee). As Dana Adams Schmidt wrote in the *New York Times*, "The declared objectives of the Hula draining project were two-fold: the addition of arable land and the eradication of malaria. Additional perceived benefits were to be an increase in the water potential of the newly

As the new Israeli government quickly named party loyalists to military leadership, Aluf (Admiral) Shulman found himself "kicked upstairs." Soon after, he retired from the navy. Then he and Saunder "Sandy" Finard (one of Shulman's instructors) set up a company to bid on large-scale construction projects in Israel. From left to right: Tzvi, Paul's oldest son; Sandy Finard and his son, Joel; and Shulman. *COURTESY MIRIAM FINARD*

established state by reducing evaporation losses, and utilization of peat as fertilizer and for industry. The ten-year project would add 4,000 acres of land for farming and some 5,000 acres of improved land suitable for building."[7]

The Galilee region, at least until 1948, was sparsely populated. In the fertile Jezreel valley, thousands of dunams (1 dunam = 2.25 acres) were being farmed by Arab-Palestinian tenants employed by absentee landlords. When the landlords sold their properties to the Histadrut Labor Federation, the tenant farmers often lost their jobs to Jewish settlers of the communes that were being developed. After the War of Independence, Israel annexed parts of the Golan region as part of the demilitarized zone between Israel and Syria. Thousands of Arab Palestinians fled or were forced out, and some four hundred villages were depopulated, according to the UN Truce Supervision Commission. More important, Israel gained access to water that originated in the Golan Heights. Thus began the "water war" between Israel and Syria that would overflow into the 1967 Six Days' War.

According to Israeli historian Shlomo Ben Ami, Ben-Gurion argued for the National Water Carrier project, even though certain members of the Israeli government questioned the economic and environmental benefits of draining the swamplands. The Jewish National Fund launched the project in July 1951. By late 1952 National Engineering and other contractors began working on one component of the Water Carrier project. This was to create the channels that would drain the marshy areas into feeder streams that flowed into the Jordan River. To accommodate the increased flow of water, the project called for deepening and straightening the Jordan River itself, which flowed south into Lake Kinneret.[8] It is not clear how much progress National Engineering made, because in 1953 the Jewish National Fund (JNF) awarded the second phase of the project to Construction Aggregates, an American firm based in Chicago. In a statement, the JNF said that the Chicago firm had more experience handling large-scale projects. "It was felt that the Israeli contracting concern . . . lacked the technical equipment such as floating dredges, to continue the job."[9] Criticism was growing, too, within the Israeli government. Those opposed to the project complained about the environmental impact of draining the swamps and doubted the quantity and quality of water that could be available. The Syrian government vigorously opposed the entire project. Syria's foreign minister complained to the UN Security Council that the project infringed on lands Syria claimed in the Golan Heights. In December 1953 UN Security Council Resolution 100 called on Israel to halt all work on the project, pending a thorough investigation. According to historian Shlomo Ben-Ami, "It was the overwhelming pressure from the two superpowers, the United States and the Soviet Union, as well as the Security Council, that forced Israel to interrupt the project."[10]

By the late 1950s, Shulman's partner, Saunder Finard, decided he'd had enough of National Engineering and Israel. Years later his widow, Miriam, recalled, "We remained in Israel for ten years. But as the business had some economic problems and prospects, at that time (poor vision on our part) my husband felt it necessary to return to the U.S.—to 'make some money.'"[11]

Despite losing the Hula contract, National Engineering stayed busy up through the 1960s. In his oral history Shulman recalled, "Together with a British company we worked on a sewage disposal plant in Haifa. We built housing and port facilities in Djibouti. We built about three hundred miles of roads in Ethiopia."[12] National Engineering was also involved with numerous military projects: in Ethiopia, a communications station and three airfields; in Iran, an underground monitoring station that listened for earthquakes, and for nuclear explosions in the Soviet Union. Soon after, Shulman sold National Engineering to Solel Boneh, the contracting division of the Histadrut Labor federation. But he was not out of business, not yet.

In his oral history Shulman made only a vague reference to his next ven-
ture: "I became President of the American company."[13] He offered only a few
more details in the draft of a biographical profile he prepared for the Technion Institute, on whose board of governors he sat. Shulman wrote that he
became the "principal shareholder and president of the Reynolds Construction Company, with headquarters in New York."[14] It is likely that Reynolds
Construction saw Shulman's expertise as a valuable asset to its plans for the
Middle East.

Reynolds Construction itself seems to have been formed in an unusual
manner. According to Wilbur Crane Eveland, in his book, *Ropes of Sand:
America's Failure in the Middle East*, Solel Boneh was actually behind the formation of the American company. Eveland wrote that he uncovered this
"truth" while he was employed as a consultant, working for the Vinnell
Construction Company. Vinnell was another American company also bidding
on large-scale construction projects throughout Israel and the Middle East.
Eveland discovered that contracts that had been awarded to Vinnell were
suddenly and without any notice, "on Washington's orders, given to a firm
that was neither American nor qualified to build the projects. The Reynolds
Construction Company, we learned, was actually Israeli."[15] Incorporated in
Delaware in 1959, six years later, in 1965 Reynolds received a Certificate
of Authority allowing it to operate in New York.[16] Eveland concluded that
Reynolds, from its New York "headquarters," could qualify to bid on projects
funded by American foreign aid.

Shulman, the Israeli navy's former commander in chief, no longer had
direct access to classified intelligence summaries prepared for the Israeli Defense
Forces. However, he and other former military leaders could not be blind to
tensions building again between Israel and Egypt as well as between Israel and
Syria. These tensions with Israel's northern neighbor erupted in April 1967
when Israeli jet fighter planes shot down Syrian jets over the Golan Heights.
Diplomatic initiatives went nowhere. The aptly named Six Days' War was
over almost as soon as it began. By June 13 Israel had captured the Golan
Heights. Israeli forces reunited Jordanian-held Jerusalem with Israel. In the
south, Israeli forces occupied the Sinai desert and set up defensive positions
along the Suez Canal. Shulman could not have been more proud to learn that
Israeli naval forces had captured the Egyptian naval base at Sharm El-Sheikh,
which overlooked the Straits of Tiran. Israel's naval victory ensured that merchant ships would have access through the straits and into the Gulf of Aqaba,
which led to Israel's southern port of Eilat. As the navy's first commander in
chief, Aluf Shulman had been a forceful advocate for a strong naval presence
in Eilat. Long before Israel had won freedom of the seas he believed that Israel

should have a naval squadron based in its southernmost city, even if it meant hauling armed patrol boats overland, across the Negev desert, to Eilat.

Whatever Shulman's feelings of pride in the successes of the Israeli navy, the former U.S. Navy lieutenant (junior grade) was greatly distressed by Israel's attack on the USS *Liberty* (AGTR-5). On June 8, 1967, the U.S. Navy's intelligence-gathering vessel was cruising in international waters off the coast of Israel when it was attacked by Israeli jet fighters and torpedo boats. Thirty-six American sailors were killed. More than one hundred, including civilian intelligence analysts, were injured. Israel offered the United States a lame apology for attacking the ship, saying they thought the vessel was an "out-of-service Egyptian horse carrier."[17] Israeli intelligence, was, of course, well aware that the *Liberty* was a U.S. intelligence-gathering vessel that had been sent to the Middle East to monitor the war situation between Israel and Egypt.[18] At the time of the attack Shulman probably did not have direct knowledge of the truth behind the incident. Still, he wrote a letter to the U.S. Navy's chief of naval operations, Admiral David L. McDonald. Shulman expressed his dismay over the "accident" (quotes in original) that cost the lives of so many "in their struggle of the freedom of the Seas." Shulman's letter concluded, "Sincerely, we hope that [the] nature of world affairs will soon permit men of the sea to sail in peaceful pursuit and that such tragedies will not be repeated."[19]

By 1967 Paul and Rose Shulman's firstborn son, Tzvi, now nineteen (he had been sent back to the United States three years earlier), had graduated from the Cheshire Academy, his father's alma mater. Said to be quiet and introspective like his father, he had been accepted at an American college, where he planned to major in psychology. The Shulman's second son, David, was sixteen. The youngest, Jonathan, had just celebrated his thirteenth birthday.

Paul became actively involved with Technion, Israel's renowned technical institute located in Haifa. He served for many years as chairman of the Student Affairs Committee of the Board of Governors. He pushed for lower tuition and fees, urged an easing of the heavy academic burden about which students complained, called for construction of more dormitories, and pleaded for better faculty-student relations. Carl Alpert, Technion's historian, recalled the frustration Paul endured getting the board to take action: "Most [board] members were interested in such matters as academic standards, budgets, construction on campus, public relations and other such matters."[20] It would seem that Paul's desire to see improvements in the quality of life for the student body remained a low priority. It was not until after Paul had died in 1994 that the Technion Board of Governors adopted at least a resolution of support for his ideas, if not putting them into practice. In a letter to Rose Shulman, Technion president Zehev Tadmore wrote, "I am sure that it will please you to know that the subjects of improving teaching at the Technion and substantially reducing the excessive study load, that were so dear to Paul, were at the focal point of discussion at the Board meeting. The significance of these subjects is being increasingly recognized at all levels and it is becoming an important factor in promoting discussion. It is indeed sad that Paul did not live to see his vision gradually become reality, but I know that both present and future students at the Technion will remember his name with gratitude."[21]

The Shulman house on Vitkin Street became a gathering place for the Shulmans' many Israeli and American friends. Among those who visited from time to time, from their home in Mexico, were Paul's brother, Mark, and his family. Mark recalled that discussions were always lively. "Paul was one of those persons who did not suffer the opinions of those who had not been there." About his older brother, Mark recalled, "Here was a person who had graduated from the naval academy and had seen combat, who could have been something of a 'hawk.' What struck me was that he . . . didn't have a lot of respect for people who were 'hawks.'"[22]

The Six Days' War saw Israeli forces retake the West Bank and reunite the Holy City of Jerusalem with the nation of Israel. Finally, it became possible to reopen the Hadassah Medical Center on Jerusalem's Mount Scopus. Paul's mother, Rebecca Shulman, had been closely associated with the medical center since it opened in 1934. She was deeply involved in the quality of training of and living conditions for the nursing staff. Rebecca had been in Tel Aviv during the 1948 War of Independence when Arab forces captured the mountain-top medical facility. She heard about the Arab massacre of a convoy of seventy-eight doctors and nurses who were trying to reach the hospital. Upon her return to New York she told the Hadassah board of directors, "I doubt whether we will be able to use Scopus again. I recommend that we start building somewhere else."[23]

After the War of Independence, Hadassah did open a medical facility in Ein Kerem, a neighborhood just below Mount Scopus. Over the next nineteen years, a security guard kept watch on the deserted medical campus, but the facility deteriorated. Rebecca Shulman was again in Israel during the Six Days' War. After Jerusalem was reunited with Israel, she was with the Hadassah delegation that accompanied Prime Minister Levi Eshkol up to Mount Scopus to raise the Israeli and Hadassah flags atop the hospital building. She was eager to see the facility returned to its former excellence and called on her son to help out.

Paul came down from Haifa and spent three days at Mount Scopus, assessing damage to the medical complex. He proposed a reconstruction program

Miriam "Mimi" Finard and Sandy Finard, and Paul and Rose Shulman, at a Purim
festival in the 1950s. Paul's brother, Mark, said that Paul never forgot the "human
cost" of suffering, and did not have a lot of respect for self-proclaimed "hawks." The
Purim festival celebrates the miracle of Jewish survival. COURTESY MIRIAM FINARD

that would include young volunteers from abroad, who would work alongside construction professionals to renovate the facility. Hadassah leaders in
Jerusalem worried that the Histadrut Labor Federation would insist that only
adult Israeli workers be employed. Labor Minister Yigal Allon sent a telegram
to Hadassah, saying that he "accepts wholeheartedly these plans" proposed by
Paul Shulman. Renovations took several months. Shulman never submitted
a bill for his services. A report by Hadassah concluded, "Mr. Shulman's warm
and friendly approach to the young people, his understanding of their interest . . . immediately influenced each of them to try to overcome the apparent
difficulties and to throw themselves into the job. . . . They considered it an
honor to work on Scopus." By February 1968 the work that Shulman managed
was far enough along that the medical center could operate on a limited basis.
During a ceremony that month Paul paid tribute to Hadassah "and to one special Hadassah lady, the chairman of this meeting, my mother." In his remarks
Shulman defined a volunteer as "one who enters into any service of his own
free well, or offers himself for service without legal obligation to do so."[24]

   In November 1970 Shulman was approached by Lawrence Schacht, president of the New York–based Schacht Steel Construction Company. That year
Larry Schacht was also chairman of the United Jewish Appeal. Schacht knew

that Shulman had experience managing large-scale construction projects. When they met in Haifa, he hired Paul to serve as managing director of a new Schacht subsidiary, Eastern Dredging. The new company submitted plans to the government to reclaim a little more than a mile (two kilometers) of Haifa shorefront south of the city for beaches. Schacht also planned to build $10- to $15-million worth of recreational facilities that would include "floatels," or houseboat-type accommodations for tourists.[25]

On the Shulman family's periodic visits to the United States, they would stay with Paul's mother, now living full-time at their Stamford home. Rebecca Shulman, then in her eighties, was no longer active with Hadassah, but she kept in touch with the organization, sometimes being chauffeur-driven into Manhattan for lunch with friends. As much as she treasured the peace and quiet of her personal wing added on to the house, she loved gatherings of her family—children, grandchildren, cousins, nieces, and nephews. Mark Shulman recalled that the summer visits to Haviland Court were like "command performances." According to Paul's nephew, David, whenever Paul himself came home, "he was kind of solitary. He wouldn't talk, but would kind of park himself in front of the TV and lose himself in sports." When Mark (who had served in the U.S. Army) was there, the two men, David recalled, would engage in "trash talk" about who would win that year's Army-Navy football game.[26] Paul's visits sometimes generated some local excitement. "Whenever 'the Admiral' did come," recalled Patricia Palkimas, a neighbor who lived across the lane, "it was quite an event. There was lots of activity and the house was full of guests."[27] Paul, she recalled, was always gracious with guests. However, Paul's wife, Rose, preferred to stay with her sister in New Jersey.

In the 1980s Paul purchased a company that had developed a process to protect metallic surfaces from rusting and corroding by applying a fused-on coating of metallic powders. When applied to a ship's hull, the coating helped to prevent barnacles from forming. The company did business with merchant shipping companies and the Israeli navy. Paul eventually brought his sons into the company, grooming them to take over. Paul joined the Carmel Yacht Club, and enjoyed commanding nothing more than his thirty-foot sailboat, *Rose of Sharon*, on the waters of Haifa bay.

Among visitors to the Shulman's Vitkin Street home in Haifa was Charles Sobel. Also a member of the U.S. Naval Academy class commissioned in 1944, Sobel knew of Shulman mainly through his "Shulman's Fighting Ships" features published in *The Log*. On a trip to Israel in the 1970s, Sobel and his wife paid a social call on the Shulmans. The two men shared stories about their years at "the Yard" (Annapolis), about the Navy, and life in Israel. A friendship was born that would last until Shulman's death in 1994.[28] In 1984

Charles Sobel's son, Lawrence, took a job with a technology company located near Haifa. He, too, called on his father's friend and found that Paul took to him almost like a son. "I would visit and [Paul] would give me lots of advice. Most of all he would take me out to dinner. Both he and his wife knew every restaurant in the country." Larry Sobel said that he "pretty much lived [at the Shulmans'] on the weekends for two or three years."[29] He and Paul's oldest son, Tzvi, then in his late thirties, became close. Their friendship, however, was destined not to last.

Chapter 12

A POSTMORTEM

In my own defense, I can seek solace in the fact that at 25 years of age, I did my BEST.

—PAUL SHULMAN, MAY 1988

No longer even indirectly involved with the Israeli navy by 1988, Paul Shulman began to collect his thoughts about his legacy to the naval service and his homeland of choice. Like maybe a dozen other of the American volunteers, he did not return home to the United States. He remained a U.S. citizen and did not make Aliyah; that is, he did not apply for Israeli citizenship. Perhaps it was because in the passage of his years in Israel he did not—or could not—embrace the changes that had come over the nation that he had helped to fight for. In particular, Paul had the feeling—a fear almost—that soon the service rendered by the volunteers from abroad would be forgotten. No one would care, or even remember that they had answered the call. Israel of the 1980s seemed no longer to be *their* homeland.

The Shulman house on Vitkin Street had become a gathering place, like an unofficial "O-Club" (social club on a military base for commissioned officers) for the graying naval volunteers. Some visited from as close as Haifa; some motored up the new coastal highway from Tel Aviv and Jerusalem. Others arrived at Ben-Gurion International Airport on a visit from America, to attend a grandson's ceremonial, coming-of-age bar mitzvah or a granddaughter's bat mitzvah. Or, perhaps, they were on a group tour with their synagogue. If the tour included Haifa and a visit to the Clandestine Immigration and Naval Museum, the old veterans might also call to see if the "Aluf"—their admiral—was available. Rose, as always the gracious hostess, provided snacks and drinks. The men might start out talking about the present "situation" in Israel, but inevitably they would lapse back in time and retell "sea stories" about the old days and their exploits. A visitor might ask after someone, or mention seeing a memorial obituary of a volunteer in the newsletter of the AACI—Association of Americans and Canadians in Israel—or in the bulletin of the AVI—American Veterans of Israel.

An always-welcome visitor from Jerusalem was Murray S. Greenfield, a former officer in the U.S. Merchant Marine. Following World War II, Greenfield served as a volunteer on a war-surplus Canadian icebreaker that had been converted into a refugee carrier and named *Hatikvah*.[1] Like Rose and Paul Shulman, after the War of Independence Murray Greenfield and his wife settled in Israel. He wrote articles for English-language magazines and then established Gefen Publishing. Gefen would go on to become the largest publisher in Israel of English-language books. By the 1980s Greenfield, too, had become concerned that the contributions of the Volunteers from Abroad—especially those who had served in the navy—would be forgotten. He began to collect oral histories, letters, and photos from American, British, Canadian, Australian, and South African volunteers who had manned the Aliyah Bet vessels and served in the Israeli navy. Greenfield dug through state and military archives for official histories of the ships, their crews, and their missions. He collaborated with Joseph Hochstein to write *The Jews' Secret Fleet*. Murray Greenfield asked Paul Shulman to write the foreword.

For forty years Shulman had been intimately linked to Israel. He had watched as the nation took its first steps and the navy became a hard-charging force manned by trained professionals. His feelings show in the foreword's opening lines:

> When this century finally finds itself in the pages of history it will probably, and sadly, not be recalled for the achievements in science and technology, or medicine, nor for the broadening of cultural interest in all its forms. No doubt our century will be remembered for two dominant features: continuous warfare and the individual's struggle for material advancement. . . . People of our generation and probably that of our children built upon the achievement of our fathers in seeking higher education and pursuing remunerative professions. . . . In their success they contributed financially to many worthy causes. . . . Surely one of these causes was the Zionist aspiration and the support of Jewish refugees. . . . The men whose stories are found in this book were not satisfied with the mere giving of money. . . . Perhaps they had little to give. . . . They saw the futility of the printed word and of well-turned speeches. They believed [that] direct action and personal involvement were morally imperative.[2]

Yet, for Paul, by then his direct action and his personal involvement in the affairs of the state had taken a backseat to personal involvement with his family and thoughts about his legacy. He was asked to write an article for an Israeli military publication. His working title was, "From My Point of View: Recollections on the Israeli Navy Forty Years Ago." Shulman began by asking readers to indulge him and his commentary. "Are you ever annoyed by the self-righteousness and glory-seeking of most writers of their memories?" Then, Shulman wrote about how he believed the fledgling Israeli navy veered off course in 1948 and 1949. "There was little understanding by the General Headquarters, where some of the officers, many from the PALMACH, openly opposed the . . . navy as ordered by Ben-Gurion. . . .When, then, did all the bad-mouthing begin?" Paul believed that it began right after the Israeli navy was established in March 1948 out of the spars of the old Palyam. "When the news reached the headquarters of the PALMACH there was an 'open revolt.' Israel Galili is reported to have said that he would fight this decision openly and in every way possible. . . . If the PALMACH could not control [the navy] the [Haganah] didn't want it"[3] (capitals in original).

Summing up, Shulman recalled, "David Ben-Gurion once advised me to the effect: 'We are by nature a vindictive, critical people who seldom offer praise but are free to express criticism of our fellows. Under such conditions, each must find self satisfaction in one's own accomplishments.'" Shulman concluded his article with, "Perhaps the criticism of some of my comrades-in-arms is out of place. Doesn't a bad carpenter blame his tools? In my own defense, I can seek solace in the fact that at 25 years of age, I did my BEST."[4]

Forty years later, apparently, his best was still not good enough for the Ministry of Defense. On May 15, 1988, Israel marked the fortieth anniversary of the state. At the annual military rally, held at the national stadium in Tel Aviv, Gershon Zaq was given an award for his role in helping to establish Israel's navy.[5] The very next day, Rose Shulman wrote an angry letter to the director of the Haganah museum. Writing "out of loyalty to my husband and without his knowledge," she demanded to know why Zaq had been given an award and cited as having been the "first commander" when he was "never in the Navy and only appeared . . . as a government adviser for a short time until my husband's arrival." Rose considered the slight as "shameful and painful that modern history can not be accurately recorded and that such hurtful mistakes are being made constantly." She fired a broadside at the system that rewarded the party faithful but ignored outsiders: "These young and courageous men, like Sandy Finard, Richard Rosenberg, Alan Burke [sic] of England and Hal Gershoni came from abroad to serve to the best of their ability, and it is painful that they should have been ignored after 40 years.

. . . I beg you to tell me why these devoted sons should have been forgotten and ignored."[6]

What Shulman thought about the award to Gershon Zaq has not been recorded. In the first in a series of family letters to friends, Paul covered up his true feelings with a wry comment about his role in that 1988 National Military Rally. Twenty of the original military commanders entered the stadium in Jeeps while their names and exploits were announced. Writing about himself in the third person (as if it might appear unseemly to refer to himself as "I"), Paul quipped, "Suffice it to say that Paul did not fall out of the Jeep. . . . Twelve months from now will see yet another Independence Day . . . at which time we will be escorted into the stadium in ambulances and not Jeeps."[7] If Paul ever learned of Rose's secret letter, what he thought of it and his wife's involvement in his affairs is suggested in that first letter, dated the day after Israel's fortieth anniversary commemoration. In it, Paul waxed philosophic: "Of course, there are divers opinions and much incrimination within the Jewish world and within this nation, as well within this house, as to the means of achieving peace . . . which will release energies and resources to strengthen and improve society and render Israel a Light Unto All nations. . . . Despite the self-criticism and that from abroad about shortcomings in government or in society, there are many things for which we can be justly proud."[8]

This first Shulman letter is exceptionally well thought out—Paul was always a good writer. He marked the difference between Israel's Independence Day and Memorial Day, which precedes it: "[Memorial Day] is a painful reminder that there is a costly price for Independence, and that the survival of this country is not given as a prize, but one won by the ongoing struggle and sacrifice of those who are prepared to bear arms in the defense of what they hold dear."[9] In the view of Israeli political historian Maoz Azaryahu, "Independence Day is linked to sentiments of national belonging and [the people's] willingness to defend (and be sacrificed for) the nation. Given how often and consistently the parade was opposed by the country's military elites the procession seemed to have suited the interests of the civilian elites."[10]

Perhaps to make amends for the Ministry of Defense slight, that year the Association of Americans and Canadians in Israel honored Shulman. At the 1988 AACI awards ceremony, which was attended by Israeli president Chaim Herzog and the American and Canadian ambassadors, Shulman and four others from North America were honored for their contributions to Israel. In her introduction AACI president Natalie Gordon remarked, "It's not always easy to succeed as immigrants, let alone excel in areas that positively affect the lives of all Israelis."[11]

Even this modest recognition could not raise Shulman's spirits, because a personal tragedy loomed. Two weeks after his first family letter, on June 1, 1988, Paul again wrote to "Dear Friend," "The most significant event in our lives has been our Tzvi's war with cancer. We are sure that many of you have experienced illness in your family. For us it is something new. Tzvi has had surgery to remove a chain of lymph glands. . . . It is a source of strength to us to see the courage and determination with which Tzvi and his family accepts this challenge. We are sure he will be successful in his fight. It is now two weeks since the surgery, which was a success."[12]

There may have been other letters written to family and friends over the next three years. The next to surface was dated January 8, 1991. The first Gulf War had been under way since August 1990. By January 1991 Iraq ignored the United Nations' demand to withdraw from Kuwait, which Iraqi leader Saddam Hussein claimed to have "annexed." When Hussein refused to withdraw, the U.S.-led military coalition launched Operation Desert Storm to destroy the Iraqi army. In retaliation, Iraq launched Russian-made SCUD missiles against Israel, hoping to divide coalition forces. Iraq had used chemical warfare in 1988 against its Kurdish minorities. All Israel was on high alert. Adults and children had been issued and practiced using gas masks and had conducted air raid drills in bomb-proof shelters. Paul's letter was dark with the portent of a "doomsday." A week later, on January 17, the U.S.-led military coalition launched its massive Operation Desert Storm. The very next day, Iraq began launching Russian-made SCUD missiles into Israel. Over the next six weeks, more than three hundred missiles fell on Tel Aviv and Haifa.[13]

In his January 8 letter Shulman wrote, "With the potential 'doomsday' just one week away, Rose and I feel an urgent desire to communicate. . . . I ask myself why this 'urgent' desire at this special moment? Probably psychologically a wish to break the bands of isolation in which the people of Israel finds itself [sic]." Though clearly worried for his family, Paul managed an apt nautical metaphor to express what he felt about the latest attempt to wipe Israel off the map:

The world is asking Israel to keep "a low profile" on a small craft in a turbulent sea whose waves are generated by an Arab madman confronted by a U.S. president and his equally WASPish Secretary of State. The madman sees standing up to the West and the destruction of Israel as his "passport to eternity" with the glory of the Arab world on route. As for the WASP twins,* they are busy trying to find Iraq [a] "face saving" tool that will convince the madman to accept an

American mandate, thus giving the President all he wants without the wrath of part of a nation reluctant to fight a potentially unpopular war. Both are willing to sacrifice the interest and security of Israel as a means to obtain their ends.[14]

Shulman himself was experiencing similar "bands of isolation." His letter continued: "The large-scale immigration is of epic proportions. There is a new second language heard on the streets. There is a new labor force ready and eager. . . . [It is] changing and need no longer be based on Arabs. Integration is not easy, and some conflicts with some levels of society are to be expected. . . . The bureaucracy and political ineptitude cannot deal with 2,000 newcomers a day and this causes some resentment."[15]

The resentment was like a rash that no salve could heal. Since the days of Ben-Gurion's Mapai political organization, Israel had been turning away from its socialist origins. Following Israel's stunning victory in the 1967 Six Days' War, Israelis became filled with a feeling of righteousness. They had fought, and won, and they felt they had earned a right to their place under the sun. *Their* place, however, did not necessarily include a place for those unlike themselves: the Palestinian and immigrant population of mostly semiskilled laborers that found itself shut out of Israel's market for skilled workers. Shulman, as an employer of numerous construction crews, was aware that the labor force "need no longer be based on Arabs."

In what the Israeli Ministry of Foreign Affairs called the "Great Awakening," starting around 1990 there began a huge influx of immigrants from the Soviet Union. But not all were the Russians that Israel needed or wanted. Many of the better-educated Russians who left had already emigrated to the United States and other countries. Not all the Russians who did settle in Israel experienced the "full social and political equality of all Israel's citizens" that Ben-Gurion had promised and assured years before.

As Paul Shulman's letter noted, "There is a new second language heard on the streets." And, there was a "second society" as well. According to social

---

*White Anglo-Saxon Protestant. President George Herbert Walker Bush and his father, Senator Prescott Bush, were from a white, upper-middle-class, New England family. George H. W. Bush was educated at exclusive private academies. Following his U.S. Navy service in World War II he attended Yale University. There he pledged to the one-hundred-year-old fraternity, Delta Kappa Epsilon (DKE—"the Dekes"). As was his father before him, he was initiated into the Skull and Bones secret society, before graduating as a member of the Phi Beta Kappa society. George H. W. Bush served in the House of Representatives, and then was elected U.S. president in 1988. His secretary of state was James A. Baker III. Not all WASPs are actually Protestants. The term is usually applied, with disdain, to a type of person who aspires to a lifestyle of power, influence, and wealth.

scientist Larissa Remenick, the Russians tended to see themselves not as new Israelis but more as "trans-national Russians." Their assimilation "empowers the weakest and least integrated segments of the Russian community, attenuating their dependency on the host society [and] hampers economic and social integration . . . and reinforces cultural conflict between the newcomers and old-timers in Israel."[16] Paul Shulman was well aware that he had become one of the "old-timers." Yet, problems with the labor force and the multiple languages heard on the street had become a mere irritant in his life. His letter of January 8, 1991, concluded, "Last month we had the second anniversary of our Tzvi's death. It is still most painful and always will be."[17]

On February 15, 1992, Paul completed writing a memorial to "My Dear and Beloved Family. This letter is intended to greet you on January First, 2000." He wrote, however, that he had "no assurance" he would be around by the turn of the century. This letter is clearly written to his children: "Each of you . . . have been a source of great pleasure. You have given much, for which you have earned our respect and admiration. . . . As an older generation, we had hoped to will to you a better world, a more human and honorable nation. . . . There is some doubt that my generation has done a creditable job." Shulman's words are then directed to his and Rose's grandchildren: "First, you, too have been sources of love and pride, and we are grateful and proud. Your parents have been excellent examples to follow, but it must be your aim to build on these worthy examples and to equip yourselves with education, intellectual interests and worldly knowledge, all of which, as much as your earning skills, will lead you to a full and meaningful life for yourselves and your future families. . . . I should end by asking forgiveness for anything which I might have done wrong, and to extend whole-hearted wishes for your aspirations. With much love, D A D."[18]

Paul Shulman died on May 14, 1994—one day short of Israel's forty-fifth anniversary, as reckoned on the Julian calendar. Rose had long known of the great disappointment that her husband harbored silently in not being given the recognition he felt he deserved. As commander in chief of the fledgling Israeli navy in 1948, he had been called Aluf, equivalent to being addressed respectfully as "the Old Man." But Shulman did not have the rank of Aluf to go with it. Until 1949, when official ranks were established for the navy, the highest rank he could have held was Sgan Mishne, or captain, equivalent to a U.S. Navy captain or U.S. Marine Corps colonel. Israel's highest general rank at the time, Rav Aluf, or major general, was reserved for army officers only.[19] Rose began a letter-writing campaign to persuade the Israeli Defense Forces and the government to recognize her husband's contribution. Nearly a year after Paul died, on January 8, 1995, Prime Minister Yitzak Rabin

authorized the posthumous rank of major general to Shaul Ben-Zvi. The award
was presented to his widow, Rose. The Cheshire Academy's ablest navigator
had finally made admiral.

Shortly after Paul's, death his cousins, Albert and Allan Bildner, spear-
headed a fund-raising drive to establish a chapel at the U.S. Naval Academy
at Annapolis, where Jewish midshipmen could attend services. At a memorial service held in Dahlgren Hall on May 12, 1995, Rose and the two surviving Shulman sons were among those honored. Rose Shulman spoke to family,
friends, supporters, and hundreds of the former Volunteers from Abroad who
had gathered from all over the world to honor Aluf Shulman.[20] With her New
York accent intact, Rose spoke of Paul's legacy: "His pride in having attended
the naval academy never ended. . . . His loyalty to Ben-Gurion endured his
entire life. . . . He was part of the pages of the history of Israel."[21]

Chapter 13

THE PAGES OF HISTORY

His loyalty to Ben-Gurion endured his entire life.He [Paul] was part of the pages of the history of Israel.

—ROSE SHULMAN, MAY 12, 1995

At the memorial service for Paul Shulman, held at the U.S. Naval Academy in May 1995, a year after his death, Rose Shulman said that her late husband belonged to the pages of Israel's history. Yes, but which Israel? Whose Israel?

Genesis 15:18–21 informs that Eretz Yisrael, the Land of Israel, was promised as an everlasting possession to the descendants of Hebrew patriarchs, a land "from the [Nile] river of Egypt as far as the great river the Euphrates" in what is modern-day Iran. However, in the view of historian Daniel Cil Brecher, "There is no place in the historical area of settlement where Jews have lived continuously. The Jewish groups who stayed here throughout the centuries were subject to the same migratory factors as other diaspora communities. The Jews' link to their original homeland, which Zionism relies on, had long ago assumed a spiritual character, and the historical 'Land of Israel' was less a concrete than a mythic place."[1] Brecher maintains that the historical Israel was hardly "settled" by Jews, and that the "building of the nation was primarily an act of colonization and subjugation of the land. . . . The goal was to settle Jews who would create the economic, political and territorial conditions to settle even more Jews."[2] The modern real estate that today is Israel has far more modest boundaries than in the biblical outline, and the state came together in a much-less miraculous fashion. Even the name of the pre-state region was fought over. Zionists wanted it called Eretz Yisrael, "The Land of Israel." British Mandate authorities insisted that the territory be called "Palestina." In twentieth-century usage the "Land of Israel" usually denotes only those parts of the region that came under British Mandate, which in 1948 included part of Trans-Jordan (now Jordan).

The emergence of modern-day Zionism in the middle of the nineteenth century is said to have emerged from within the European culture of anti-Semitism. Even the powerful Catholic Church promulgated the idea that Jews could not and would never be totally assimilated into Western European culture and thus would remain as an eternally stateless people. This gave impetus to a small group of articulate Jewish thinkers to re-create the biblical Zion elsewhere. According to *Israel, a Country Study*, written by Helen Chapin Metz and published by the Federal Research Division of the Library of Congress, "The Zionists sought to solve the Jewish problem by creating a Jewish entity outside Europe but modeled after the European nation-state. . . . West European Jewry had become distanced from both the ritual and culture of traditional Judaism. Thus, Zionism in its West European Jewish context envisioned a purely political solution to the Jewish problem: a state of Jews rather than a Jewish state."[3]

It was Theodor Herzl, a journalist, who saw that the solution to the "Jewish problem" would be the establishment of a Jewish state in any available territory to which the majority of European Jewry could emigrate. It was Herzl who, in 1897, convened the First Zionist Congress, in Basel, Switzerland. The conference established as its mandate "to create for the Jewish people a home in Palestine, secured by Public Law."[4] Between 1882 and 1903 some 35,000 Jews fled Europe to begin settlements in Palestine, which was then a Turkish province on the outskirts of the despotic Ottoman Empire. Groups of settlers of this First Aliyah (return to the Homeland) established collective agricultural communities called moshavim (singular: moshav), whose organization is similar to that of kibbutzim (singular: kibbutz), or communes.[5] The first true kibbutz, Degania Aleph, was established in 1902, near Lake Kinneret.

However harsh the political and social climate had been back in the immigrants' countries of origin, the physical conditions in Palestine were grim. For one thing the weather could be brutally hot. Living conditions were primitive. Also, the rock-hard land had to be cleared and tilled by hand. By 1903 half of the settlers from the First Aliyah had returned to their homes of origin because the socialist-imbued Moshav way of life provided meager spiritual and economic rewards. A man who was skilled at a trade was expected to clear the land alongside a common laborer and was paid the same as the laborer. Some settlers who stayed migrated to cities such as Jaffa, Jerusalem, and Haifa, where there were more opportunities for them to use their skills and ply their trades. In the early years of the twentieth century, relations between Arabs and the Jewish settlers were amicable, at least until the number of Jews began to outnumber Arab interests.

From 1903 to 1914, the period of the so-called Second Aliyah, another 40,000 Jews came by sea and overland to settle in what they hoped would be their new homeland. Among those arriving in 1906 from Poland (then part of Russia) was twenty-year-old David Grün. He was already imbued with the socialist philosophies of Theodore Herzl and his dream of a Zionist homeland in Palestine. Grün took the Hebrew surname Ben-Gurion (lion cub). After studying law at the University of Istanbul, in 1915 he made his way to the United States. In New York City he began building a network of contacts with influential Americans, to get them involved with the Zionist dream. Ben-Gurion would later call on this network of supporters when he began the quest to establish the State of Israel.

After serving in the Jewish Legion of the British Army during World War I, David Ben-Gurion returned to Palestine. Along with Berl Katznelson, his friend and socialist soul mate, Ben-Gurion established the Labor Zionist movement. One of Ben-Gurion's biographers said that his philosophy was clear from the start. In a 1922 speech before the Zionist organization, Ben-Gurion declared, "We are conquerors of the land facing an iron wall, and we have to break through it. . . . We will be able to carry out this conquest of the land by the Jewish worker. . . . The creation of a new Zionist movement . . . is the prerequisite for the fulfillment of Zionism."[6] Through shrewd political maneuvering Ben-Gurion amalgamated several small Zionist groups into the labor federation that became known as Histadrut. This organization would provide Ben-Gurion with enormous political resources during Israel's early decades because it was Histadrut that controlled access to jobs and capital.

Waves of immigrants continued to arrive right up to the eve of World War II. By 1940 the population of Jews in Palestine had risen to 554,000 from 84,000 in 1926. More important, this growth represented a population increase of Jews of more than 800 percent in rural areas and over 500 percent in urban areas.[7] It was among these communities that Ben-Gurion built his political base, the left-of-center Mapai party.[8] In the 1930s Ben-Gurion and the Mapai could be considered moderate, if that organization were compared with the politically right-wing and more militarily aggressive Irgun Tsvai Leumi movement, whose chief proponent was Menachem Begin. Yet, however "moderate" Mapai might have seemed, Ben-Gurion understood the need for a defense force and formed the quasi-official, mostly volunteer Haganah, which would be able to protect the domestic, agricultural, and economic enclaves the settlers had created in Palestine. Mapai leaders had no illusions about continuing an amicable relationship with Arabs in Palestine.

Between 1936 and 1939, in fact right up until the start of World War II in 1940, discontent among Arabs remaining in Palestine simmered and boiled over numerous times. Their aspirations stifled by the oppressive Mandatory government, the Arabs attacked British installations and property owned by Jews, as well. The Mapai was complicit in helping the British suppress civil disobedience by Arabs because the Mandatory authorities found it convenient to tacitly accept help from the Haganah to quell the violence. According to historian Shlomo Ben-Ami, the reality of the suppression was that Ben-Gurion and the Zionists had no intention of seeking peace and accommodation with the Arabs. "Of course Ben-Gurion knew only too well that the full realization of Zionism in terms of territory and immigration meant that there could be no peace, for the Arabs would never reconcile themselves to such Zionist objectives."[9]

The non-Jewish residents of Palestine also had reason to fear the Histadrut-financed purchases of land from individual farmers, and from the absentee owners who held large tracts of land and employed *fellahin* peasants to work the land. The Zionists took the position that only those Jewish settlers who tilled the land themselves should be seen as the rightful owners. The *fellahin* understood that as soon as the land they worked was sold to Jews, they would lose their jobs. They also feared that they would become disenfranchised from the place that they had long considered to be *their* homeland. Historian Shlomo Ben-Ami claims, "Tribal and local loyalties, more than a defined national identity with a clear notion of its territorial horizons, characterized the Palestinian[s]."[10]

In the years following World War I, both the British and the Zionists had dreams, aspirations, and plans for Palestine. In 1917 British foreign secretary Arthur James, Lord Balfour sent a letter to Lord Rothschild, a leader of England's Jewish community. The letter stated, in part, "His Majesty's Government view with favour the establishment in Palestine of a national home for the Jewish people." The next sentence, however, clearly qualified the government's "favour": "it being clearly understood that nothing shall be done which may prejudice the civil and religious rights of existing non-Jewish communities in Palestine."[11] This so-called "Balfour Declaration" set the stage for the Zionists' drive for a Homeland for Jews the world over. Once and for all time, the Homeland would end the centuries-old Jewish Diaspora, or worldwide dispersion, of the Jewish people. The Arabs feared any partition of the territory, in particular if it were coupled with the unlimited immigration of Jews, which could force the Arabs into a minority.

In 1922—the year Paul Shulman was born—the League of Nations voted to give Great Britain a Mandate to govern Palestine. Under the mandate, Great Britain saw its role as being the benevolent administrator of a territory in which two groups of mutually distrustful "children"—the Jews and Arabs— attempted to cohabitate. Great Britain, not willing to upset the neighboring

Arab states (and endanger British access to Middle East oil), steadily back-pedaled on its support for the 1917 Balfour Declaration. By the late 1930s, British governmental and public sentiment had turned away from the plight of the Jewish people. In May 1939 Foreign Secretary Ernest Bevin published a White Paper—an official statement of policy—that repudiated the Balfour Declaration. The White Paper declared that Palestine "should [not] be con-verted into a Jewish State against the will of the Arab population." The White Paper also limited legal Jewish immigration to Palestine to a total of 75,000 men, women, and children over the next five years. After that, immigration of Jews would be "contingent on Arab consent."[12] Not only did Great Britain renege on admitting the promised 75,000 immigrants to Palestine, but the British government also issued only 58,000 entry visas and, by May 1944, sus-pended legal immigration.

At one point after World War II, Great Britain proposed dividing Palestine into four regions, like a commonwealth, which would be administered by a regent governor. Jerusalem would be an international city. The idea had the support of Chaim Weitzman, who was then president of the World Zionist Organization. Ben-Gurion, then chairman of the Executive Committee of the Jewish Agency for Palestine, vociferously objected to the scheme. Speaking before the 1946 annual convention of Hadassah, Ben-Gurion declared, "The only thing that can replace the Mandate with our consent or agreement—and no settlement in Palestine is possible without our agreement—is the establish-ment of a Jewish state, which will rebuild the country for the benefit of the Jewish settlers and the present Arab population."[13]

Ben-Gurion understood that if there were to be a Jewish state, then the Zionists would do whatever was necessary to terminate Palestinian interests, and those of Great Britain as well. He was quoted as saying, "We will fight with the British against Hitler as if there were no White Paper. [We] will fight the White Paper as if there were no war."[14] In a disagreement over policy, Weitzman soon resigned as president of the World Zionist Organization. He would later be called upon to fill the mostly ceremonial position of president of the State of Israel, with Ben-Gurion as its first prime minister.

The Franklin D. Roosevelt administration did little to protest or oppose British opposition to Jewish immigration. In fact, Breckinridge Long, during World War II assistant secretary of state with jurisdiction over immigration and refugee problems, was the major obstacle to the United States admit-ting war refugees to America. Long's well-known racial biases set the tone for the anti-Jewish culture within the Department of State during the latter years of the Roosevelt administration and early years of the administration of President Harry S. Truman, Roosevelt's successor. This bias influenced President

Truman's decision to go along with the State Department–authored embargo of the sale of American-made military hardware to the Middle East. (Even barbed wire was embargoed!) Further, U.S.-flagged cargo ships were forbidden to carry war materiel to the Middle East. These restrictions would greatly hinder Israel's ability to defend itself in the 1948 War of Independence.[15]

In his seminal work, *The Abandonment of the Jews*, historian David Wyman leveled harsh criticism at the Roosevelt administration and how it failed the Jewish people. For example, by November 1943 Washington had firsthand, verified, eyewitness accounts of the mass extermination of the Jews by the Nazis. Only then did FDR condemn Nazi atrocities in general, and that mainly to quiet a general public outcry over the lack of the government's rescue policy for survivors of the genocide. In one notorious incident that was hushed up until after the war in Europe was over, the War Department refused to let American B-24 aircraft bomb the Auschwitz extermination center and railroad, yet okayed a raid on a power plant only five miles away. When pressed for an explanation, the administration's public response was that America didn't want to be accused of bombing and killing "innocent civilians." Wyman is no less critical of the American Jewish community. "[The Jewish organizations'] effectiveness was diminished by their inability to mount a sustained or unified drive for governmental action; and by fighting among the several [Jewish] organizations."[16]

Ben-Gurion and the Jewish Agency knew it had to overcome this internal divisiveness if it wanted to mobilize American support to counter what they perceived as America's ambivalence at best—and outright bigotry at worst—toward the world's Jewish people. A hard-nosed pragmatist, Ben-Gurion knew that the Jewish people would have to go it alone in their fight for the Jewish state of Israel. He was a leader who inspired (and demanded) loyalty from his party faithful and military commanders. During the War of Independence "B. G." could be personally loyal to Rebecca Shulman's son because he needed Paul to help train, launch, and lead the Israeli navy. But Prime Minister Ben-Gurion's first loyalty was to "his" Jewish people. The leitmotif of Ben-Gurion's leadership was his pledge to "uphold the full social and political equality of all [Israel's] citizens, without distinction of race, creed or sex." What would this Israel look like? In the view of historian Helen Chapin Metz, Ben-Gurion and the Mapai faithful foresaw an Israel in which "the socialist Labor Zionists assumed that the Jewish society of Israel would be egalitarian, free of the class divisions that plagued Europe. Instead, along with the growing industrially fueled economy came the usual divisions of class, stratification, and socioeconomic inequality. [These] seemed to coincide with ethnic divisions. . . .

For utopian thinkers, the persistence of Jewish ethnic groups was troubling enough; their stratification into a class structure was unthinkable."[17]

Israel's new Labor government could not have been unaware of the consequences of the tsunami of humanity that would soon be arriving on the shores of Israel, and the cultural dislocation that could result from such a mass immigration. Yet in July 1950 Israel's parliament, the Knesset, approved the Law of Return. This far-reaching act "declares that Israel constitutes a home not only for the inhabitants of the State, but also for all . . . Jews . . . everywhere. . . . The law declares to the Jewish people and to the world that the State of Israel welcomes the Jews of the world to return to their ancient homeland."[18]

Before long, however, Israel's population began to tilt away from the Eurocentric Ashkenazim and toward the Sephardim—Jews who came from all over the Middle East. The new settlers arrived in a new nation that was financially broke, had IOUs to creditors all over the world, and was struggling to build an infrastructure to house, feed, and employ its new citizens. This ingathering of exiles included a sizable number of Jews living in Egypt, and all but a few of Morocco's 265,000 Jews. The new settlers included Bene Yisrael Jews from India, and more than 9,000 Black Jews of Ethiopia's Bete Israel sect.[19] In 1948 and 1949 Alaska Airlines and other air carriers were contracted to mount operation Magic Carpet, to airlift almost all of Yemen's 49,000 Jews to the new state. The new Israelis also included thousands of disaffected Jews from the United States.

As the Palestinian Arabs had prophesied, they became disenfranchised. They lost their land, their livelihood, and, in some instances, their Israeli citizenship. Of the estimated 1.3 million Palestinian Arabs who had lived in the pre-State region, about 175,000 remained after the War of Independence. For these, according to Helen Chapin Metz, "their civil rights were always precarious. Israel's Arab residents were seen both by Jewish Israelis and by themselves as aliens in a foreign country."[20]

For many of the newcomers the promise of their new homeland was, literally, lost in translation. Few spoke Hebrew. Many had come from or been uprooted from "primitive" villages and ancestral farmlands. In Israel, most were initially settled in transition camps—huge tent cities—some of which were a far remove from Israel's urban centers and lush coastal regions. The Ashkenazim, most of whom had come from Europe, began to refer to the new settlers, somewhat pejoratively and without regard to their country of origin, as "Oriental" Jews, or "the Orientals" (Hebrew: *Edot Mizrah*, communities of the East).

The better-educated and more-highly trained European immigrants grav-
itated toward communities inhabited by *landsmen*—Jews from their home
country, or province, or city—who had preceded them to Israel. The established settlers formed robust, mutual self-help organizations to assist the newcomers in finding work or plying their trades. The Orientals, however, lacked
the strong organizational skills of the European settlers and their preexisting
social networks. Most were processed through "absorption centers" to accli-
mate them to life in Israel. They were required to attend *ulpan*—immersion
language schools—to learn to speak and read Hebrew. They were shown how
to weave themselves into fabric of everyday Israeli life. Yet, despite Ben-
Gurion's public promise of a society that would "uphold the full social and
political equality of all citizens, without distinction of race, creed or sex," the
Oriental underclass found itself with limited opportunities for social integration and upward mobility into the cultural landscape. There were few choices
other than work in the service industries, doing construction work, or as day
laborers on the Moshavim and Kibbutzim communities.

In his oral history Paul Shulman sounded incredulous when responding to
the question whether he had gone through an absorption center or attended
an *ulpan*. "I never had the benefits of the absorption centers," he replied in a
carefully controlled voice. As for learning to speak Hebrew, he conceded, "I
never had time to go to ulpan." There was little incentive for him to become
fluent. While running the Israeli naval academy, Shulman communicated with
his staff in English. He and the instructors taught in English or used interpreters.[21] Later, as president of National Engineering, he and his managers could
always hire interpreters when doing business throughout the Middle East. To
keep up with world affairs, there was always the English-language *Jerusalem
Post* and the *International Herald Tribune*.[22]

The stress and alienation felt by Orientals of the so-called "Second Israel"
(read: second-class Israelis) boiled over in June 1959, in Haifa. What began
as demonstrations by Jewish workers from Morocco, who were protesting ethnic discrimination and what they felt was the repressive rule of the Mapai,
degenerated into full-scale rioting. Gangs destroyed private and public property. They started in the commercial areas, then made their way up Mount
Carmel to the affluent residential neighborhoods. The municipal government
in Haifa responded by demolishing the old Arab quarter and moving the residents to new neighborhoods farther out from the center of the city.

Paul Shulman was not affected by the civil unrest, at least not personally. In his business operations he said that his company "employed many
Moroccans in our factories and construction work. . . . We have found
that the Moroccans, if you treat them with understanding and respect,

they are excellent workers. They do not deserve the bad reputation they frequently have."[23]

Shulman could afford to be politically correct in his 1993 oral history. But back in the 1950s and 1960s, a fundamental change was sculpting a new social order in Israel. Historian Daniel Cil Brecher provided one analysis:

> Within a few years, the core of the settler society—at the time of the establishment of the state, some six hundred thousand mainly non-religious Jews from Eastern Europe—faced double the number of newcomers, who were mostly poor and "underdeveloped" in the eyes of the old-timers. The Arab culture of these groups clashed with the emerging identity of the "Israeli," which began to be defined in contrast to the . . . non-Jew, but also in contrast to the "Arab"—the hated opponent in the territorial conflict. The suppression of the Arab-Jewish culture that now followed was done in the name of progress and "in the best interest" of the immigrants themselves.[24]

Other analysts of Israel's social and political history have observed that it was the steady coalescence of the non-Ashkenazim population blocs—the Sephardim as well as the Orientals—that began to erode influence of the Labor government and its Zionist precursors. Palestinian Arabs, those born in Palestine and who were eligible to hold Israeli citizenship, resented European Jews, who, they felt, saw Israel as a homeland for only themselves. According to Israeli sociologist Baruch Kimmerling, "The [Arabs] perceived the Jewish claims of ownership over the land, based on a distant and ambiguous past, and on some holy scriptures, as unjust and ridiculous."[25]

In her country study of Israel, Helen Chapin Metz wrote, "Many Orientals came to see the Labor party as unresponsive to their needs, and also blamed Labor for the indignities of the transition camps." These disaffected peoples wanted only to be included in the mainstream of Israeli society, to have parity in education and in the workforce, and even to be able to serve in the Israeli Defense Force. By the mid-1960s the non-Ashkenazim were turning thumbs down on Labor and were throwing their support toward Herut, the political party led by Menachem Begin, which was a successor to the Irgun. According to Metz, Herut's "right-wing populism and ultra-nationalist, anti-Arab national security posture appealed to the 'Orientals.'"[26]

When contemporary observers of Israel's history—a group sometimes regarded as the "new historians"[27]—look back at the period when David Ben-Gurion reigned supreme, they see a man whose vision for Israel was shaped by a practical need to form a nation of people—*the* People; the

Chosen. His preferred name for the land, Eretz Yisrael—the Greater Israel—acknowledged that the land belonged to more than just the pioneering settlers who founded the early communes and collective communities. And yet, and perhaps because of Ben-Gurion's vision, in some ways Israel had become an "us-them" society.

The leaders of Labor Zionism had foreseen and planned a nation that (as Metz put it) "would be egalitarian, free of the class distinctions that plagued Europe." Now, they had to deal with a calcified society whose members increasingly were defined by national origin *and* by how "Jewish" they were, at least as "Jewishness" was being defined by the nation's powerful Orthodox Rabbis, who were exercising increasing political power, as well. These religious leaders were not content to follow the "law" as enshrined within Torah, to be studied in the abstract. They worked assiduously to get their interpretations of Halakhah, or Jewish religious law, enacted into public statutes.[28] For example, in the early years of the Law of Return, it was enough for a person to register with the Ministry of the Interior and get an identification card to be considered a Jew. By the 1960s, ultraorthodox Jews in the Knesset forced a law that said, basically, that a Jew needed to show proof of being "born of a Jewish mother, and did not belong to any other religion."[29]

The issue of who was or who could be a Jew, however crucial it was to the Rabbinate, paled before the gathering storms that threatened from Egypt in the south and Syria in the north. Egyptian president Gamal Abdel Nasser was equipping his military forces with Soviet-supplied arms. Israel feared a defeat by Egypt less than the Tel Aviv government feared that such a regional conflict would draw in the superpower, the United States, as a peacekeeping force. In the opinion of Shlomo Ben-Ami, this "would shatter beyond redemption the IDF's deterrence and with it Israel's entire security doctrine."[30]

In the north of Israel, long-standing animosities with Syria began to heat up over water rights. Control of water that originated in Syria's Golan Heights, and Israel's diversion of that water into its National Water Carrier, was pushing Syria closer to the conflict with Israel that would ultimately lead to the Six Days' War in 1967. But was it Syria that provoked the military action? Papers of Yitzak Rabin (in 1966, chief of staff of the IDF) strongly suggest that Rabin believed Israel needed the Golan Heights, because control of the heights was the only way to stop attacks on Israel by Palestinian Fatah forces entrenched in Syria.[31] Israel's stunning victory in the 1967 Six Days' War, which reunited Jerusalem and the West Bank with the whole of Israel, had a dramatic impact on Israel's national morale. As Helen Chapin Metz saw it, "The capture of Jerusalem unleashed a wave of religious nationalism throughout Israel. The war was widely viewed . . . as a vindication of Zionism; the defenseless Jew of the Shtetl, oppressed by the Tsar and slaughtered by the Nazis, had become the courageous soldier of the IDF, who . . . had won a miraculous victory."[32] And yet, it was mainly Israel's European Jews—the so-called "Holocaust Jews"—and their native-born offspring, the Sabra, who shared in the national euphoria. For them, defense of the Homeland was paramount.

Israel's victory in the Six Days' War also had a dramatic impact on the nation's economy. An analysis in *Middle East Review of International Affairs* showed that, "After the [1967] war; with its ambitions stoked by its fantastic victory, Israel began to produce sophisticated weapons systems including fighter jets, tanks, and missiles."[33] Before the conflict, defense spending had been about 10 percent of Gross National Product. Afterward, spending for military hardware and infrastructure shot up to about 20 percent of GNP by 1969, and up to 32 percent between 1973 and 1976. David Ben-Gurion, who had resigned as prime minister in 1953, then made a dramatic return to public service in 1955 as minister of defense under Prime Minister Moshe Sharett, whom Ben-Gurion saw as too moderate in his policies toward Israel's enemies.[34] After Sharett resigned in 1956, Ben-Gurion again became prime minister and oversaw the buildup of Israel's military forces, at least until he relinquished the position to Levi Eshkol, another moderate. Yet under intense behind-the-scenes criticism by Ben-Gurion and leaders of the old Mapai party, Eshkol relinquished his position as defense minister to Moshe Dayan, who had been given major credit for Israel's victory in the Six Days' War. After Prime Minister Levi Eshkol died suddenly in March 1969, his foreign minister, Golda Meir, (Hebrew for "illuminate.") was elected prime minister.

Meir had long been a vocal proponent of increased immigration of Jews from the Soviet Union, which had doled out only a few thousands of exit visas during the 1960s. Now, under policies set in motion by the "Iron Lady," Moscow's closed-door policy was met by carefully articulated protests worldwide. In cities around the world Jews took to the streets to show how they felt about the Soviet Union and its repression of Jews who wanted only to live in peace. According to Israeli historian Howard Sachar, Golda Meir "announced that [Israel] would openly champion the cause of Soviet-Jewish emigration. By the spring of 1970 . . . mass protest rallies . . . were conducted in Buenos Aires, Melbourne, Johannesburg, Rome [and] New York. . . . On April 26, tens of thousands of Jews shared in a Passover "Exodus March" that began at the Soviet mission to the United Nations."[35]

Soviet authorities responded by opening the gates wide in the 1970s. Among the thousands of Russians who emigrated were educated, experienced professionals. However, when these new settlers reached Israel, many found it daunting to make their way on the rocky social and economic playing field.

The power of the Rabbinate and the sometimes suffocating dominance of the Eurocentric citizenry created roadblocks for the Russian Jews to feel that they were a part of mainstream society. As historian Daniel Cil Brecher saw it, "The increasing political use of the Holocaust . . . as a symbol of the common identity of all Jews must have appeared to many Orientals as a demand to give up their separate cultural and religious identities and accept solidarity with the dominant Europeans."[36]

The difficulties faced by the legions of new immigrants might have been a nettlesome worry to the Israeli government. To borrow from a sports metaphor, Israel was still suffused with the "thrill of victory" from the Six Days' War, but had yet to taste the "agony of defeat" that loomed, in the form of another attempt by Egypt to regain its Sinai Peninsula. In the view of Shlomo Ben Ami, Prime Minister Golda Meir was "a self-righteous, intransigent and stubborn iron lady . . . [who] turned political inaction into a system of government. Her unwillingness to question the position of the complacent [Israeli] military . . . made her premiership one of almost inevitable decline towards war."[37]

During the run-up to the 1973 Yom Kippur War, Egypt used incessant artillery attacks against Israeli forces occupying the Sinai. Egypt's objective was to keep up pressure on IDF units to withdraw from their fortified positions along the Israeli-Egyptian border. Golda Meir was not willing to let the IDF be drawn into a sustained conflict with Egypt, yet she rejected initiatives to pull back from the Sinai and work toward a negotiated settlement. Meir is said to have brushed off a political solution suggested by the United States (which, anyway, was more concerned with containing the growing Soviet influence in the Middle East). Meir also had to face critics in the Knesset because she had ignored peace initiatives put forward in February 1971 by Egyptian prime minister Anwar Sadat. That spring, as the Soviet Union increased its military aid to Egypt, Meir instead traveled to Washington to meet with Secretary of State Henry Kissinger. She presented her shopping list for American military hardware powerful enough to counter the Russian-supplied Egyptian forces. The United States did respond, but only with foreign aid and loans.

Although another war loomed, Meir refused to allow her defense minister, Moshe Dayan, to order a preemptive, cross–Suez Canal strike against Egypt, because Meir did not want Israel to be seen as the "aggressor." While initially suffering reverses in the twenty-three-day-long Yom Kippur War, Israel did prevail in the Sinai region against Egypt, as well as in the north against Syrian strikes designed to regain control of the Golan Heights. Still, Israelis now felt anything but victorious. Ami Isseroff, a leading proponent of Israeli coexistence with the Palestinians, wrote in 2006:

The war shattered the Israeli self-image of invincibility that had been cultivated since 1967 [the Six Days' War]. . . . The failure [was] of Golda Meir to take [Egyptian president Anwar] Sadat's peace propos- als seriously. . . . If Israel did not believe Sadat wanted peace, then obviously it should have been prepared for war, but it was not. . . . While the war set the stage for peace with Egypt a few years later, it also set in motion a political process that moved Israel to the right. The faith of the nation in the wisdom of the founding generation was broken. The power of the Israel Labor Party was eroded both by resentment and distrust . . . and the failure of the government to address social problems.[38]

Though Israel's military-industrial sector remained stable and even pros- pered during the 1970s and up through the 1990s, this growth was forged at the expense of the country's social growth: compulsory military service for young men and women delayed their entry into the commercial and eco- nomic spheres of Israeli life. And, wrote Linda Sharaby, in *Middle East Review of International Affairs*, "The enormous investment in Israel's defense budget came at the expense of a redistribution of income to the weaker segments of society, namely Jews whose ancestors came from Arab and Muslim countries, not to mention Israeli Arabs. These communities have remained underprivi- leged as inequality persisted and grew."[39]

The year 1988 was, in many ways, a watershed for Israel. In the year that Paul Shulman and others from North America were honored for their ser- vice to Israel, in February President Ronald Reagan approved a plan whereby Secretary of State George Shultz would come to Israel to try to get Israel and the Palestinian Authority to the negotiating table. In what would later be called Shultz's "shuttle diplomacy" the idea was to get both powers to come to terms on the situation in Gaza and the West Bank. Then, in December 1988, Yasir Arafat, chairman of the Palestine Liberation Organization, dropped a bombshell. He declared that the PLO would finally accept UN Resolution 242, regarding Israel's right to exist as a state. Further, Arafat also declared that the PLO would renounce all forms of terrorism.

Although the 1991 Madrid Peace Conference was to have moved a nego- tiated settlement forward, Israel's Likud government under Yitzak Shamir balked at the prospect that Israel would have to withdraw from and give up the territories it had occupied since 1967. Following the 1992 elections, which returned the Labor government to power, Prime Minister Yitzak Rabin proposed a "Land for Peace" solution. This went nowhere. The Palestinian

Authority read the proposal as peace in return for some land, that is, acreage in Gaza and the West Bank that Palestinians had occupied until being forced out by Israeli settlers and the IDF after 1967. The Oslo Accord of September 1993 laid out an interim arrangement whereby sections of the West Bank and Gaza would be offered to the Palestinians. The Palestinian Authority, in a clever turnabout, used an old phrase to discredit the solution. To them, getting the West Bank and Gaza was like getting "a land without a people for a people without a land."[40]

Paul Shulman died on May 14, 1994, one day before Israel marked its forty-fifth year as a nation. The question remains today: Which people? Whose Land?

CODA

In March 1948 Paul Shulman was putting together an academy to train and lead the Israeli navy. Somewhere in the Jezreel valley an American volunteer named Ralph Lowenstein was serving with the Israeli 79th Armored Regiment in its encounters against Syrian forces. Unlike Shulman who stayed on in Israel, Lowenstein returned to the United States after fulfilling his contract. Ralph Lowenstein went on to a distinguished career as a journalist. He then became a professor of journalism at the University of Florida at Gainesville and finally, dean of its journalism department.

In 1966 Lowenstein published a novel, A Time of War. Its chief character is an American volunteer named "Evan Copperman," who was not unlike Lowenstein himself. The novel has lots of action, but the novel's central theme is how Copperman's appreciation of his Israeli comrades matures as he follows and sees them fighting to retake more than just the hilly terrain; they are fighting for what they believe is their God-given place on Earth. As his volunteer military service comes to an end, Copperman's unit members give him a send-off party. On the eve of his departure for the United States and home he reflects on his Israeli comrades and their new homeland:

> They were a nation that had proclaimed the Law of the Return, and then reached out to bring the oppressed seed from afar, while the citizen in Haifa was apprehensive that there would soon be more dark Jews in the country than light ones and that one of them might move next door. How would historians a thousand years from now see this land, as Lilliput or Brobdingnag—or nothing? For it wasn't too difficult to believe that the feats of this little nation, in the eyes of historians, would be eclipsed by the massive horror

of the extended Dark Ages during when they were accomplished. The Twentieth Century was the miserable climax to a black millennium. . . . Among it all, the re-birth of the Jewish state would be as insignificant as the exodus of the Hebrews from Egypt had been to the historians of ancient Egypt.[41]

APPENDIX
From *Argosy* to *Abril*

Following [*Abril's*] publicity bash . . . our sources closed up like a soundproofed door.

—DAVID MACAROV, *AVI BULLETIN*, SPRING 2005

As far as the Jewish Agency for Palestine was concerned, Menachem Begin had long been a stone in David Ben-Gurion's sandal. Begin's position, as head of the Irgun Tsvai Leumi organization, was considerably to the right of Ben-Gurion's Mapai. The Irgun was willing to take more measures that were more aggressive to get the British out of Palestine. It was the Irgun, helped by the even more radical organization known as the "Stern Gang," that engineered the July 1946 bombing of the British Mandatory administration's headquarters, housed in one wing of Jerusalem's King David Hotel. Ninety persons were killed in the bomb blast, a loss that undoubtedly helped decide the British to pack it in.

The Irgun, like the Jewish Agency, had its supporters in the United States. Among its front organizations was the American League for a Free Palestine. The ALFP's president (in public, at least) was Senator Guy Gillette, a Democrat from Iowa. he inspiration behind the ALFP was Hillel Kook, who, in the United States, took the name Peter Bergson. A politically conservative Zionist, Kook/Bergson was also an experienced promoter and publicist. He came up with the idea that the ALFP should also launch a refugee sealift. Unlike the Mossad le Aliyah Bet, which tried to operate below the U.S. government's surveillance, the ALFP broadcast its mission to the world.

The vessel they acquired in 1946—as is—was a rusting, listing hulk tied up in a backwater of the Gowanus Canal in Brooklyn, New York. The vessel had traveled a long way since its launch and had followed an interesting if unusual odyssey under its several owners. The 150-foot, 800-ton ship had been built in 1931 by Germany's Krupp Iron Works as a private, personal yacht for American financier Charles Stone. He christened her the *Argosy*. She was powered by twin diesel engines and had sophisticated navigation and communications equipment. A crew of twelve served a lounge, dining room, and a dozen staterooms fitted out with exotic wood furnishings and marble sinks with gold-plated fixtures. For reasons that are not clear Stone never took title to his ship and sold it a year later to Thomas Octave Murdoch Sopwith.

T. O. M. Sopwith was a British aviation pioneer who became famous for the design of his World War I–era biplane, the "Sopwith Camel" fighter plane, that helped to devastate Germany's air aces in their Fokker flying machines. Sopwith, an experienced yacht skipper, renamed the boat *Vita* and turned it into the mother ship for Great Britain's Americas Cup ocean yacht racing syndicate.

The boat, like a child in foster care, was then sold to an American of Filipino origin whose sympathies lay with Spain's Republican government. Following the Spanish Civil war and the overthrow of the government by Franco's Nationalists, the vessel, now named *Abril*, carried remnants of the Republican leadership and $50 to $60 millions worth of looted jewels and money across the Atlantic to Mexico. There, under Mexico's sympathetic regime, the former Republicans planned to set up a Spanish government in exile. *Abril* reached Vera Cruz in March 1939. Under cover of night and heavy guard, more than 150 wooden packing crates filled with the loot were put on a special train to, well, no one seems to know what happened to it after that, and the government in exile never happened, either. Eventually, the ship's registered owner put it up for sale.

Enter now the U.S. Navy, which purchased the vessel at auction for $150,000 and accepted it into service (but did not commission the ship). The vessel's sleek, clipper ship bow was removed, and the ship gained a 20-mm deck cannon. She was painted haze gray and got under way as the patrol yacht, PY-31, *Cythera II*. The vessel cruised up and down the East Coast of the United States, looking for enemy submarines. Its skipper must not have been terribly vigilant, because he ran her aground on a sand bar. Following World War II the War Shipping Administration was eager to dump her on the commercial market and sold the hulk to a broker for $36,000, who parked it in a backwater of Brooklyn's Gowanus Canal. He flipped the ship, selling it to the ALFP's paper corporation, Tyre Shipping, for $50,000.

The ALFP felt it didn't need to resort to the sort of secretive financing employed by the Sonneborn Institute, which collected millions of dollars to purchase and rehabilitate a dozen ships for the Mossad le Aliyah Bet. Instead, the ALFP went to Hollywood. Peter Bergson asked screenwriter Ben Hecht to write a play whose proceeds would be used to support the Irgun's objectives in Palestine. Bergson also enlisted the aid of prominent entertainers, writers,

Launched in 1931 as *Argosy*, the once-posh vessel served many masters. She is shown here as PY-31 *Cythera II*, a U.S. Navy patrol craft. In 1946 the ship, named *Ben Hecht* in honor of the playwright, carried 660 refugees, including sympathetic journalists and photographers. It became the Israeli navy's K-24 *Ma'oz*. *RELEASED BY THE NAVAL HISTORICAL CENTER*

and publishers in his scheme to raise millions of dollars to support a Jewish state in Palestine. This state envisioned by the ALFP, however, would operate under the politically conservative philosophies of Menachem Begin's revisionist Zionist group, the Irgun.

The "Bergson Boys" had among its supporters such writers as Dorothy Parker, the witty but caustic columnist for the *New Yorker* magazine; Thomas Mann, the German, anti-Nazi author; Langston Hughes, the Black American poet and playwright; former First Lady Eleanor Roosevelt; composer Leonard Bernstein; and the humorist Will Rogers Jr. Others who endorsed the project included an A-list of entertainment luminaries: Milton Berle, Perry Como, Bob Hope, Groucho and Harpo Marx, Carl Reiner, Paul Robeson, and Frank Sinatra.

Ben Hecht had written or collaborated on thirty-five books, seventy screenplays, and a dozen plays for Broadway, including *The Front Page*. Hecht's 1943 pageant, *We Will Never Die*, dramatically recited the history of the Jewish people since the time of Abraham. The play's point was that even Hitler could not exterminate the Jews. For the ALFP Hecht wrote a play called *A Flag Is Born*, which advocated a Homeland in Palestine for all Jews of the Diaspora. Composer Kurt Weill (who composed music for Bertold

Brecht's *Threepenny Opera*) wrote the musical score. Quentin Reynolds, a World War II radio correspondent, agreed to serve as the play's narrator. Actor Paul Muni signed on, as did Celia Adler, sister of Actors' Studio cofounder Stella Adler. To round out the cast, director Luther Adler hired a rising young actor—Marlon Brando.

Hyped by full-page display advertisements in the New York papers, the play opened on September 4, 1946, at the old Alvin Theater. The curtain went up on a scene that showed a graveyard somewhere. In his deep and sonorous voice Reynolds intoned, "Of all the things that happened in that time—our time—the slaughter of the Jews of Europe was the only thing that counted forever in the annals of man. The proud oration of heroes and conquerors will be a footnote in history beside the great silence that watched the slaughter."[1] Muni and Adler portrayed Tevya and Zelda, two postwar elderly survivors of Treblinka, the Nazi-run extermination center in Poland that wiped out more than 850,000 Jews and other "undesirables." Brando portrayed David, a young and angry concentration camp survivor. The three are attempting to make their way to Palestine. It is a Friday night, and Zelda has lit the Sabbath candles. Later, in his sleep, Tevya dreams of a "Council of the Mighty," to which he makes a plea for a homeland for the Jews. The Council of the Mighty was a guarded reference to the United Nations' newly established Security Council. The next morning Tevya finds that Zelda has died. Despondent, Tevya bids David a farewell. Now feeling abandoned, David is "rescued" by three Jewish soldiers, who plan to spirit him off to Palestine. Before the young survivor makes his final exit, he comes to the edge of the stage, where he angrily exclaims, "Where were you—Jews—when the killing was going on? Where was your voice crying out against the slaughter?" One reviewer said that Brando's delivery was so powerful that men and women in the audience openly wept. The four-week run in New York was extended to ten weeks before the ALFP took the show on the road to six other cities. *A Flag Is Born* raised nearly a half million dollars for the American League for a Free Palestine.

However successful *Flag* was, it made the Jewish Agency for Palestine and the Mossad cringe (and, maybe, a little jealous). David Macarov, who had handled and moved money for the Mossad's Danny Schind, recalled, "Following the publicity bash for the [*Abril's*] send off, our sources closed up like a soundproof door. People and firms who had been providing us with material as gifts, at reduced prices, or even on the open market, refused to deal with us. Everyone was afraid of some sort of pressure or retribution from the American government, and took no chances. We couldn't buy a can of beans, a blanket, or an anchor." More important, Macarov wrote, foreign consuls would no longer meet with Mossad representatives, or discuss ship charter arrangements.[2]

The *Abril* sailed from New York the day after Christmas 1946. On board in addition to the crew were Wallace Litwin, a freelance photographer; Shepard Rifkin, a novelist; and the investigative journalist, I. F. Stone. As a columnist for *The Nation*, Izzy Stone had uncovered bigotry and racism in J. Edgar Hoover's FBI. After the magazine fired him in 1946, he joined the liberal New York newspaper, *P.M.*, where he held forth on "fascism" in the United States. In the ship's hold, according to a *New York Times* article, were "a thousand mess kits of an army type . . . and 1,500 standard type lifejackets. Her stores list indicated she would take on passengers in number far in excess of any journey in her previous history."[3]

Now flying a Honduran flag, once in international waters, its Brooklyn-born captain, Robert Levitan, christened the vessel *Ben Hecht*, to honor the playwright. *Abril* reached Port du Bouc, France, where its staterooms were torn out and replaced with sleeping shelves for some six hundred refugees. The ship got under way for Palestine in March 1947 and was almost immediately tailed by a destroyer from the Royal Navy's Palestine Patrol. The *Abril/Ben Hecht* got within twelve miles of Tel Aviv before the British, fearful that the captain would try to beach the ship, came alongside and boarded. The crew disabled the engines, forcing the British destroyer to tow her to Haifa. There, the refugees were put on a British "comfort" ship headed for the internment camp on Cyprus. The Americans, including Wallace Litwin, Shepard Rifkin, and I. F. Stone, were turned over to American authorities. Another photographer on board, Robert Nicolai, managed to hold on to his camera and later published an article in *Pageant* magazine.[4] Shepard Rifkin went on to write a novel, *What Ship? Where Bound?* The *Abril*, like others of the impounded refugee vessels, was tied up inside the Haifa harbor breakwater and left to rust, until Paul Shulman showed up and requisitioned her for Israel's navy. Now designated as the K-26 *Ma'oz*, she took part in the raid on the Egyptian warships at Gaza.

The former *Argosy/Vita/Abril/Cythera II/Abril/Ben Hecht/Ma'oz* was known to be still steaming in the late 1990s, having been renamed *Santa Maria del Mare*, and working as a ferry between Naples, Italy, and the island of Stromboli.

NOTES

Prelude

1. Israeli Ministry of Foreign Affairs, "Declaration of the Establishment of the State of Israel, May 14, 1948," www.mfa.gov.il.

Chapter 1: Truce and Consequences

1. Attributed to Sidney Rabinowitz, a former U.S. Navy radar operator who volunteered to serve in the Israeli navy. His quote is recalled by David Genn, another American volunteer, in an interview with the author, August 2, 2005.
2. Murray Greenfield and Joseph Hochstein, *The Jews' Secret Fleet* (Jerusalem: Gefen Publishing, 1987), 55–63. Greenfield gives an extensive account of the purchase of the former HMCS *Beauharnois* by the Haganah, its role as an Aliyah Bet refugee ship, and its service as K-18 *Josiah Wedgwood* in the Israeli navy.
3. Robert Gardiner and Roger Chesneau, *Conway's All the World's Fighting Ships 1922–1946* (London: Brassey's Military Histories, 1980), 401. The *Al Emir Farouq* and another sloop, *Al Amir Fawzia*, were built in 1929 for the Egyptian Royal Navy.
4. Jacques Soustelle, *The Long March of Israel* (New York: American Heritage Press, 1969), 196. Soustelle attributes the remark to the rector of El-Azhar University, Cairo, whose words were broadcast over Radio Cairo for weeks in March 1948, leading up to the Arab invasion of Israel.
5. Stanton Griffis, U.S. ambassador to Egypt, secret telegram, October 21, 1948, to Robert A. Lovett, acting U.S. secretary of state. The cablegram also detailed successes by the Israeli air force flying smuggled B-17 bombers and Czech-made Messerschmitt ME-109 fighters used by the Luftwaffe (College Park, Md.: National Archives and Records Administration, Record Group 59); Hereafter NARA, RG 59).
6. Craig Weiss and Jeffrey Weiss, *I Am My Brother's Keeper: American Volunteers in Israel's War for Independence* (Atgen, Pa.: Schiffer Military Publishing, 1998), 236.
7. Samuel Katz, *The Night Raiders: Israel's Naval Commandos at War* (New York: Pocket Books, 1997), 161. Katz describes the so-called "explosive boat unit," led

by Yochai Bin Nun, as one of three units within Shayetet 13, a semiautonomous commando group within the Israeli navy. Bin Nun's unit was so secretive that many in the navy did not know it existed.

8. *Palestine Post*, Friday, October 23, 1948, 1.

9. Among those at the ceremony were Paul's wife, Rose, and Henry Morgenthau Jr., a former U.S. secretary of the Treasury. Morgenthau was then in Israel as chairman of the United Jewish Appeal. The UJA had asked him to assess how the millions of dollars contributed by American Jews were being put to use in Israel. Morgenthau was among the close personal friends of Paul Shulman's late father, Herman.

10. Carl Alpert, "From Lieutenant to Admiral in 3 Years," *Jewish Review*, March 27, 1967. Alpert, a historian of Haifa's Technion, said that Shulman served as the volunteer chairperson of Technion's Student Affairs Committee and advised on the welfare of students studying at Israel's prestigious science institute.

Chapter 2: The Ablest Navigator

1. Mark Shulman, along with his wife, Peggy, and their children, David Shulman and Judith S. Roth, interview, July 22, 2006.

2. The Columbia Grammar School began as a site for student teachers from Columbia Teachers' College. By the time the Shulman children attended in the mid-1930s, it was an independently chartered private school.

3. Mark Shulman, 2006.

4. Ruth Halprin Kaslove, interview, October 11, 2005. "[Herman Shulman] was the lowest man on the totem pole in his law firm. So, the firm decided that if anybody was going to lose the case they should give it to Herman."

5. "The Magpie Sings the Great Depression: Selections from DeWitt Clinton High School's Literary Magazine, 1929–1942." Archived and reproduced by the New Deal Network, an online database of more than 20,000 items, which were originated during President Franklin D. Roosevelt's New Deal period. www.newdeal. feri.org/magpie, accessed January 10, 2006.

6. Mark Shulman, 2006.

7. George Dyas, "A History of the Academy," *Rolling Stone* (Cheshire, Conn.: Cheshire Academy), Spring 1939. *Rolling Stone* was the student yearbook. Dyas was in the class of 1930. The Cheshire Academy was established in 1796 as an academy to "propagate the learning of the [Episcopal] Church in the New World." Even in 1938 the bishop and instructors adhered to the Toleration Act of 1708, which "permitted the right of public worship to sober dissidents."

8. Albert Bildner, interview, October 28, 2003. Bildner was one of Paul Shulman's cousins. Paul was fascinated with submarines and hoped to join the ranks of the U.S. Navy's "Silent Service."

9. Robert S. Coleman, captain, USNR (Ret.) (source and date not shown). Courtesy of C. Downing Tait, captain, USN (Ret.). Mr. Tait was one of Shulman's

classmates. He and other classmates of that first NROTC course at the University of Virginia, who were interviewed for this work, could not confirm that the top five cadets were offered "commissions" at the Naval Academy.

10. Paul Shulman, oral history, transcript, page 1, recorded May 13, 1993 (hereafter: Shulman, OH). Shulman's oral history is one of scores of interviews in the "North Americans in Israel" series, sponsored jointly by the Association of Americans and Canadians in Israel (AACI) and the American Jewish Committee Oral History Collection. The tape and transcript can be found in the New York Public Library, Dorot Division of Jewish History.

11. Regulations Governing the Admission of Candidates into the United States Naval Academy as Midshipmen, 5.

12. Albert Bildner believes that to help Paul get into Annapolis, his father, Herman, "had a deal" with his friend Sumner Welles, then the U.S. undersecretary of state. If so, it would not have been uncommon for Welles to send a personal note to Representative Baldwin, asking him to do a "favor" for his friend, Herman, and his son.

13. Oath of Office, United States Naval Academy, courtesy, Academic Archives, U.S. Naval Academy.

Chapter 3: Shulman's Fighting Ships

1. Wayne Whittaker, "Annapolis at War," *Popular Mechanics*, August 1943, 6.
2. Donald T. Poe, rear admiral, USN (Ret.), letter to the author, September 12, 2006. At the time of this letter, Rear Admiral Poe was corresponding secretary of the U.S. Naval Academy Class of 1945 Alumni Association.
3. Jonathan Leff, commander, USN (Ret.), interview, August 2, 2005. Leff arrived in Israel in September 1948 and served as a gunnery instructor at the naval academy established by Shulman.
4. Shulman, OH, 3.
5. Arthur A. Ageton, lieutenant, USN, "Annapolis, Cradle of the Navy," *National Geographic*, July 1936, 789–800.
6. Lawrence Shaffer, commander, USN (Ret.), interview, May 16, 2003. Larry Shaffer roomed with Shulman during their second, or "youngster" year.
7. Ibid.
8. The notion of an "our crowd" atmosphere was brilliantly delineated in Stephen Birmingham's 1987 novel, *Our Crowd*. Birmingham, however, was writing about the exclusionary tendency among prominent Jewish families in New York City in the late nineteenth and early twentieth centuries. Paul's brilliant, wealthy, art-collecting father, Herman, and Paul's politically-active mother, Rebecca, may have aspired to their own "our crowd" life. In a 2006 interview, Paul's brother, Mark, hinted that their parents did not see their children as "academically gifted." Paul's inability to reach his father's expectations for him may also have weighed him down.

9. Joel I. Holwitt, "The Judaic Experience at the U.S. Naval Academy," December 2002. Master's thesis submitted to the Department of History, in partial fulfillment of the requirements for a degree with honors. Two years before, in 2000, the Friends of the Jewish Chapel at the Naval Academy announced construction of a Jewish chapel. The chapel opened in 2005 next to Mitscher Hall.

10. In his oral history Shulman said that, except for attending a Jewish academy when he was a child, he had no formal, structured Jewish education. His parents also were "secular" in their practice of Judaism, one that did not adhere strictly to Judaic teachings, or require regular observance at synagogue. They leaned more toward the philosophy of Zionism than to strict Talmudic precepts.

11. Commendation from Captain C. R. Cole Jr. to Paul Shulman, September 13, 1943. Courtesy of the U.S. Naval Academy Academic Archives. Unfortunately, Midshipman Shulman was informed that his eyesight was not up to the requirements for duty in the submarine service.

12. On board U.S. Navy ships, the sleeping compartments and offices for commissioned officers are known as "officers' country."

13. The Curtiss SB2C Helldiver was a carrier-based dive-bomber produced for the U.S. Navy during World War II. It replaced the Douglas SBD Dauntless in U.S. Navy service. Despite it being larger and heavier, the SB2C was much faster than the Dauntless. Pilots referred to the Helldiver as "the Big-Tailed Beast" (or just "Beast"), and "Son-of-a-Bitch 2nd Class."

14. R. M. Tucker, "Professional Notes," *The Log*, May 19, 1944, 13. The Academy's Nimitz Memorial Library holds *The Log*.

15. Of the 1,100 midshipmen who began with the class of 1945 (accelerated), 914 graduated. Paul Shulman was ranked number 835.

Chapter 4: On the *Hunt*

1. *New York Times*, March 2, 1943, 1. The "United Nations" that Herman Shulman referred to was a precursor to the United Nations chartered in 1946. President Roosevelt devised the term "United Nations" to refer to the "Big Three"—the United States, Great Britain, and the Union of Soviet Socialist Republics— that were fighting the Axis powers. A chief reason why the United States is said to have done "nothing" to save Jews from the Nazi's "Final Solution" was that one official in the Department of State was able to thwart the president's will. Breckinridge Long was said to be extremely paranoid about what he perceived as a threat by legions of eastern Europeans flooding the United States. In 1940 Long was an undersecretary of state in charge of the visa division. He was able, through threats and intimidation within his division, to greatly reduce the number of visas issued that would admit immigrants to the United States. In a 1943 intradepartment memo Long wrote that the State Department "could delay and effectively stop for a temporary period of indefinite length the number of immigrants coming in to the United States . . . by simply advising our consuls to put every obstacle

in the way . . . and resort to various administrative devices which would postpone and postpone and postpone the granting of visas." Long's anti-Semitism also sabotaged a U.S. government attempt to save thousands of Hungarian and Romanian Jews. Finally, President Roosevelt, believed to fear losing the Jewish vote in the coming 1944 election, fired Breckinridge Long, but the damage had been done.

2. *New York Times*, October 26, 1943, 8. The *Times's* correspondent (probably William Blair, who covered international affairs) reported that Hadassah withdrew from the influential American Jewish Committee because it thought that group was focused too much on the international political situation regarding Jews, while it disregarded the domestic needs of American Jews.

3. "The Jewish Home in Palestine," Hearings on HR418 and HR419, Seventy-Eighth Congress, February 8–16, 1944. Published in *The Jewish National Home in Palestine* (New York: KTAV Publishing, 1970). Often overlooked by Zionist leaders was that Lord Balfour's "declaration" included the phrase that a Jewish Homeland was "contingent on Arab support."

4. The wardroom is the main gathering and dining space for the ship's commissioned officers. The executive officer is the wardroom's mess president, who collects dues and enforces etiquette. Politics, religion, and sex are taboo subjects, and talk about one's professional business is not encouraged. The commanding officer is not usually a member of the mess, but is, of course, invited to the table. Large warships may have several wardrooms, for flag-rank, senior, and junior officers. On aircraft carriers each of the embarked squadrons usually has its own wardroom and mess separate from the ship's company. The term "mess" comes from the Old English word "*mes*," which is derived from the Latin "*mas*," "to put in place."

5. Don Steffins, letter to the author, May 3, 2003. Steffins was one of the petty officers in the USS *Hunt*'s "Power Gang."

6. On U.S. Navy ships the "quarterdeck" is any place on the main deck where people come on board the vessel. Depending on how and where the vessel is tied up, it could be amidships, or at the rear of the vessel, near the fantail. A uniformed service member first salutes the ensign (American flag), then the OOD, then asks, "Request permission to come aboard" (or "Request permission to go ashore"). The commanding officer's comings and goings are broadcast on the public address system, as "*Hunt*, arriving" (or "departing"). Flag-rank officers and dignitaries are "piped aboard" by sideboys, with the boatswain blowing the appropriate call on his bos'un pipe.

7. Alan Kahn, lieutenant, USNR, letter to the author, June 29, 2003.

8. James L. Wilson, commander, USNR (Ret.), telephone interview, May 1, 2003.

9. Dominic Legato, gunner's mate 2nd class, USN. Petty officer Legato's complete story can be read on the USS *Hunt*'s alumni Web site, http://members.aol.com/dlegato/storm.

10. Several books have been written about Typhoon Cobra, including: *Typhoon: The Other Enemy*, by Raymond C. Calhoun; and *The Typhoon That Stopped a War*, by Edwin P. Hoyt. A Court of Inquiry convened by Admiral Chester Nimitz,

commander in chief of the U.S. Pacific Fleet, found that inadequate weather information, which arrived hours too late to be helpful, prevented Halsey from ordering his ships to take evasive action. Nonetheless, Admiral Halsey was cited for ordering his ships to remain on a course for Japan, with disastrous consequences.

11. Halford Knoertzer, commander, USN (Ret.), "Anti-Aircraft Action by U.S.S. Hunt on 18 March, 1945," NARA, RG 38.

12. Before the Allied Tactical Publication was enacted in 1949, navies of the world used their own system of signal flags to communicate tactical and administrative information among ships operating at sea. During World War II, the U.S. Navy signaled a "well-done" with the flags "Tare," "Victor," and "George," which were the spoken words for *T*, *V*, and *G*. In 1949 the U.S. Navy and all others shifted to a two-letter signal code system and adopted the International Phonetic Alphabet's designation for the spoken names of the signal flags. Thus, "Bravo" stood for the letter *B* and "Zulu" stood for the letter *Z*. The U.S. Navy assigned Bravo to administrative matters. Zulu was reserved for actions well done; hence, "Bravo Zulu."

13. Gene Moore, "Ulithi Atoll, Largest Anchorage in the Pacific," Attleboro, Mass., *Sun-Chronicle*, November 6, 2000. At the time of this article Moore was a correspondent for the newspaper.

14. James L. Wilson, commander, USNR (Ret.), "A Lucky Ship: Recollections of the First Cruise of USS *Hunt*" (unpublished). During a 2003 interview, Jim Wilson, by then practicing law, showed this author a mangled piece of aluminum from the aircraft's wing, his "souvenir" of the kamikaze suicide attack.

15. City and County of San Francisco, Marriage License No. 71284, July 18, 1945. Certified copy obtained on January 17, 2006. The ceremony was performed by Chaplain Rabbi H. Kepshaus, lieutenant commander, USNR.

Chapter 5: Two New Years, One Resolution

1. Carl Nolte, "The Dark Side of San Francisco," *San Francisco Chronicle*, August 15, 2005. Of all the cities in the United States that celebrated V-J day, San Francisco was the only one that suffered from riots.

2. Ray Shilka, letter to the author, September 8, 2003. Shilka was an enlisted member of the crew and had other run-ins with Lieutenant (j.g.) Shulman. When Shilka knew he would be late returning to the ship at the end of one Christmas leave because weather forced travel delays, he called the USS *Massey*'s executive officer and asked for and was granted a delay in reporting back. When Shilka reached the ship, Mister Shulman was on duty as officer of the deck and attempted to put the petty officer on report for being "absent over leave." Shilka said that the exec vouched for his phone call, then tore up the citation.

3. USS *Massey* deck log, April 15, 1946, NARA, RG 38.

4. Ehud Avriel, *Open the Gates! The Dramatic Personal Story of "Illegal" Immigration to Israel* (New York: Athaeneum, 1975), 278–86.

5. James Reston, "Illegal Palestine Immigrants Will Be Detained on Cyprus," *New York Times*, August 8, 1946, 1. The British Foreign Office's announcement set off civil unrest and rioting in Palestine. In Haifa mobs, urged on by broadcasts from the Haganah's clandestine "Voice of Israel" radio station, surged into the port area in an attempt to stop the British from shipping 1,300 immigrants to the internment camps on the island of Cyprus. British forces fired on the crowd, killing at least three persons. The Jewish Agency stated that there was no legal validity to restricting the number of immigrants or detaining them in the camps on Cyprus. The British Foreign Office issued a statement saying that the United States had no business questioning the British action. The Foreign Office also criticized the *New York Times* for allowing full-page advertisements in support of what the British insisted was an illegal operation by the Haganah.

6. Officer's Fitness Report for the period of February–August 1946. From a private source.

7. Martin Zenni, captain, USN (Ret.), letter to the author, November 1, 2006.

8. USS *Massey* deck log, Monday, September 30, 1946, NARA, RG 38.

9. Chaim Stern, ed., *Gates of Repentance*, The New Union Prayer Book for the Days of Awe (New York: Central Conference of American Rabbis, 1978), 106–8.

10. Navy Department news release, August 15, 1945.

11. Although concerned with having subordinates follow Navy regulations, protocol, and etiquette, Lieutenant (j.g.) Shulman evidently was not above bending certain traditions to suit his needs. While en route to Peru and Chile in November 1946 on an official goodwill cruise, the USS *Massey* crossed the equator. Members of a U.S. Navy warship's crew—both enlisted and commissioned—who have crossed the equator are known as "Shellbacks." Those who have not crossed the equator are known as "Polywogs." According to an age-old tradition, the Polywogs are invited to join the realm of the "Kingdom of Neptune" and become a Shellback. In a time-honored ceremony, the Polywogs endure some disgusting but harmless hazing by the Shellbacks. Rank has no privilege during the ceremony. The ship's commanding officer is as likely to be hazed (with some modification) as the most junior seaman apprentice. When anointed as dutiful members of King Neptune's realm, an ornate (if unofficial) certificate is then entered into a sailor's military service record. A photo exists that shows Mister Shulman, in costume, taking part in the ceremonies, but as a Shellback—on the giving end. According to USS *Massey* crew member Ray Shilka, the destroyer's ship's clerk could find no record of Shulman having previously been initiated. This author's correspondence with crew members of Shulman's former ship, the USS *Hunt*, shows that from the time he reported for duty in November 1944, to the time it was on its way home from the Western Pacific in June 1945, the ship always operated north of the equator. Thus, Shulman could not have become a Shellback.

12. Martin Zenni, letter to the author, October 12, 2005. The hotel was the Francis Marion, on King Street, across from Calhoun Square.

Chapter 6: Hotel Fourteen

1. Lois Slott, "I Became a Zionist on the Top Floor," *American Jewish Women and the Zionist Enterprise,* Shulamit Reinharz and Mark Raider, eds. (Waltham, Mass.: Brandeis University Press, 2005), chapter 22.

2. Leonard Slater, *The Pledge* (New York: Simon & Shuster, 1971), 82.

3. Robbyn Swann and Anthony Summers, *Sinatra: The Life* (New York: Knopf, 2005). Although not widely known at the time, Sinatra was highly critical of anti-Semitism in America and the government's unwillingness to support the Zionists. By September 1947 Teddy Kollek had taken charge of the Haganah's New York office. Late one evening, Kollek approached Sinatra at the Copacabana's bar. Kollek had a favor to ask. Could Frank deliver a "package" to a certain individual? Sinatra nodded. Kollek used an unmarked door from the club to the hotel. In a few minutes he returned carrying a brown paper bag. Sinatra finished his drink, left the club by the same door, and delivered one million dollars in cash to Kollek's contact, waiting by a ship at a pier in Brooklyn.

4. John Loftus and Mark Aarons, *The Secret War against the Jews* (New York: Saint Martin's Press, 1994), 183. Loftus, a former CIA operative, relied, in large part, on "confidential interviews" with former officers of the National Security Agency, former consultants on communications security, and former officers of the U.S. Army Security Agency.

    According to Raymond Batvinis, in his book, *Origins of FBI Counter-Intelligence* (Lawrence: University of Kansas Press, 2007), 189, FBI Director J. Edgar Hoover expected that the British would want increased intelligence access in the United States. "British intelligence access to rich data on issues was critical to [British intelligence] missions. Good relations [with the United States] would also help ensure the amicable settlement of conflicts rising from inadequate coordination, while minimizing the political risks to President Roosevelt associated with exposure of a foreign intelligence and counterintelligence service operating at cross purposes on U.S. soil. Roosevelt endorsed the British proposal for closer intelligence cooperation without hesitation."

5. Paul Shulman, OH, 3; and Mark Shulman, 2006.

6. Slater, *The Pledge,* 75. In Israel, Rabinovitch would take the name Shlomo Shamir and would succeed Shulman as commander in chief of Israel's navy.

7. Akiva Skidell was born in Poland. His family and he emigrated to Canada, then to the United States, where they applied for and were granted U.S. citizenship. Skidell served in the U.S. Army and fought in Europe. After his discharge, he and his wife settled in Israel on an American-founded kibbutz at Kfar Blum. The village is in northern Israel, at the edge of the fertile Jezreel valley. Skidell, deeply involved with the Zionist plan for a Jewish national homeland, was assigned to the Haganah operation in New York City. Skidell's military career is detailed in *GI Jew,* by historian Deborah Dash Moore (Cambridge, Mass.: Belknap Press, 2004).

8. Slater, *The Pledge*, 211.

9. There can be little doubt that Shulman knew he might be flouting the law. Like all midshipmen at the Naval Academy, he had listened many times as the "Articles for the Government of the Navy" were read at assemblies. These principles enjoined naval officers to "guard against and suppress all dissolute and immoral practices," lest they ruin their careers on legal "rocks and shoals." Before the Uniform Code of Military Justice was enacted in 1951, violations of the "rocks and shoals" Articles of Government could bring a Navy officer immediate summary court-martial and punishment, which could include reduction in rank to seaman second class. Donald I. Thomas, captain, USN (Ret.), "Rocks and Shoals," *Shipmate* 54, no. 7 (September 31, 1991). *Shipmate* is the publication of the U.S. Naval Academy Alumni Association.

10. David C. Holly, *Exodus 47* (Annapolis: Naval Institute Press, revised, 1995), 112. Holly's claim that Shulman helped to "evaluate" the *President Warfield* is difficult to substantiate. Captain William C. Ash, a licensed, professional marine surveyor, did the primary evaluation. In January 1947 Shulman was still on active duty, on board the USS *Massey*, which was at the Charleston Naval Shipyard. The *President Warfield* departed from Baltimore on January 25 for its initial sea trials, and almost sank. By the time Shulman was released from active duty in March 1947, the *President Warfield* was already crossing the Atlantic Ocean, heading for Marseilles, France. There, it was converted into a refugee carrier and christened *Haganah Ship Exodus 1947*, after it sailed in June with more than 4,550 refugees on board.

11. *New York Times*, June 4, 1947, 55.

Chapter 7: The Pans as Pawns

1. "The Meeting between Jewish Soldiers from Eretz Israel and the Surviving Remnants," presented by historian Yoav Gelber, to the Yad Vashem Sixth International Conference on the Holocaust, in 1985. Since 1943 Schind had been among a group from the Haganah involved in attempts to rescue Jews from Eastern Europe who had *not* been caught in the Nazi's mass murder scheme. Schind reported to Ben-Gurion and the Mapai organization's central committee that after the war "the survivors were less concerned with reaching the promised homeland. Their primary concern was to be able to live on equal footing with [European] Gentiles, to be rid of the Yellow Star [of David] that they were forced to wear, and an end to the ban on travel." Gelber's article was published by the Shoah Resource Center, International School for Holocaust Studies. Schind also understood the problems associated with moving hundreds of thousands of displaced persons from European DP camps to Palestine. According to Yosef Grodzinsky in his study, "Historical Commission in the DP Camps: The Resilience of Jewish Identity," by summer 1946 there were only about 250,000 Jews remaining in the DP camps. By 1948 some 48 percent had immigrated, legally or otherwise, to Israel, while 36 percent had immigrated to the United States.

2. Mordechai Naor, *Ha'apalah: Clandestine Immigration* (Jerusalem: State of Israel, Ministry of Defense, English ed., 1987), 43. Of the 116 vessels used before, during, and after World War II in the clandestine immigration sealift, only one remains. It is a former tank-landing craft used by the British. Renamed *Al-af-pi-chen* ("In spite of"), it made one voyage from Italy at the end of September 1947, carrying 434 refugees, including one woman who turned out to be a spy for the British. When the ship was intercepted by the Royal Navy's Palestine Patrol, she identified many of the crew who were members of the Haganah. They and the refugees were interned at Cyprus. In the 1960s the landing craft itself was "rescued" and began its new mission as part of the Clandestine Immigration and Naval Museum in Haifa. The craft was cut into sections then reassembled at the museum to show the privations endured by refugees trying to reach Palestine.

3. Fritz Liebreich, *Britain's Naval and Political Reaction to Illegal Immigration of Jews to Palestine, 1945–1948* (London: Routledge, 2005), 75.

4. David Macarov, e-mail to the author, July 4, 2008. Macarov served as a liaison between the Mossad and the Waterman Steamship Company and hand-delivered the bank check in full payment. Macarov sometimes was called on to be the courier for unmarked envelopes filled with cash, to be handed to reluctant officials as "incentives" to accomplish an otherwise impossible piece of business.

5. Other sources suggest that "F. B." was to honor Fannie Barnett, who, with her husband, Rudy, owned and managed Hotel Fourteen.

6. Ze'ev Hadari and Ze'ev Tsahor, *Voyage to Freedom* (London: Vallentine Mitchell, 1985), 28. Hadari based the recollection of this celebration on a report Danny Schind made to the Haganah. That report, in Hebrew, is filed in the Archives of the History of the Haganah, in Tel Aviv.

7. Naor, *Ha'apalah: Clandestine Immigration*, 111.

8. Baruch Kimmerling a professor of sociology at Hebrew University in Jerusalem, wrote, "Few observers at the time knew that many of the refugees from the *Exodus* had applied for visas to the United States, and were hardly anxious to settle in Israel. By dramatizing the fate of the survivors in whom [Ben-Gurion] had little interest except as future residents of the state he was building, Ben-Gurion helped to make Israel the world's chief power broker over Jewish affairs. . . . Israel acquired the right to speak not only for living Jews but for the six million exterminated Jews, to whom Ben-Gurion suggested granting symbolic citizenship—in effect, turning them into martyrs for the Jewish state." *The Nation*, January 10, 2005.

9. Voyage Record Cards for *Pan Crescent* and *Pan York*, 1947, Lloyd's Shipping Index, Courtesy of Guildhall Library, London, England.

10. From this center the Mossad "established routes [for the refugees' escape] across Europe, [set up] truck and rail facilities, and [sought] the active assistance of officials in the French government" (Hadari and Tsahor, *Voyage to Freedom*). According to Ben Dunkelman, who was in charge of a Canadian battalion of volunteers, "Training would not be intensive: volunteers were all supposedly combat veterans, and they would need little more than some exercise to get back in

shape, and some practice to familiarize themselves with the weapons they would be using. The main thing would be for them to get to know each other, and get used to functioning as a unit." Quoted in Ben Dunkelman, *Dual Allegiance* (New York: Crown, 1976), 162. It was from this transit camp at St. Jerome that most of the volunteers joined refugees on board the Aliyah Bet ships, which departed from small ports and fishing villages along the coast of France and Italy.

11. Shulman, OH, 4.

12. Hadari and Tsahor, *Voyage to Freedom*, 32.

13. *Gazzettino di Venezia,* September 3, 1947. Courtesy of Captain Rudy Guastadisegni, director, Museu Storico Navale, Venice, October 12, 2005.

14. Lionel Kenneth Philip Crabb was renowned within British naval circles. After World War II, "Crabbie," as he was known, was the Royal Navy's principal diving officer for northern Italy and headed a team that cleared Venice Lagoon and its shipping channels of mines. He served in Palestine, leading a Navy team charged with removing terrorist mines from British warships and police launches. In the early 1990s Fritz Liebreich, a British researcher, interviewed retired members of the Mossad le Aliyah Bet who had direct knowledge of the sabotage. They said that Crabb had hired an Italian dockworker to place a bomb with a delayed fuse inside a hold at the ship's stern, causing the vessel to sink to the bottom of the waterway. Only the fact that repairs to the *Pan Crescent* were behind schedule, which delayed its departure, prevented the 4,570-ton ship from going down on the open sea (Liebreich, *Britain's Naval and Political Reaction*, 279n).

15. Hadari and Tsahor, *Voyage to Freedom*, 126.

16. Avriel, *Open the Gates!* 296.

17. Idith Zertal, *From Catastrophe to Power* (Berkeley: University of California Press, 1998), 278.

18. "Panama Asks Data on Refugee Ships," *New York Times* (via Reuter), October 27, 1947, 45.

19. Charles Weiss, interview with the author, January 31, 2007.

20. Greenfield and Hochstein, *The Jews' Secret Fleet*, 149–50.

21. Zertal, *From Catastrophe to Power*, 83. Idith Zertal believes, however, that the *Exodus* voyage was not planned to end as it did. As it turned out, the Zionists were more nimble and adept at taking advantage of the British blunder in trying to return the refugees to France. The Jewish Agency played the propaganda game with brilliant success.

22. Hadari and Tsahor, *Voyage to Freedom*, 99–100.

23. Charles Egan, "Red Agents May Infiltrate Palestine Ships Now in Rumanian Ports, British Tell U.S.," *New York Times*, November 13, 1947, 13.

24. Charles Weiss, January 31, 2007. Weiss recalled that while he was in the internment camp he was able to get out, because the Haganah gave him the identity of another volunteer who had come through before, on another ship. Weiss says he departed as that person, not as himself. He and the other Americans spent only a few weeks in the internment camp on Cyprus. British authorities, working with

U.S. officials, arranged for the Americans to be issued one-way travel documents, which permitted them to return to the United States.

25. Hadari and Tsahor, *Voyage to Freedom*, 126.

26. Craig Weiss and Jeffrey Weiss, *I Am My Brother's Keeper*, 136.

27. Hadari and Tsahor, *Voyage to Freedom*, 211.

Chapter 8: The "Bathtub Corps"

1. Pan African Airways was a cover company set up by the Haganah through which to purchase aircraft for Israel's air force. The air service would later become El Al, the Israeli state airline. These aircraft were separate from the B-17 bombers and Czech-built fighter planes that were smuggled into Israel by Al Schwimmer. See also chapter 10, this book.

2. The Haganah was operating out of Tel Aviv, but the nearby airfield at Lydda remained under British control until June 11, 1948. Michaelis field was the only facility in the northern part of Palestine into which Shulman could fly.

3. The exodus of Arabs began in January 1948, after the Arab High Committee began to persuade their people to leave as soon as possible. They would be able to return, they were promised, after "the victorious Arab armies liberated Palestine from the Jews." By mid-April British forces had pulled out of Haifa and were embarked on warships sent to bring them home. In late April, Arab unrest in Haifa exploded. Gangs stormed the Jewish section on Mount Carmel. Only a massive counterattack by Haganah and Irgun forces pushed the Arabs back, causing Arab military leaders to flee and leaving their forces vulnerable.

4. By December 1947 the Haganah had secretly purchased six trawler-type vessels in Europe and registered them under foreign flags of convenience. The Haganah then purchased arms and munitions from Czechoslovakian manufacturers, as well as other military hardware bought at war-surplus marketplaces. The munitions were packed and labeled as "household goods" and "agriculture equipment." Three of the ships evaded the British naval blockade and were able to offload some 1,500 tons of arms and munitions. In Palestine, as well, a huge clandestine underground (literally) cottage industry turned out homemade bullets, bombs, and mortars.

5. Benny Morris, "The Capture of Haifa," in *The Birth of the Palestinian Refugee Problem, 1947–1949* (Cambridge, UK: Cambridge University Press, 1987), 64. To the Arabs, and even to some Palestine-born Jews, the siege of Haifa was known then—and today—as *Naqba*—"the taking."

6. Among the delegation that met Shulman was Lee Harris, an American and also an ex–U.S. Navy officer. Harris had been in Palestine since February 1947, working for the Palestine Economic Commission. He would become an ally of Shulman and would later take up the cause of the Machal Volunteers from Abroad from America and Canada. He recalled that the trip from Haifa to Tel Aviv was diffi-

cult. The old coastal road was filled with potholes. They had to watch for bands of trigger-happy Arabs who were likely to take potshots at the car.

7. Zertal, *From Catastrophe to Power*, 161, *passim*.

8. Naval Company of the Palmach/Haganah, www.palyam.org.

9. Liebreich, *Britain's Naval and Political Reaction*, 194. Fritz Liebreich recalls that the British naval commander in Haifa "embarked in HMS *Phoebe* while Seafire (aircraft) circled overhead. The defiant presence of the warships managed to veil the impotence of the [Royal Navy]. The major British naval demonstration . . . was meant to alleviate the bitterness [the British] felt. At the time, it seemed appropriate to 'cock a snook' (British slang for thumbing one's nose) at the triumphant Zionists. The show of force thus softened the shock of abandoning the commitments so solemnly undertaken, and disengage the Mandate from an embarrassing entanglement."

10. David Ben-Gurion, *Israel: A Personal History* (Tel Aviv: American-Israeli Publishing Co., 1971; English edition, New York: Funk & Wagnalls, 1971), 185. Ben-Gurion was writing in his war diary for June 30, 1948.

11. *New York Times*, June 2, 1948, 4.

12. At the time of Israel's founding, the Haganah did not even have a Hebrew word for navy. The naval force was initially called Cheyl Hayam, "Army of the Sea." Official ranks would not be instituted for several months. At the beginning, there were not even badges of rank that Shulman could wear on his hand-me-down, ex–Palestine Police uniforms. Within a year Shulman's rank and title would be adjusted to captain, or Sgan Mishne. As such, and out of respect, he was addressed by the title, "Aluf Shulman," roughly equivalent to calling a leader the "Old Man."

13. Shulman, OH, 8; and Greenfield and Hochstein, *The Jews' Secret Fleet*, 144.

14. Harold Shugar, interview, August 16, 2005. Shugar recalled that the gun mount had no mechanism for elevation or traverse. The gunners had to anticipate the up-and-down motion of the vessel when firing, then hope that the shell's trajectory would cause it to hit something. After a few rounds, the cannon got stuck at a 45-degree angle.

15. Richard Rosenberg, letter to the author, April 28, 2003.

16. Ibid. Richard Rosenberg had been a lieutenant in the U.S. Navy, and served as a radar and communications officer on a U.S. destroyer-escort. He served as one of Shulman's instructors, and later headed up the Israeli navy's communications systems.

17. Fritz Liebreich, *The Israeli Navy during the War of Independence 1948–1949: Politicking, Struggle for Control, and the Early Operations* (Master's thesis, 1994). Liebreich maintains that Gershon Zaq, whom he called a "stalwart" in Ben-Gurion's political party, was not a seafaring man. His background was in educational administration.

18. Shulman didn't need to remind the Sonneborn Institute that Israel would not be getting any support from the United States, which had embargoed shipment of

military hardware to the Middle East. Most of Israel's arms and munitions came from war surplus markets in Europe.

19. Shulman chose "Shaul Ben Zvi" as his Hebrew name to honor his late father, Herman, whose Hebrew name was Zvi.

20. Paul and Rose Shulman were able to move into Peter Cooper Village, at 531 East 20th Street, on November 1, 1947. They vacated the apartment in August 1948 but kept the lease until 1956, according to Patricia McCarthy of Rose Associates Town & Country. In 2006 Rose Associates was the management company for Peter Cooper Village.

21. Rosenberg, letter to the author, August 18, 2005. Rosenberg and his wife arrived in September 1948. After completing his obligation to the Israeli navy in 1952, he and his family settled in Israel. He became a professor and taught at Haifa University.

22. Marvin Broder, commander, USNR (Ret.), interview with the author, December 17, 2004.

23. Miriam Finard, letter, April 18, 1992, to Ralph Lowenstein, director, American Veterans of Israel Archives, University of Florida at Gainesville. Marvin Broder and Sandy Finard, and their wives and children, sailed for Israel on the *Marine Carp*, a former troop ship chartered by the U.S. Maritime Administration. They arrived in September 1948, but were not welcomed with open arms. Gershon Zaq, the Ben-Gurion loyalist, is said to have resented Shulman's move to bring in foreign instructors instead of using Jewish officers. Zaq believed that Shulman's effort was an attempt to denigrate his prerogative as Sea Service commander. The fact that there were no trained Israelis who had experience with command and control was lost on the former educational administrator.

24. Leff, 2005.

25. Ibid.

26. Haim Gershoni (Harold Gershenow), *Israel: The Way It Was* (New York: Herzl Press, 1989), 46.

27. Ibid., 52.

28. The Honorable Josiah Wedgwood served as a British minister of Parliament from 1906 to 1943. His passionate support for the Zionist cause helped shape the 1917 Balfour Declaration that called for a Jewish national homeland. Yet later, Wedgwood came to advocate armed resistance against British repression of the Jews in Palestine.

29. Greenfield and Hochstein, *The Jews' Secret Fleet*, 62. The question is moot as to whether the vessel *Josiah Wedgwood*, owned by the "Weston Trading Company," was seized in international waters or the "territorial" waters of Palestine. Before there was a State of Israel, Palestine itself was not sovereign. A former Turkish colony, it was merely administered by the British Mandatory government. Nevertheless, the Royal Navy's interdiction and seizure of the *Josiah Wedgwood*, which was flying a Honduran flag in international waters, violated the maritime Law of the Sea and could, therefore, have been considered illegal. In any case, the

Jewish Agency for Palestine had no intention of suing the Royal Navy or Great Britain.

30. The provisional government found itself in something of a dilemma. Several intercepted Aliyah Bet vessels were interned at Haifa by the British, but none was abandoned—legally, at least. Each ship had been purchased by a Mossad company, however fictitious that shell company was, or that each company had been dissolved after buying one or two ships. The vessels were *still* owned by some legal entity, and were still registered under some nation's maritime flag of convenience. In order for them to be legally accepted into the Israeli Naval Service, the provisional government had to repurchase them from the former Mossad companies; in other words, from Israel itself.

31. Gershoni, *Israel: The Way It Was*, 47.

32. Liebreich, *Britain's Naval and Political Reaction*, 14.

33. Ben-Gurion, *Israel: A Personal History*, 247. Marcus, a West Point graduate who served on General Eisenhower's staff after World War II, is credited with bringing order and tactical unity to the Haganah units fighting Arab forces during the War of Independence. It was Marcus's idea to create a "Burma Road"—a one-lane track bulldozed through the hills to bypass the sole highway that went through the Bab-al-Wad gorge, from Tel Aviv to Jerusalem. The Burma Road enabled Israeli forces and vehicles to go around Arab gunners that regularly shot up relief convoys. Marcus was "accidentally" shot and killed by a sentry. Marcus might have forgotten that night's password, but he spoke little Hebrew and may not have understood the challenge by the sentry, who spoke no English. Publicly, Ben-Gurion accepted Mickey Marcus's death as accidental, but he never gave up suspicion that the shooting had been *no* accident. His appointment of Marcus as commander of the Jerusalem front infuriated Palmach commanders, who wanted no outsider telling them how to fight their war. An investigation raised more questions than it answered. According to author Dan Kurzman, "Several shots were heard, although the guard fired only once. A doctor testified that the fatal bullet appeared to have been fired from a Sten gun, not the guard's Czech rifle." Dan Kurzman, *Genesis 1948* (Cambridge, Mass.: Da Capo Press, 1992), 291.

34. Liebreich, *The Israeli Navy during the War of Independence 1948–1949*, 14.

35. Liebreich, *Britain's Naval and Political Reaction*, 22.

36. Leff, letter to the author, April 4, 2008. Leff included a copy of the five-page, single-spaced "Outline of Report Submitted to Army Chief of Staff Concerning Deplorable State of Navy of Israel, dated January 18, 1949."

37. Quoted in Liebreich, *Britain's Naval and Political Reaction*, 32.

Chapter 9: The Consequence of Truth

1. Rosenberg, 2004.

2. Broder, 2005.

3. Shulman, OH, 5.

4. Leff, letter to the author, June 6, 2008.

5. Jacques Soustelle, *The Long March to Israel* (New York: American Heritage Press, 1969), 37. After World War II, Great Britain sold more than forty-five attack and support ships to Egypt and trained the navy's crews. In December 1947 the United States, not wanting to appear to publicly support one faction over another, embargoed the sale and shipment of all military items from the United States to the Middle East. The U.S. embargo, initiated by the conspicuously anti-Zionist Department of State, hamstrung the Israeli provisional government from equipping and supplying its military forces.

6. *Palestine Post*, June 6, 1948. The report indicated that Egyptian warships had previously shelled a Palyam training facility at Caesarea, north of Tel Aviv.

7. Jonathan Leff, interview with the author, August 2, 2005.

8. *LST-138* took part in the invasion of Normandy. It was decommissioned, then struck from the naval register in December 1945. Sold to a ship repair company, it was converted to merchant service. The Irgun purchased her in early 1948. The 328-foot-long, flat-bottomed vessel drew only four feet of water at its bow, even with a 500-ton load. This allowed her to go right up onto an invasion beach, open its watertight bow doors, drop a ramp onto the sand, and unload its tracked vehicles and supplies right onto the beach. Menachem Begin named the LST *Altalena* to honor the memory of Ze'ev Jabotinsky, who wrote under the pen name, Altalena. Jabotinsky, who died in 1940, influenced the ideals of the Irgun Tsvai Leumi, the revisionist voice of Zionism.

9. The UN Truce Commission seemed as vigilant as the Royal Navy's Palestine Patrol in keeping Aliyah Bet ships from bringing in refugees, now as *legal* immigrants. The *Pan Crescent* and *Pan York* both arrived in Haifa in July 1948. About half of the 5,089 males on board the two ships were male individuals of military age, or "MIMAs" in commission jargon. The MIMAs were interned in temporary holding camps, lest the Israeli Defense Force recruit them. The UN Truce Commission did not restrict the Arabs from reinforcing their fighting forces.

10. Under Menachem Begin, the Irgun carried out aggressive measures against the British. The Irgun's most notorious act was to blow up the British Mandatory Government's headquarters, housed in Jerusalem's King David Hotel. Ben-Gurion (in Paris at the time) denounced the bombing. Conveniently overlooked was evidence that the instructions to carry out the act came from Moshe Sneh, then commander in chief of the Haganah central command.

11. Dan Kurzman, *Genesis 1948* (Cambridge, Mass.: Da Capo Press, 1992), 471.

12. Ben-Gurion, *Israel: A Personal History*, 172. Ben-Gurion's recollection was supposedly taken from daily entries in his war diary. Irgun historians, however, insist that the *Altalena*'s commanding officer, Monroe Fein, radioed for a doctor to treat those wounded by shore gunfire, but no doctors were available. Another anomaly in accounts of the attack on the *Altalena* appears in a footnote to Craig and Jeffrey Weiss's book, *I Am My Brother's Keeper: American Volunteers in the Fight*

for Israel. The Weiss brothers claim that a gunner on the *Josiah Wedgwood* told them he would not fire on fellow Jews and removed the firing pin from the gun.

13. A photograph shows the *Altalena* off Tel Aviv's Frischmann Street beach, on fire, with its bow pointed toward the city. This seems to belie both Kurzman's and Ben-Gurion's accounts that the LST had tried to head out to sea, and that, as Ben-Gurion claimed, the Israeli ships "were three to four miles from the shore."

14. Lee Harris, oral history, December 2, 1979, 14. Courtesy of the American Veterans of Israel archives at the University of Florida at Gainesville. Used by permission.

15. Ben-Gurion, *Israel: A Personal History*, 192. It is unlikely Paul Shulman would have been offered a commission in the Israeli navy if he had *not* made some sort of official commitment. Several American volunteers claimed that though they had taken an oath, it was to their immediate unit commander and *not* to the State of Israel; thus, they believed that they had not violated any U.S. laws, which stated that it was illegal to join and serve the military forces of a foreign nation.

16. "Early Operations of Israeli Intelligence" lecture given by Doron Geller (date and place unknown). Part of the lecture was based on reporting by authors Samuel Katz and Dan Kurzman.

17. Ben-Gurion, *Israel: A Personal History*, 247–48. In the months leading up to the War of Independence Ben-Gurion incessantly questioned his military commanders about their understanding of how to conduct warfare against well-trained enemy troops, in particular against units that fought with mechanized armor, which the Israeli units did not possess. One critic of Ben-Gurion's war policies identified what he called a weakness in his military policies. In an article, "Speaking Out for Palestine and Peace," published in *Mideast Web Opinion Forum* (www.mideastweb.org/Palestine), August 2003, Israeli historian Ami Isseroff concluded that Ben-Gurion put less trust in commanders whose battlefield playbook came out of their experiences as hit-and-run commandos. The minister of defense put more trust in the abilities of the British-trained officers who were then fighting for and leading the Haganah. It was this reliance that persuaded Ben-Gurion initially to rely on David M. "Mickey" Marcus to train Haganah units and Paul Shulman to train navy officers.

18. Ben-Gurion, *Israel: A Personal History*, 240.

19. Lee Harris, letter of December 12, 1948, to "Chief of Staff, Israeli Navy." The letter was sent via Shulman's chief of staff, Avraham Zakai. Courtesy of the American Veterans of Israel archive, University of Florida at Gainesville.

20. "Report Submitted to Army Chief of Staff Concerning Deplorable State of Navy in Israel," January 18, 1949. Courtesy of Jonathan Leff. Leff said that Paul Shulman could not attach his name to the document, but he did set up the meeting between the group and Yaacov Dori, chief of staff of the Central Command. Leff recalled that they were driven to Tel Aviv, blindfolded, and changed cars several times before reaching Dori's headquarters. According to Haim Gershoni in his book, *Israel: The Way It Was*, Dori is said to have told them, "I know what's wrong. I agree wholeheartedly with everything you've said, but you don't understand my

problem. I know what's wrong but I don't know what to do about it. We don't have proper equipment or money to buy it. We do not even know what we need. On top of this we have no broad base of highly trained experts."

21. Shulman, OH, 7. When Shulman referred to the navy's "direct access" to Ben-Gurion, he was talking about his own personal accessibility to the Israeli leader.

22. "Army Day Marked by Israeli Forces," New York Times, July 18, 1949, 3.

23. Shulman, OH, 9. The reference to "half a Nelson" is to Admiral Lord Horatio Nelson and his victory in 1813 over the French fleet at Trafalgar.

24. Shlomo Shamir (nee Rabinovitch) had been a major in the British army's Jewish Brigade during World War II. Unknown to the British, he was also the leader of all Haganah members in the brigade. After the war, he was sent to New York City to head up the Haganah's operation based at Hotel Fourteen. It was here that he met Paul Shulman. Shamir returned to Palestine in January 1948, bringing Mickey Marcus, and was promoted to the rank of colonel in the Haganah. In the War of Independence, he commanded the Seventh Mechanized Brigade. This unit made five unsuccessful attempts to dislodge enemy forces that held the fortress at Latrun, which blocked the only road to Jerusalem.

25. Shulman, OH, 9.

Chapter 10: Passport Problems

1. Slater, The Pledge, 210–11.

2. Philip D. Caine, American Pilots in the RAF (Dulles, Va.: Brassey's, 1998), 42. In the 1970s the U.S. Supreme Court ruled that those Americans could not be stripped of their citizenship because they had joined the military service of a foreign power.

3. Macarov, e-mail to the author, July 10, 2006.

4. Craig and Jeffrey Weiss, I Am My Brother's Keeper, 67.

5. Dr. Jason Fenton, "The Machal Story, Chapter 2" Source: www.sabra.net/machal/section2, accessed February 12, 2007.

6. Shulman, OH, 6.

7. Department of State message no. 452, June 2, 1949. Obtained through the author's Freedom of Information Act request (hereafter: Author's FoIA). In fact, the State Department knew that since October 1948 Paul Shulman had served as commander in chief—in other words, the head of the Israeli navy.

8. Thomas S. Bloodworth, letter, July 2, 1949, to secretary of state. Author's FoIA.

9. David Ben-Gurion, letter, "To Whom It May Concern," June 28, 1949. Author's FoIA. Hakirya is the section of Tel Aviv where the Ministry of Defense was located in the 1940s.

10. Airgram, July 15, 1949, classified SECRET, from Secretary of State Acheson to American consul, Haifa. Author's FoIA.

11. Shulman, OH, 11. There is no doubt that Shulman led the Israeli naval squadron, whose commandos attacked and sank the Egyptian vessel Al Emir

Farouk. The *Jerusalem Post* reported the action, and it showed up as an item in a UN Security Council memorandum of action, on October 25, 1948. This author has not been able to confirm that a formal complaint was ever lodged, by Egypt, against the United States, because of Shulman's actions.

12. Broder, 2004.

13. Rosenberg, 2004.

14. The Czech-made Messerschmitt aircraft could not carry enough fuel to fly from Czechoslovakia to Israel. So, the planes were taken apart and shipped in wooden crates labeled "household goods." The ammunition was packed in crates labeled "canned goods."

15. (a) Tom Tugend, "Whom Pardons Are Made For," *Jewish Journal of Greater Los Angeles*, March 9, 2003; (b) U.S. v. Adolph W. Schwimmer, Case No. 20636, U.S. District Court of Los Angeles, October 1949–February 1950.

16. Paul Shulman, Supplementary Affidavit, June 21, 1951. Author's FoIA.

17. Charles B. Hinton, "Guardian of American Passports," *New York Times Magazine*, April 27, 1941, 21.

18. W. H. Young, memorandum, July 11, 1951. Author's FoIA.

19. Department of State telegram, July 24, 1951. Author's FoIA.

20. Paul and Rose Shulman moved into Apartment 6-G on November 1, 1947, and held a lease on the apartment until July 1956. E-mail, September 8, 2006, from Patricia McCarthy, Rose Associates Town and Village LLC (in 2006 the managing agent for Peter Cooper Village).

21. Paul Shulman, letter to U.S. Department of State, December 13, 1951. Author's FoIA.

Chapter 11: Forty Years

1. In 1949 Israel signed an armistice with Egypt, on February 24; with Lebanon, on March 23; with Trans-Jordan, on April 3; and with Syria, on July 20.

2. Lee Harris, letter, February 11, 1949, to D. Lou Harris (no relation), Palestine Economic Corporation. Courtesy of the AVI Archive, University of Florida at Gainesville. Lee Harris was an ex–U.S. Navy personnel officer who had helped to demobilize U.S. Navy personnel in Europe after World War II. He was hired by the Palestine Economic Corporation to manage its banking operations. In February 1947 Harris set up an office in Tel Aviv. As more Americans and Canadians volunteered and came up against difficulties in dealing with the Israeli way of doing things, Harris became the de facto "go-to guy" to help them solve such problems as speaking and reading Hebrew, of dealing with government officials, getting travel documents, sending and receiving mail, and getting paid on time. Harris also helped to set up Club Semidar, a recreation center in Tel Aviv for English-speaking Machal from Australia, Canada, Holland, South Africa, the United Kingdom, and the United States.

3. Ibid.

4. Lee Harris, oral history, December 2, 1979, 13. Courtesy of the AVI Archives, University of Florida, Gainesville. Used by permission.

5. David Macarov, e-mail to the author, September 1, 2005.

6. What the Israelis saw as taking back Haifa, the Arabs called *Naqba*, simply, "the taking." According to the UN Truce Supervision Commission, more than four hundred Arab villages were depopulated. Approximately 750,000 Palestinian Arabs fled or were expelled from their homes. Muslims were offered a "right of return," but only if they agreed to take an oath of allegiance to Israel. Most refused. Aubrey Lippincott, the American consul general in Haifa, issued a strongly worded "demand" that called on Israel to return Arab property. Instead, the provisional government set up an organization to take inventory of all Arab property left behind. In his report Lippincott wrote, "Houses are inspected and furnishings are put in. An invoice is made and the [new] occupants sign promissory notes for one year in advance. . . . A local bank collects rents and credits them to the proper owners. All the money in the Arab property transaction is merely a credit. Most of the money will not be paid to the Arabs now. Eventual compensation will be worked out by act of the Israeli Parliament." Aubrey Lippincott, letter to U.S. Secretary of State, NARA, RG 84.

7. Dana Adams Schmidt, "Israel Is Draining Swamps for Farms," *New York Times*, August 18, 1953, 6.

8. Tamar Zohary and K. David Hambright, "Lake Hula—Lake Agmon." The citation is published by the Jewish Virtual Library (www.us-israel.org/source/Society&Culture/geo/Hula). Shulman believed that he would be able to leverage National Engineering's work on the Hula project into work on the larger All-Israel Plan, which included the National Water Carrier. This aqueduct was envisioned to carry water from the Galilee to agricultural developments planned as far south as in the arid Negev desert.

9. Ibid.

10. Shlomo Ben-Ami, *Scars of War, Sounds of Peace: The Israeli-Arab Tragedy* (London: Oxford University Press, English ed., 2007), 73–74.

11. Miriam Finard, letter, April 8, 2002, to Ralph Lowenstein, director, American Veterans of Israel Archive. Courtesy of Ralph Lowenstein. Used by permission.

12. Shulman, OH, 12.

13. Ibid., 11.

14. Typed copy of Shulman's biographical profile (no date). Courtesy of Carl Alpert, historian of the Technion, June 6, 2003.

15. Wilbur Crane Eveland, *Ropes of Sand: America's Failure in the Middle East* (New York: W.W. Norton, 1980), 320–21 and 322n. Eveland worked for the Central Intelligence Agency in the Middle East, using Vinnell Construction as his cover. Eveland wrote that Solel Boneh hired Clark Clifford, former counsel to President Harry Truman, to turn Reynolds into an "American company." Clifford reportedly acquired the charter of the defunct Reynolds Ball Point Pen Company, and then modified it to make it look as if Reynolds was a construction firm. The new

Reynolds Construction Company was incorporated in Delaware on August 6, 1959. On August 23, 1965, Reynolds obtained a Certificate of Authority, which permitted it to operate in New York. Eveland wrote that the name "was used by Solel Boneh as a front for bids prepared in Haifa and mailed from New York."

16. (a) State of Delaware, Division of Corporations, copy of certificate of incorporation; (b) State of New York, Division of Corporations, copy of certificate of authority to operate in New York.

17. USS *Liberty* Memorial (www.agtr5.org). The incident caused a major rift in U.S.-Israeli military and diplomatic relations.

18. In *Ropes of Sand* (p. 325) author Wilbur Crane Eveland, a retired top CIA operative, stated, "Message intercepts by the [USS] *Liberty* made it clear that Israel had never intended to limit its attack to Egypt. To destroy . . . incriminating evidence, Minister of Defense, Moshe Dayan ordered his jets and torpedo boats to destroy the *Liberty* immediately." Ten U.S. military investigations of the incident found no culpability on Israel's part. The United States accepted Israel's formal apology for the "accident," as well as some $13 million in reparations paid to victims' family members.

19. Draft of letter by Paul Shulman to Admiral David L. MacDonald, U.S. Navy chief of naval operations (no date). There is no indication that Shulman completed or sent the letter. From a private source.

20. Carl Alpert, e-mail to the author, May 31, 2003.

21. Zehev Tadmore, president of the Technion, letter to Rose Shulman, July 7, 1994. Courtesy of Colonel David Teperson, director, Machal Museum, Latrun, Israel.

22. Mark Shulman, interview, July 22, 2006.

23. Marlin Levin, *Balm in Gilead: The Story of Hadassah* (New York: Schocken Books, 1973), 215.

24. Paul Shulman, quoted in the May 25, 1968, Hadassah report of the renovation of Mount Scopus, Hadassah Archives, American Jewish Historical Society, New York.

25. *Jerusalem Post*, November 3, 1970.

26. David Shulman, interview with the author, July 22, 2006.

27. Patricia Palkimas, interview with the author, March 17, 2006.

28. Charles Sobel, interview with the author, May 22, 2003. Sobel would go on to serve as the Shulman family financial adviser, guiding the investments and trust funds of the Shulman children and grandchildren.

29. Lawrence Sobel, telephone interview with the author, June 22, 2006. Larry Sobel claims that Paul Shulman, through his contacts with the Israeli Defense Force, was able to get him, a U.S. Army reservist, assigned to a U.S. Navy unit in Haifa, with which he could perform his weekend and annual training.

Chapter 12: A Postmortem

1. Greenfield and Hochstein, *The Jews' Secret Fleet*, 105–16. As with other of the Aliyah Bet vessels that attempted to make the run across the Mediterranean to Palestine, the *Hatikvah* was intercepted by British warships. Along with the refugees, Greenfield and other Americans among the crew were interned in the British camps on Cyprus. However, Haganah operatives in the camps created false identities on forged documents, so that Americans would not be separated out and turned over to American authorities for repatriation to the United States. In July 1947 Greenfield and the other Americans arrived in Haifa on the British "comfort" ship, *Empire Lifeguard*. Hidden among their personal effects were the makings of a bomb. Before the ship offloaded the refugees, one among the group assembled the bomb and placed it deep into the hold and set its timed fuse. After all the refugees were safely ashore, the bomb detonated, and the ship sank in Haifa harbor.

2. Greenfield and Hochstein, *The Jews' Secret Fleet*, xiii.

3. Shulman, technically, is not correct when he blames the Palmach for fighting the establishment of the navy; it was the Haganah Central Command under Israel Galili. In 1948 he was adamant that the Haganah be in control of the navy, the command of which should be vested in an Israeli Jew, and specifically not in Paul Shulman. The Haganah had been the military arm of the Jewish Agency for Palestine since the 1930s. The Palmach, or "strike force," was established in May 1941. Many of its leaders had served in the Jewish Brigade of the British army or had matured politically through the kibbutz movement. This social framework was considered to build the philosophical core of the Sabra, or native-born Israeli. It was Gershon Zaq who was named the first commander of the Sea Service. Shulman's title initially was chief of staff for training. See also chapter 8, this book.

4. Paul Shulman, mimeograph typescript of the article, dated "Haifa, December 1987." Courtesy of Albert Bildner. There is no indication that the article was ever published. In notes for his article, prepared in August 1986, Shulman initially wrote that he saw his service with the Israel navy "as a PERIOD OF COMPROMISE AND OF PERSUASION and not of regulations and chain of command" (capitals in original).

5. A contemporary summary history of the Israeli navy, published by the Israeli Defense Forces, says that Ben-Gurion established the navy on March 17, 1948. This present-day capsule history makes no mention of the role played by Paul Shulman. It says only that the "naval service [would be] under the command of naval captain Gershon Zak [sic]." Most sources say that Zaq held a civilian title that was equivalent to the secretary of the navy. He is not known to have held a commission in the Israeli navy. His background was in educational administration.

6. Rose Shulman, letter to Meir Pe'el, director, Haganah Museum, Tel Aviv, May 16, 1988. From a private source.

7. Shulman family letter, May 16, 1988. Courtesy of Albert Bildner.

8. Ibid.

9. Ibid.

10. Maoz Azaryahu, "The Independence Day Military Parade: A Political History of a Patriotic Ritual," *The Military and Militarism in Israel*, Edna Lomsky-Feder and Eyal Ben-Ami, eds. (New York: SUNY Press, 2003).

11. Courtesy of the AACI archives, Tel Aviv. AACI president Natalie Gordon found it prudent to cross out one line in her remarks, that the honorees had similarly been recognized "in celebration of the 40th anniversary of the State of Israel, and in recognition of the role *olim* have played in [Israel's] survival." The reality, as she and many others knew, was that Israel barely recognized the contributions of the nearly four thousand "volunteers from abroad." The Hebrew word *olim* means immigrants. The singular, "immigrant," is *oleh*.

12. Shulman family letter, June 1, 1988. Courtesy of Albert Bildner. Used by permission.

13. According to several but conflicting estimates, there were eighteen missile attacks over a thirty-nine-day period. The hardest hit was the Ramat Gan section of Tel Aviv, where many government and military offices were located. There were 13 deaths and anywhere from 165 to 334 wounded. "Needless Deaths in Gulf War," New York, Human Rights Watch, 1991 (www.hrw.org/reports/1991/gulfwar), accessed August 22, 2008.

14. Shulman family letter, January 8, 1991. Courtesy of Albert Bildner. Used by permission.

15. Ibid.

16. Larissa Remenick, "Trans-national Community in the Making: Russian-Jewish Immigrants in Israel in the 1990s." *Journal of Ethnic and Migration Studies* 28, no 2 (2002): 515–30. At the time of this writing Remenick was an associate professor of social sciences and anthropology at Bar-Ilan University.

17. Shulman family letter, 1991.

18. Shulman family letter, February 15, 1992. Courtesy of Albert Bildner. Used by permission.

19. The Hebrew word *Aluf* means "commander of thousands" of personnel. Following Shulman's "elevation" to be Ben-Gurion's special adviser, he took the title of "chief of naval headquarters." Gershon Zaq continued to hold the position as "chief of naval service," roughly equivalent to the American secretary of the Navy. Shlomo Shamir replaced Shulman as navy commander in chief.

20. Visitors to the stately campus of the Naval Academy should explore the Uriah P. Levy chapel, the Navy's acknowledgment of the contribution of Jewish naval officers. Levy was the first Jewish midshipman to graduate from the Academy. He rose to the rank of commodore, but faced courts-martial six times for fighting anti-Semitism in the navy. A naval Court of Inquiry finally restored him to the rank of commodore. The Naval Academy would produce other notable Jewish officers who held flag rank. These include Rear Admiral Hershal Goldberg, chief

of the navy's supply system; Vice Admiral Bernard Kauderer, who commanded both the Atlantic and Pacific fleets; Rear Admiral Sumner Shapiro, director of naval intelligence; Rear Admiral Aaron Landes, director of naval chaplains; Admiral Hyman Rickover, "father" of the United States' nuclear-powered Navy; and Admiral Jeremy "Mike" Boorda, chief of naval operations. Boorda had risen up from the ranks as an enlisted man. *Washington Post* writer Benjamin Forgey described the chapel as "like a miniature Gothic cathedral—all light and uplift. . . . The wall behind the bimah (the raised platform from which services are conducted) is sheathed in Jerusalem stone . . . to resemble the ancient stones of the Western Wall of the Second Temple of the Israelites." Forgey concluded that the synagogue is "a fitting historical gesture that symbolically unites [Uriah P. Levy] and the principles of freedom and tolerance he believed in."

21. Rose Shulman, transcript of notes from a video presentation made at the U.S. Naval Academy memorial service, May 12, 1995. Videotape courtesy of Murray Shear.

Chapter 13: The Pages of History

1. Daniel Cil Brecher, *A Stranger in the Land: Jewish Identity beyond Nationalism* (New York: Other Press, 2007), 106.
2. Ibid., 107.
3. Helen Chapin Metz, *Israel, a Country Study* (Washington, D.C.: Federal Research Division, Library of Congress, 1988), 12.
4. Ibid., 15. Thedor Herzl foresaw a state that would combine both a modern Jewish culture with the best that Europe could offer. At the same time Herzl foresaw the Jewish Temple being resurrected in Jerusalem he also envisioned a Palace of Peace, which would arbitrate international disputes. However lofty his vision, Herzl also believed that the land in Palestine should be expropriated from the Arabs, and they should be encouraged to leave, because they would be denied the right to live and work in the new Jewish homeland.
5. Many Jews view Aliyah as a return to the Promised Land and regard it as the fulfillment of God's biblical promise to Abraham, Isaac, and Jacob.
6. Ze'ev Sternhell, *The Founding Myths of Israel* (Princeton, N.J.: Princeton University Press; English edition, 1998), 2–36.
7. The figures are from *L'Experience Sioniste,* by George Reutt; quoted in Soustelle, *The Long March to Israel,* 164.
8. This is an acronym for Mifleget Poalei Eretz Yisrael, or The Land of Israel Workers Party. Mapai absorbed several other socialist groups that included Ben-Gurion's own Labor Zionist movement.
9. Ben-Ami, *Scars of War, Sounds of Peace,* 14.
10. Ibid., 94–95.
11. "Balfour Declaration of 1917." Israeli Ministry of Foreign Affairs (www.mfa.gov.il).

12. "British White Paper of 1939." Jewish Virtual Library (www. Jewishvirtuallibrary.org).

13. David Ben-Gurion, quoted in William Blair, "Ben-Gurion Scores Palestine Policy," *New York Times*, November, 11, 1946, 12.

14. Ben-Ami, *Scars of War, Sounds of Peace*, 27. Original source not known.

15. Breckrinridge Long was so notoriously anti-Semitic that President Franklin D. Roosevelt, under extreme pressure from American Jewish organizations (and fearful that he would lose the "Jewish vote" in the upcoming 1944 election), demoted Long, who soon retired from public service. Simon Wiesenthal would later write that Long "obstructed rescue attempts, drastically restricted immigration, and falsified figures of refugees admitted." Wiesthenthal founded the Wiesenthal Center, an international Jewish human rights organization.

16. David S. Wyman, *The Abandonment of the Jews* (New York: Pantheon/ Random House, 1984), x, xi.

17. Metz, *Israel, a Country Study*, 57.

18. The 1950 Law of Return was intended to encourage Jews to return to their new homeland, to what would be called Eretz Yisrael, the Land of Israel. Supporters of the Law of Return claim that in order to understand the Law, one must comprehend the political context in which it was written: Only five years had passed since the end of World War II. The Holocaust caused huge losses of families and destroyed communities and livelihoods. In this context, the Law of Return was intended to redress persecution of Jews in practically the entire Jewish Diaspora.

19. The Bete Israel was also known, somewhat pejoratively, as Falasha, meaning "exile" or "stranger." By 1984 some 90,000, or 85 percent, of Ethiopian Jews had been airlifted to Israel during "Operation Moses." The new immigrants included the Falasha Mura, a smaller sect of Abyssinian Jews. Citizenship was granted to those who could show that their grandparents were Jews.

20. Metz, *Israel, a Country Study*, 30.

21. Jonathan Leff, gunnery officer on board one ship of the Israeli navy's squadron, told this author that he had to write the text of radio messages in English. These were then translated into Hebrew before being transmitted. Replies in Hebrew had to be translated back into English so that Shulman could carry out an order.

22. Shulman, OH, 15. Shulman spoke enough Hebrew to get by in casual conversation. With business associates he preferred to rely on translators and interpreters for formal business communications.

23. Ibid., 16.

24. Brecher, *A Stranger in the Land*, 67.

25. Baruch Kimmerling, "Israel's Culture of Martyrdom," a review of *Israel's Holocaust and the Politics of Nationhood*, by Idith Zertal (New York: Cambridge University Press, English ed., 2005). Kimmerling was a professor of sociology at Hebrew University of Jerusalem. Until his death in 2007, he was regarded as a leading voice among a group of critics known as Israel's "new historians." Though

describing himself as a committed Zionist who favored a "secular" Jewish state, he was, nonetheless, an outspoken critic of Israel's politics. His review appeared in *The Nation*, January 10, 2005.

26. Metz, *Israel, a Country Study*, 96.

27. The so-called "new historians" is a loosely defined group of historians who publish new and controversial views concerning Israel, its beginning, and its evolution as a modern nation-state. Much of their work is based on declassified government documents. Although some of their critics liked to hang the term "revisionist" around their neck, the new historians are more concerned with presenting a view of Israel not shrouded in the myth of the state as Eretz Israel—the Land of Israel. They contend that Israel was possible only through expulsion of the Arab populations.

28. The term "Torah" (without the grammatical article "the" before the proper noun) comprises the five books of Moses, of what Christians call the Old Testament: Genesis, Exodus, Leviticus, Numbers, and Deuteronomy. Torah includes 613 biblical "commandments," of which 365 instruct Jews what not to do, and 248 tell them what they may do. Jewish religious law, or Halakhah, includes both rabbinic and Talmudic law, as well as traditions and customs. In eighteenth- and nineteenth-century European Jewish shtetl, or communities, Halakhah was a body of enforceable religious and civil law. In modern times, compliance with Halakhah is voluntary, although strongly encouraged. Adherence to Halakhah varies among the several practices of the Judaic experience, from ultra-Orthodox, to Conservative, Reform, and Reconstructionist Judaism.

29. The word Halakhah comes from the Hebrew word meaning "the path" or "the way of walking." Halakhic law guides not only religious practices and beliefs but also numerous aspects of everyday living. In Israel, many aspects of family and personal status law are governed by rabbinic interpretations of Halakhah.

30. Ben-Ami, *Scars of War, Sounds of Peace*, 104.

31. *Yitzak Rabin, Prime Minister of Israel, Selection of Papers from His Life*. Referenced in Ben-Ami, *Scars of War, Sounds of Peace*, 100.

32. Metz, *Israel, a Country Study*, 33. The shtetl is a small town with a large Jewish population. In pre-Holocaust central and eastern Europe, the shtetl was a haven where pious Orthodox Jews could follow their traditional ways, despite social and political turmoil outside the community.

33. Linda Sharaby, "Israel's Economic Growth: Success Without Security," *MERIA: Middle East Review of International Affairs* 6, no. 3 (September 2002): 4. (http://meria.idc.ac.il). At the time Sharaby wrote this article, she was an assistant editor at *MERIA*.

34. Born Moshe Shertok, he emigrated to Palestine in 1906 and studied economics at the London School of Economics. He served as secretary of the Jewish Agency's Political Department and since 1933 was the head of the agency until the founding of Israel, with Ben-Gurion as chairman of its executive committee. Shertok always felt that armed retaliation was not the best way for the Zionists to

achieve their goals. After he took Sharrett as his Hebrew name, he was appointed Ben-Gurion's successor by the Mapai party. He also retained the foreign affairs portfolio. Ben-Gurion remained politically active behind the scenes throughout Sharett's two-year term as prime minister. This took place against the backdrop of growing concern over massive arms acquisition by the Arab countries, supplied by the Soviet bloc, as well as mounting international pressure on Israel to make far-reaching concessions on water rights, while still showing restraint in response to attacks from across the borders. Ben-Gurion perceived Sharett as being too moderate in retaliation against incursions and attacks on Israeli citizens, while Sharett considered it important to maintain his policy of moderation and de-escalation of the Arab-Israel conflict. Source: Israel Ministry of Foreign Affairs, www.mfa.gov.il.

35. Howard Sachar, A History of the Jews in the Modern World (New York: Knopf, 2005), 725.

36. Brecher, A Stranger in the Land, 213.

37. Ben-Ami, Scars of War, Sounds of Peace, 130–31.

38. Ami Isseroff, "The Yom Kippur War," 24; 2005, Zionism and Israel Information Center (Zionism-Israel.com/dic/YomKippurWar). Dr. Isseroff was then director, MidEastWeb for Coexistence.

39. Sharaby, "Israel's Economic Growth," 7.

40. The phrase has often been attributed to early Zionist leaders, who saw the territory along the Mediterranean as a place where they had a historical, even biblical right to create a nation for the world's Jews. Yet, according to historian Diana Muir, writing in Middle East Quarterly (15, no. 2 [Spring 2008]), there is no evidence that early Zionist leaders adopted this 1844 slogan to justify their right to establish a nation in the territory, which was well known to have been long inhabited by indigenous Arab peoples. Still, the slogan has suited different factions for different reasons.

41. Ralph Lowenstein, A Time of War (New York: Lancer Books, 1996), 228. Used by permission.

Appendix: From *Argosy* to *Abril*

1. Medoff, Rafael, "Ben Hecht's 'A Flag Is Born,' A Play That Changed History." David S. Wyman Institute for Holocaust Studies. www.wymaninstitute.org/articles, accessed March 7, 2005. Mr. Medoff is executive director of the Wyman Institute.

2. David Macarov, letter to the editor, Bulletin of the American Veterans of Israel, Summer, 2005. Macarov was responding to this author's article in the AVI newsletter, "The Mighty Ma'oz," in the Spring 2005 issue, www.israelvets.org.

3. George Horne, New York Times, January 18, 1947, 5.

4. The article appeared in Pageant 3, no. 7 (August 1947); www.haganah.us/harchives.

GLOSSARY

Aliyah   (Hebrew: "ascent." Pronounced: "Ah-lee-YAH.") *Scars of War, Sounds of Peace* Historically, a return to the biblical Jerusalem. Also, a basic tenet of Zionist ideology, later written into the Law of Return, which permits Jews to immigrate to Israel and become Israeli citizens.

Aluf   (Hebrew. Pronounced: "ah-loof," as in "hoof.") Israeli Defense Force rank equivalent to the U.S. Army rank of major general. In 1948 ranks for the new Israeli Naval Service had not been established, so army ranks were assigned to naval officers. *Rav Aluf* is admiral.

Apparatchik   (Russian: "apparat," a government function, plus "chik," agent.) A full-time, professional functionary of the Communist Party. Now, often derogatory, to describe a person likely to cause bureaucratic bottlenecks in an otherwise efficient function.

Ashkenazi   (Hebrew; plural: *Ashkenazim*.) Originally, Jews from the Alsace region of southern Germany. Starting around the sixteenth century many Ashkenazim migrated to eastern Europe, replicating the tight-knit communities called shtetl. However, facing persecution wherever they settled, the Jews formed a movement to establish a homeland in Palestine, which they believed was—and again should be—their National Homeland. See also *Sephardi*.

Bricha   (Hebrew: "escape." Pronounced: "brick-ah.") An organization within the Jewish Agency that coordinated movements of refugees from Europe to coastal ports in France, Italy, and Romania, where they were put on the Aliyah Bet vessels for transport to Palestine. An estimated 40,000 to 80,000 refugees passed through the Bricha pipeline from 1945 to 1948.

Cheyl Hayam   The Israeli Naval Service.

Diaspora	(Greek: "a scattering [of seeds]." Pronounced: "dye-ASP-ora.") Generally, any movement of a people who share a common national and ethnic identity. The *Jewish Diaspora* refers to the *galut*, or expulsion and exile of Jews from the pre-Christian kingdoms of Israel and Judah.
Ex-pat	Ex-patriate. A citizen of one nation who lives and works on a permanent basis in another country but retains citizenship in country of origin.
Haapalah	(Hebrew: "to go or act with force.") In Israel today, Haapalah is used to describe and remember the so-called "clandestine" immigration sealift operated by the Haganah's Mossad le Aliyah Bet organization.
Haganah	(Hebrew: "the Defense." Pronounced: "ha-gah-NAH.") A paramilitary organization formed by Jewish leaders in Palestine in the 1920s after the League of Nations mandated Great Britain to govern Palestine. Initially, the Haganah was made up of many local self-defense groups. By the late 1930s the Haganah had coalesced into a unified fighting force, with formal training and an underground supply source of light weapons. Ironically, during its early years the Mandatory authorities called on the Haganah to help quell Arab riots. (Source: Jewish Virtual Library.) See also *Palmach*.
Halakhah	(Hebrew: "The path that one walks." Pronounced: "Ha-LOCK-ha.") A set of religious laws, rules, and precepts designed to "increase the spirituality of one's life." (Source: Judaism 101, www.jewfaq.org/halakhah.)
Hatikvah	(Hebrew: "The Hope.") Based on a tone poem, *Hatikvah* was adopted as the Zionists' anthem in 1897 at the First World Zionist conference. Though sung as an anthem since 1948, it was not officially sanctioned by the Knesset until 2004.
Irgun	(Hebrew: acronym for *Irgun Tsvai Leumi Eretz Yisrael*, the "National Military Organization in the Land of Israel.") Its founder and chief proponent was Menachim Begin, who based the Irgun's philosophy on the writings of Ze'ev Jabotinsky, who wrote under the name of "Altalena."
Kibbutz	(Hebrew: "a gathering," or "clustering.") Generally, people who live on, or are associated with the communal community known as a kibbutz. With the Russian suffix "*nik*" added, Kibbutznik refers to a person who supports or is associated with

	a political cause or cultural attitude. Often used in a derogatory fashion, as in the American word, "Beatnik."
Krystallnacht	(Yiddish: "Night of Broken Glass.") Refers to a period in November 1938 when Nazis desecrated and destroyed hundreds of synagogues throughout Europe.
Kvarnit	An Israeli Defense Force rank, equivalent to U.S. Army lieutenant colonel or U.S. Navy commander.
Machal	(Hebrew: "workers from outside the land of Israel." Pronounced: "MAH-kahl." Acronym for "Mitnadvei Hutz LaAretz.") The term was applied to the estimated 3,500 men and women volunteers from all over the world who came to help Israel secure its independence.
Machal West	An organization for veterans of the Machal—Volunteers from Abroad—who currently live in the western half of the United States. A similar organization, World Machal, has members throughout Europe, in South Africa, and in Israel.
Moshav	(Hebrew: "a village," or "settlement.") Similar to a kibbutz, the moshav differs in that it is run as cooperative settlement. Members own their farm plot and house and produce food and goods for the members but may keep profits for their own use. A moshav leadership council, however, buys commonly used materials for the benefit of all members.
Mossad le Aliyah Bet	(Hebrew: Mossad is "department," or "institute." Aliyah is a return to Israel. Bet is the second letter of the Hebrew alphabet; in this usage, it corresponds to "Plan B.") This Haganah organization purchased war surplus vessels, then converted them to transport Jewish immigrants from Europe to Palestine before Israel became a nation. The British declared the immigration project illegal. To the Mossad it was merely "clandestine."
Orientals	(Hebrew: *Edot Mizrah*, "Communities of the East.") Generally, immigrants and settlers from eastern Europe and the Middle East. Because they arrived often less socially adept than immigrants from western Europe, or they still adhered to a tribal culture, many had difficulty in being absorbed into the dominant European structure that was Israeli society. See also *Sephardim*.
Palmach	(Hebrew: "strike force." Pronounced: "Pol-MOCK.") The Haganah had been around since the 1920s, but the better-trained and better-armed Strike Force units were organized in the 1940s. In the 1948 War of Independence, Palmach

units were responsible for many military victories over Arab invaders.

Palyam (Hebrew: "Sea Company." Acronym for "Plugat haYam.") The Palyam was formed in 1943 out of Jewish veterans, many of whom had served in the British Royal Navy. In Palestine, small groups of Palyam commandos carried out sabotage against British naval bases and ships. The Palyam was absorbed into the post-1948 Israeli Naval Service.

Passover A significant Jewish Holy Day, usually in March or April, that commemorates the liberation of the biblical Jews from bondage under the despotic Pharaoh, king of Egypt. See also *Seder*.

Protectzia (Hebrew: "influence.") The term combines the English word, "protect" with the Russian suffix, "*tzia*." It refers to one person's political ability or influence to shield another person from interference or censure. (Source: Judaism Without Borders, www.judaismwithoutborders.org.)

Refusenik (Russian: "otkaznik.") An unofficial term initially applied mostly to Jews in the Soviet Union who were refused permission to emigrate abroad. Today, the term is applied to almost any type of protester.

Rosh Hashanah (Hebrew: "Head of the Year.") The High Holy Days period is a commemoration, usually in September or October, of the beginning of the traditional Jewish New Year. The ten-day period begins with Rosh Hashanah and ends with Yom Kippur. The dates change each year because the Hebrew calendar is not based on the Gregorian calendar but on three naturally occurring astronomical phenomena.

Seder (Hebrew: "feast.") A ritual meal held on the first, or first two, nights of Passover in which the family or group retells the story of the biblical Jews' liberation from ancient Egypt. Foods on the Seder plate are symbolic of the tribulations endured by the ancient Israelites as they made their way to the Promised Land.

Sephardi (Hebrew; plural: *Sephardim*.) Descendants of Jewish people who inhabited the Iberian Peninsula (today's Spain and Portugal) until their expulsion by the Spanish crown beginning in 1492. Thousands were killed in the Inquisition. Thousands of Sephardim resettled all over the world, in order to keep their traditional religious and cultural practices. Those Sephardim who remained in Spain publicly embraced Catholicism but continued to follow their Jewish religious practices in secret.

(Source: Cecil Roth, *A History of the Marranos* [New York: Jewish Publication Society, 2001]).

Sgan Mishne   Equivalent to a U.S. Marine Corps colonel or captain in the U.S. Navy.

Shtetl   (Yiddish: "town"; plural: *Shetlekh*.) A self-contained community of Jews, in which social stability and order was prized and where scholarly discourse and discussion of Jewish law was paramount. Most shtetlekh were located in the Pale of Settlement, an area within the Russian Empire where Jews were permitted to live. Nearly all were destroyed in the pogroms—the organized, brutal persecution of the Jews—and by the Nazi's Final Solution of the Jews that led up to the Holocaust.

Silk Stocking District   The section of Manhattan, originally from Park Avenue to the East River, from 59th to 96th streets. In the nineteenth century, it was where most of New York's wealthiest captains of industry (who could afford to wear socks woven of pure silk) built their mansions. Later, as part of New York's Seventeenth Congressional District, the designation included the affluent Upper West Side of Manhattan.

White Paper   An authoritative, official statement or guide on key issues and how they should be resolved. Originally used by the British government; now, it is in general use for any official statement of policy.

Zionist   (also: Zionism.) A political and religious movement begun in the nineteenth century in Europe to combat racist and exclusionary treatment of European Jews. Zion is a hill in Jerusalem, on which the Temple was built, destroyed, and the Second Temple rebuilt. Today, only the Western Wall remains. To some people Zion represents the place of Heaven on Earth for the Jewish people.

BIBLIOGRAPHY

BOOKS

Avriel, Ehud. *Open the Gates: The Dramatic Personal Story of "Illegal" Immigration to Israel*. New York: Athaeneum, 1975.

Batvinis, Raymond. *Origin of FBI Counter-Intelligence*. Lawrence: University of Kansas Press, 2007.

Ben-Ami, Shlomo. *Scars of War, Sounds of Peace: The Israeli-Arab Tragedy* (English edition). London: Oxford University Press, 2007.

Ben-Gurion, David. *Israel: A Personal History* (English edition). New York: Funk & Wagnall's, 1971.

Brecher, Daniel Cil. *A Stranger in the Land: Jewish History beyond Nationalism*. New York: Other Press, 2007.

Caine, Philip D. *American Pilots in the RAF*. Dulles, Va.: Brassey's, 1998.

Dunkelman, Ben. *Dual Allegiance*. New York: Crown, 1976.

Eveland, Wilbur Crane. *Ropes of Sand: America's Failure in the Middle East*. New York: Norton, 1980.

Gardner, Robert, and Roger Chesneau. *Conway's All the World's Fighting Ships, 1922–1946*. London: Brassey's Military History, 1980.

Gershoni, Haim (Harold Gershenow). *Israel: The Way It Was*. New York: Herzl Press, 1989.

Greenfield, Murray, and Joseph Hochstein. *The Jews' Secret Fleet*. Jerusalem: Gefen Publishing, 1987.

Hadari, Ze'ev, and Ze'ev Tsahor. *Voyage to Freedom*. London: Vallentine Mitchell, 1985.

Holly, David C. *Exodus 47*. Annapolis: U.S. Naval Institute Press, Revised, 1995.

Katz, Samuel. *The Night Raiders: Israel's Naval Commandos at War*. New York: Pocket Books, 1997.

Kurzman, Dan. *Genesis 1948*. Cambridge, Mass.: Da Capo Press, 1992.

Levin, Marlin. *Balm in Gilead: The Story of Hadassah*. New York: Schocken, 1973.

Liebreich, Fritz. *Britain's Naval and Political Reaction to Illegal Immigration of Jews to Palestine 1945–1948*. London: Routledge, 2005.

Loftus, John, and Mark Aarons. *The Secret War against the Jews*. New York: St. Martin's Press, 1994.

Lowenstein, Ralph. *A Time of War*. New York: Lancer Books, 1996.

Metz, Helen Chapin. *Israel: A Country Study*. Washington, D.C.: Library of Congress, Federal Research Division, 1988.

Morris, Benny. *The Birth of the Palestinian Refugee Problem 1947–1949*. Cambridge, UK: Cambridge University Press, 1987.

Naor, Mordechai. *Ha'apalah: Clandestine Immigration* (English Edition). Jerusalem: Israeli Ministry of Defense, 1987.

Rifkin, Shepard. *What Ship? Where Bound?* New York: Knopf, 1961.

Sachar, Howard. *A History of the Jews in the Modern World*. New York: Knopf, 2005.

Slater, Leonard. *The Pledge*. New York: Simon & Shuster, 1971.

Soustelle, Jacques. *The Long March of Israel*. New York: American Heritage Press, 1969.

Stern, Chaim, ed. *Gates of Repentance: The New Union Prayer Book for the Days of Awe*. New York: Central Conference of American Rabbis, 1978.

Sternhell, Ze'ev. *The Founding Myths of Israel* (English edition). Princeton, N.J.: Princeton University Press, 1998.

Swann, Robbyn, and Anthony Summers. *Sinatra: The Life*. New York: Knopf, 2005.

Weiss, Craig, and Jeffrey Weiss. *I Am My Brother's Keeper: American Volunteers in Israel's War for Independence*. Atgen, Pa.: Schiffer Military Histories, 1998.

Wyman, David S. *The Abandonment of the Jews*. New York: Pantheon/Random House, 1984.

Zertal, Idith. *From Catastrophe to Power*. Berkeley: University of California Press, 1998.

ARTICLES

Ageton, Arthur A. "Annapolis: Cradle of the Navy." *National Geographic* (July 1936).

Alpert, Carl. "From Lieutenant to Admiral in 3 Years." *Jewish Review* (March 27, 1967).

Azaryahu, Ma'oz. "The Independence Day Parade: A Political History of a Patriotic Ritual." In *The Military and Militarism in Israel*, Edna Lomsky-Feder and Eyal Ben-Ami, eds. New York: SUNY Press, 2003.

Coleman, Robert S. "Four Nautical Years at Virginia" (n.d., n.p.) Courtesy of C. Downing Tait, captain, USN (Ret.).

Dyas, George. "A History of the Academy." *Rolling Stone* (Spring 1939). (*Rolling Stone* was the yearbook of the Cheshire Academy.)

Gelber, Yoav. "The Meeting between the Jewish Soldiers from Eretz Israel and the Surviving Remnant." In *Sherit Hapletah, 1944–1948—Rehabilitation and Political Struggle*, Jerusalem, 1990, 60–79. From Proceedings, Yad Vashem Sixth International Conference, Jerusalem, 1985.

Isseroff, Ami. "The Yom Kippur War." Zionism and Israeli Information Center, 2005; www.Zionism-Israel.com/dic/YomKippurWar, accessed March 4, 2008.

Kimmerling, Baruch. "Review of *Israel's Holocaust and the Politics of Nationhood*, by Idith Zertal." Review appeared in *The Nation* (January 10, 2005).

Muir, Diana. "A Land Without a People for a People Without a Land." *Middle East Quarterly* 15, no. 2 (Spring 2008); www.meforum.org, accessed October 14, 2009.

Nicolai, Robert (as told to Harry Rauch). "I Ran Britain's Palestine Blockade." *Pageant* 3, no. 7 (August 1947); http://haganah.us.org/harchives, accessed February 18, 2005.

Remenick, Larissa. "Trans-national Community in the Making: Russian-Jewish Immigrants in Israel in the 1990s." *Journal of Ethnic and Migration Studies* 28, no. 2 (2002): 515–30; www.tandf.co.uk/journals.

Sharaby, Linda. "Israel's Economic Growth: Success Without Security." *MERIA: Middle East Review of International Affairs* 6, no. 3 (2006), http://MERIA.idc.ac.il, accessed March 2, 2008.

Slott, Lois. "I Became a Zionist on the Top Floor." In *American Jewish Women and the Zionist Enterprise*, Reinhart, Shulamit and Mark Raider, eds. Waltham, Mass.: Brandeis University Press, 2005.

Thomas, Donald I. "Rocks and Shoals." *Shipmate* 54, no. 1 (1991): 31.

Tucker, R. M. "Professional Notes." *The Log* (May 19, 1944). U.S. Naval Academy, Nimitz Memorial Library.

Whitaker, Wayne. "Annapolis at War." *Popular Mechanics* (August 1943).

NEWSPAPER ARTICLES

"Army Day Marked by Israeli Forces." *New York Times*, July 18, 1949.

Blair, William. "Ben Gurion Scores Palestine Policy." *New York Times*, November 11, 1946.

———. "Hadassah Quits Jewish Committee." *New York Times*, October 26, 1943.

"Cabinet Orders Cease Fire as Negev and Southern Armies Link." *Palestine Post*, October 23, 1948.

Egan, Charles. "Red Agents May Infiltrate Palestine Ships Now in Roumanian Ports, British Tell U.S." *New York Times*, November 12, 1947.

"Egyptian Navy Turned Back from Coast." *Palestine Post*, June 6, 1948.

Hinton, Charles B. "Guardian of American Passports." *New York Times Magazine*, April 27, 1941.

Moore, Gene. "Ulithi Atoll, Largest Anchorage in the Pacific." *Sun-Chronicle*, Attleboro, Mass., November 6, 2000; www.sunchronicle.com, accessed February 20, 2006.

Nolte, Carl. "The Dark Side of San Francisco." *San Francisco Chronicle*, August 15, 2005; www.sfgate.com/chronicle, accessed March 1, 2006.

"Northland Is Sold to Mystery Buyer." *New York Times*, January 4, 1947.

"Panama Asks Data on Refugee Ships." *New York Times* (via Reuter), October 20, 1947.

Reston, James. "Illegal Palestine Immigrants Will Be Detained on Cyprus." *New York Times*, August 8, 1946.

"Save Doomed Jews, Huge Rally Pleads." *New York Times*, March 2, 1943.

Schmidt, Dana Adams. "Israel Draining Swamps for Farms." *New York Times*, August 18, 1953.

Tugend, Tom. "Whom Pardons Are Made For." *Jewish Journal of Greater Los Angeles*, March 9, 2003; www.jewishjournal.com, accessed December 5, 2005.

"Vessel Figured in War. Acquisition by New York Company Described in London." *New York Times*, June 4, 1947.

Zohary, Tamar, and Hambright, K. David. "Lake Hula—Lake Agmon." Jewish Virtual Library; www.us-israel.org/source/Society&Culture/geo/Hula, accessed February 6, 2004.

DISSERTATIONS

Holwitt, Joel C. "The Judaic Experience in the U.S. Naval Academy" (M.A. thesis, U.S. Naval Academy, Annapolis, 2002).

Liebreich, Fritz. "The Israeli Navy during the War of Independence, 1948–1949: Politicking, Struggle for Control and Early Operations" (M.A. thesis, King's College, University of London, London, UK, 1994).

Shulman, Paul. "From My Point of View: Recollections on the Israeli Navy Forty Years Ago." Courtesy of Albert Bildner. Used with permission.

DOCUMENTS

City and County of San Francisco, Bureau of Marriage Licenses.

Finard, Miriam. Letter, April 18, 1992, to Ralph Lowenstein, director (American Veterans of Israel archive, University of Florida, Gainesville).

———. Letter, April 8, 2002, to Ralph Lowenstein, director (American Veterans of Israel archive, University of Florida, Gainesville).

Griffis, Stanton, U.S. ambassador to Egypt. Telegram, October 21, 1948, to U.S. Department of State, NARA, RG 84.

Harris, Lee. Letter, September 12, 1948, to "Chief of Staff, Israeli Navy" (American Veterans of Israel archive, University of Florida, Gainesville).

———. Letter, February 11, 1949, to D. Lou Harris, Palestine Economic Commission (American Veterans of Israel archive, University of Florida, Gainesville).

Hearings before the Committee on Foreign Relations, House of Representatives, 78th Congress.

Knoertzer, Halford, commander, U.S. Navy. "Anti-aircraft Action. By U.S.S. *Hunt* on March 18, 1945." Deck Log, USS *Hunt*, NARA, RG 38.

Lippincott, Aubrey. Letter, August 2, 1948, to U.S. Secretary of State. NARA, RG 84.

Oath of Office, U.S. Naval Academy. Annapolis, Maryland.

Regulations Governing the Admission of Candidates into the United States Naval Academy as Midshipmen, U.S. Naval Academy, Annapolis, Maryland.

Second Session, on HR 418 and HR 419, February 1944. Testimony of Herman Shulman, pp. 356–61, in *The Jewish National Home in Palestine*. New York: KTAV Publishing, 1970.

Statement on Navy Department Personnel Release Plan, August 15, 1946 (Naval Historical Center, Washington, D.C.).

USS *Massey* Deck Log, April 15, 1946. NARA, RG 38.

U.S. v. Adolph W. Schwimmer, et al. District Court of Los Angeles, October 1949–February 1950.

FREEDOM OF INFORMATION ACT/PRIVACY REQUEST, NOVEMBER 2, 2007, TO U.S. DEPARTMENT OF STATE

Airgram, July 15, 1949, to U.S. vice consul, Haifa.

Ben-Gurion, David. Israeli minister of defense, letter, June 28, 1949.

Bloodworth, Thomas. U.S. vice consul, Haifa, letter, July 2, 1949.

DoS Message No. 452, June 2, 1949.

Shulman, Paul. Letter to Department of State, December 13, 1951.
————. Supplementary Affidavit, June 21, 1951.
Young, W. H. Memo to U.S. vice consul, Haifa, July 11, 1951.

ORAL HISTORIES

Harris, Lee. Oral History, December 2, 1979 (American Veterans of Israel archive, University of Florida, Gainesville).
Legato, Dominic. USS *Hunt* Veterans Association, http://members.aol.com/dlegato/storm, accessed April 29, 2003.
Shulman, Paul. Oral History, May 13, 1993 (New York Public Library, Dorot division of Jewish History).

WEB SITES

"Balfour Declaration of 1917." Jewish Virtual Library, www.jewishvirtual library.org/Balfour.
"Declaration of the State of Israel, May 14, 1948." State of Israel, Ministry of Foreign Affairs. www.mfa.gov.il.
Fenton, Dr. Jason. "The Machal Story, Chapter 2." www.sabra.net/machal/section 2, accessed November 4, 2004.
Geller, Doron. "Early Operations of Israeli Intelligence." Jewish Agency for Palestine, Department for Jewish Zionist Education, www.iafi.org.il/education, accessed February 6, 2004.
Isseroff, Ami. "Speaking Out for Palestine and Peace." Mideast Web Opinion Forum, www.mideastweb.org/Palestine, accessed October 12, 2008.
————. "The Yom Kippur War." Zionism and Israel Information Center, www.Zionism-Israel.com/dic/YomKippurWar.
Legato, Dominic. "Typhoon: The Hunt's Other Enemy." USS *Hunt* Alumni Association, http://members.aol.com/dlegato/storm, accessed April 29, 2003.
Macarov, David. Letter, Spring 2005 to the editor, *AVI Bulletin*, www.israelvets.org/avi. Dr. Macarov was responding to this author's article, "The Mighty Ma'oz" in the Winter 2004 *AVI Bulletin*.
"The Magpie Sings the Great Depression: Selections from DeWitt Clinton High School's literary magazine, 1929–1942." In *The New Deal Network*, www.newdeal.feri.org, accessed January 10, 2006.
Medoff, Rafael. "Ben Hecht's 'A Flag Is Born,' A Play that Changed History." David S. Wyman Institute for Holocaust Studies, www.wymaninstute.org/articles, accessed March 7, 2005. Rafael Medoff is executive director of the Wyman Institute.
Naval Company of Palmach/Haganah, www.palyam.org.

"Needless Deaths in Gulf War." Human Rights Watch, New York, 1991, www.hrw.org/reports/1991/gulfwar.

USS Liberty Memorial, www.agtr5.org, accessed June 4, 2007.

Zohary, Tamar, and K. David Hambright. "Lake Hula—Lake Agmon." Jewish Virtual Library, www.us-israel.org/source/Society&culture/geo/hula, accessed January 11, 2006.

INTERVIEWS

Bildner, Albert. October 28, 2003.

Broder, Marvin. December 17, 2004; January 18, 2005.

Kaslove, Ruth. October 11, 2005.

Leff, Jonathan. August 2, 2005.

Palkimas, Patricia. March 17, 2006.

Shaffer, Lawrence. May 16, 2003.

Shugar, Harold. August 16, 2005.

Shulman, David. July 22, 2006.

Shulman, Mark. July 22, 2006.

Sobel, Charles. May 22, 2003.

Sobel, Lawrence. June 22, 2006.

Weiss, Charles. January 31, 2007.

Wilson, James L. May 1, 2003.

INDEX

NOTE: Some vessels listed here were never accepted by Israel for the Israeli navy; they are listed by the organization that owned them, such as "Haganah" or "Irgun."

ABOUT THE AUTHOR

J. Wandres is a retired U.S. Navy public affairs specialist who holds an MS in video production and a BA in English. He has written for *Military Officer*, *Naval History*, *World War II History*, and *All Hands*. He edited two award-winning magazines and published *Pennsylvania-New Jersey Travel Smart* (Avalon, 1999). An associate with the Center for World War II History and Conflict Resolution, he has written about the Navy's World War II Norden Broadcasts and the Mulberry Harbors.

The Naval Institute Press is the book-publishing arm of the U.S. Naval Institute, a private, nonprofit, membership society for sea service professionals and others who share an interest in naval and maritime affairs. Established in 1873 at the U.S. Naval Academy in Annapolis, Maryland, where its offices remain today, the Naval Institute has members worldwide.

Members of the Naval Institute support the education programs of the society and receive the influential monthly magazine *Proceedings* or the colorful bimonthly magazine *Naval History* and discounts on fine nautical prints and on ship and aircraft photos. They also have access to the transcripts of the Institute's Oral History Program and get discounted admission to any of the Institute-sponsored seminars offered around the country.

The Naval Institute's book-publishing program, begun in 1898 with basic guides to naval practices, has broadened its scope to include books of more general interest. Now the Naval Institute Press publishes about seventy titles each year, ranging from how-to books on boating and navigation to battle histories, biographies, ship and aircraft guides, and novels. Institute members receive significant discounts on the Press's more than eight hundred books in print.

Full-time students are eligible for special half-price membership rates. Life memberships are also available.

For a free catalog describing Naval Institute Press books currently available, and for further information about joining the U.S. Naval Institute, please write to:

Member Services
U.S. Naval Institute
291 Wood Road
Annapolis, MD 21402-5034
Telephone: (800) 233-8764
Fax: (410) 571-1703
Web address: www.usni.org